D1075455

The Real Computer:
Its Influence, Uses, and Effects

The Real Computer:

 ADDISON-WESLEY PUBLISHING COMPANY

Its Influence, Uses, and Effects

FREDERIC G. WITHINGTON
Arthur D. Little, Inc.

Reading, Massachusetts • Menlo Park, California • London • Don Mills, Ontario

651.26
W82N
Cop. 2

Copyright © 1969 by Addison-Wesley Publishing Company, Inc. Philippines copyright 1969 by Addison-Wesley Publishing Company, Inc.

All rights reserved. No part of this publication may be reproduced, stored in a retrieval system, or transmitted, in any form or by any means, electronic, mechanical, photocopying, recording, or otherwise, without the prior written permission of the publisher. Printed in the United States of America. Published simultaneously in Canada. Library of Congress Catalog Card No. 74–87047.

PREFACE

Computers are causing changes in the structure and behavior of the organizations and individuals using them. This book is intended to help concerned managers control these changes and adapt to them intelligently. It presents a factual, objective study of these changes, giving a balanced picture of the computer's strengths and weaknesses and its desirable and undesirable effects. The objective guidance that is offered to the reader in this book should improve his ability to make intelligent decisions about the use of computers, and to live in a world that is becoming increasingly dependent on computer systems.

It is no longer necessary to treat this subject in a speculative manner: some 50,000 organizations are using computers; a few have done so for more than fifteen years. This book is based on a compilation and distillation of actual experience, mostly presented in the form of case studies. More than one hundred case descriptions in brief summary form are interspersed within the text. With the exception of a few hypothetical cases in the last chapter that are set in the future, all the cases are drawn from real situations with which the author is personally familiar. They are simplified for brevity and sometimes modified to conceal the identities of the organizations or individuals involved, but are otherwise factual.

The book's primary objective is to be factual; the computer is presented neither as a panacea nor as an agent of harm, but in both roles as the evidence dictates. To emphasize the fact that both good and bad accompany the computer, its positive and negative aspects are considered separately. Thus a chapter on "The Computer's Strengths" is paired with a chapter on "Compensating for the Computer's Weaknesses," and a chapter discussing "Those Who Benefit" from the computer is paired with a chapter considering "Those Who Suffer." The chapters illustrating the negative cases give examples of its failures and ill effects, and those illustrating the positive cases depict successes and benefits. The world is not black and white, however; there are few unmixed blessings or evils resulting from the computer's use. The cases themselves show this.

NOV 19 '70

v

HUNT LIBRARY
CARNEGIE-MELLON UNIVERSITY

After the presently observed effects of the computer on organizations and individuals have been explained, the book proceeds to explain the synthesis of good and bad effects that appears to be emerging in advanced computer-using organizations and services to the public. An extrapolation of these effects to the "next generation" of individuals and organizations using them is presented in Part IV. The pattern of the immediate future appears to be both less radical than many forecasters have suggested, and more radical in ways not generally appreciated.

Because of the book's objective, its tone is unemotional. The subject of the changes caused by computers is highly charged with emotion, though: those who have been hurt feel bitterness, those who have been helped feel gratification, and the thousands of pioneers among users and manufacturers alike feel pride (and sometimes disappointment) in their progress. Few technical innovations have ever grown so fast or so broadly as the computer, and few have been accompanied by such far-reaching effects and intensity of change. The field is rich, active, and confusing, yet immensely rewarding in its insight into the underlying behavioral patterns of individuals and organizations. This book should provide concrete guidance to its readers, but even if it does no more than convey a sense of this richness and insight it will have been a success.

Literally hundreds of individuals have helped make this book possible. Martin Greenberger and Arthur Nesse provided useful guidance; Judith Fisher and Beatrice Walter labored long and enthusiastically at the typewriter. Above all, though, the experiences of the author's consulting clients—their successes, failures, trials and discoveries—form the "bricks and mortar" from which the book was constructed. This is their book.

Cambridge, Mass.   F.G.W.
February 1969

CONTENTS

Part I | THE COMPUTER
UNMASKED

CHAPTER 1

THE COMPUTER'S STRENGTHS

*It is now time to apply management's knowledge of business
more fully to the planning and evaluation of computers.**
JOHN DIEBOLD

With 40,000 or more computers in use, it is obvious that they must have great
virtues of widespread appeal. It is easy to become confused about what these
virtues are, however, because most of the publicity associated with computers
dwells on their ability to do the strange and spectacular, and on experiments
that show more future promise than present performance. We are not interested here in the computer's ability to perform unusual or spectacular achieve-
ments; the unusual and spectacular are not in the repertoire of most ordinary
computers used by ordinary firms. An objective assessment of the actual
strengths of computers makes it necessary to isolate and identify the characteristics of computer systems which have accounted for their tremendous
popularity, whether they be routine and mundane or exciting and exceptional.
With these underlying strengths isolated and identified, it will be possible in
succeeding chapters to balance them against the demonstrated weaknesses of
computers, thereby making it possible to understand the impact of computers
and make intelligent decisions about their use.

ABILITY TO REPEAT ITSELF PRECISELY AND RAPIDLY

Fortunately for the computer's success, it appeared on the scene during an era
of increasing regulation, bureaucracy, and population explosion that led to a
colossal increase in paperwork—the handling and processing of masses of individual transactions in a formal, preestablished manner. As we all know from
experience, humans are by nature very poor at performing this kind of work.

---

* *Bad decisions About Computer Use, Harvard Business Review,* January–February 1969.

When a human is faced with endless repetition of simple clerical tasks, providing no variation or scope for initiative, he invariably becomes bored and inattentive, error prone, and subject to all the motivational problems that accompany unsatisfying and uninteresting work. The computer's greatest strength, unquestionably accounting for most of its success to date, is that it does not share these human failings. Once programmed to perform a set of clerical tasks, it will continue to perform them at full speed as long as its power is on. Hours of work are irrelevant—as long as it is properly maintained, the computer will work 24 hours a day, 7 days a week. Its speed is constant; it does not tire; it does not make errors in the sense of human arithmetic or clerical mistakes. As long as its programs are accurate and complete and the equipment is functioning correctly, each transaction will be processed accurately and precisely the same as every other, and if a process is duplicated a thousand times, the answer comes out identical a thousand times. This ability of the computer to function as a "robot clerk" is demonstrably its most important strength, because all studies of computer usage agree that more than three-quarters of all of the computers installed perform solely this kind of work.

The computer is also very fast. From the point of view of its use as a "robot clerk," this is not intrinsically important. If the machines were no faster than a single human clerk and were no more costly, they would be as popular as they are today. However, the computer is far more expensive than a single clerk and must be able to do the work of many in order to justify its cost. The typical business computer system costs as much as the salaries of perhaps 20 clerks. In work of a suitably routine nature, however, a computer can do the work of 30 or more clerks; it is therefore amply justified.

CASE IA

◀ The United States Internal Revenue Service uses computers to process all documents associated with individual and corporate income tax returns. The documents are received and reviewed in the 58 District Offices, which are the points of contact with the taxpayers. Then the documents are sent to seven Regional Service Centers, where punched cards are prepared containing the data to be processed. (Some corporations that use computers to prepare their payrolls send withholding statements to IRS in the form of reels of magnetic tape. This practice, which is growing, saves both parties money by eliminating the transcription of data to and from a paper document.)

Computers at the regional centers then convert the punched cards to magnetic tape, in the process checking the taxpayer's arithmetic and performing many checks and verifications of the data. If the computer finds an error, omission, or highly unusual condition, it prints a suitable report which is returned to the district. The reels of magnetic tape containing the data are then sent to the IRS's national computer center, where the tax master file is kept and accounts are processed. The files are centralized so that all information about a taxpayer can be brought together regardless of its point of origin; such illegal practices as multiple filing of requests for refunds in different regions are prevented. The tax account processing produces reels of magnetic tape containing the information required for refunds, bills, notices, and reports. The tapes are returned to the regions, where computers prepare the actual documents.

As of 1966, the IRS had 27 computers worth approximately $12,000,000.* It said that during 1966 they:

> Did the work of 12,000 people,

> Produced additional revenues of $27,000,000,

> Held back $61,000,000 in refunds to cover tax debits,

> Noted 700,000 missing returns, with potential tax collections of $156,000,000,

> Yielded $19,000,000 by discovering mathematical errors,

> Uncovered 416,000 duplicate refund claims.† ▶

This kind of strong justification for computers is particularly important because it is very expensive to "train" the computer to perform any given job. The design and production of computer programs for clerical tasks, even simple ones readily learned by average clerks, may require many years of effort by technicians. This programming of the computer system imposes an additional financial burden on its user, a high "startup" cost that must be invested in the system before any returns can be realized.

This is true for two reasons. First, since the instructions the computer can execute are minute and accomplish very little individually, thousands are likely to be needed to perform a typical clerical task. Second, the nature of the computer system usually forces its user to completely redesign the way the work is done. The devices within the computer system that store files of information, for example, operate more slowly than the computer itself. For reasons of efficiency, then, it is usually desirable to so arrange the processing procedure and file sequence that the number of file references is minimized. Another limitation is the size of the computer's working storage, where the program currently being executed is stored. In order to keep the cost of the

---

* *Inventory of Automatic Data Processing Equipment in the Federal Government,* U.S. Bureau of the Budget, July 1966.
† *Internal Revenue Service Automatic Data Processing,* Honeywell Corporation, 1967.

system down, the user will acquire as little of this costly working storage as possible, with the result that there is not enough room for all the many thousands of computer commands required to perform an entire clerical process. The program therefore will be divided into segments, each a functionally separate part of the total task. The segments will be run one after another, each performing its successive functions on each of a group or batch of transactions. (These assertions are not true in every case, because the great flexibility of computer systems makes it possible to operate otherwise, usually at higher cost. However, the great majority of computer systems used for clerical functions operate this way.)

Because this change in the way clerical work is done has a significant effect on the organization and its people, it is worthwhile to review an example of the way a typical user carries out clerical work with a computer. The following case is simplified and generalized from the actual experience of a moderate size company.

CASE 1B

◀ In 1962 a moderate size life insurance company decided to use a computer system for its premium accounting application—issuing premium notices, recording payments, recording claims and benefit payments, and the related accounting. The company ordered a computer system having a monthly rental of $7000, and with the manufacturer's assistance trained six of its most promising clerical supervisors in computer programming. They adapted a standard life insurance processing system design supplied by the manufacturer and developed the processing system shown schematically in Fig. 1-1. It shows the set of programs which, together, perform the entire application. They are designed to be run in sequence, the entire sequence to be performed once each day. The premium notices to be mailed that day are produced, and the payments and other transactions that were collected during the previous day are processed. There is also a monthly cycle and an annual cycle for the production of accounting reports, but the daily cycle is the most important.

The first computer program (1) causes punched cards containing the data to be processed, edited, and recorded on magnetic tape. The editing operation, constituting the bulk of the program, checks each punched card to verify that it represents a valid type of transaction, and that all of the expected information is present. The program causes transactions that fail its tests to be printed for human correction. The transactions that were rejected by the computer in the previous day's processing and subsequently corrected are reentered to be processed by the computer during this day's operation. Inquiries about policy status, cash value, and the like are also entered along with the transactions.

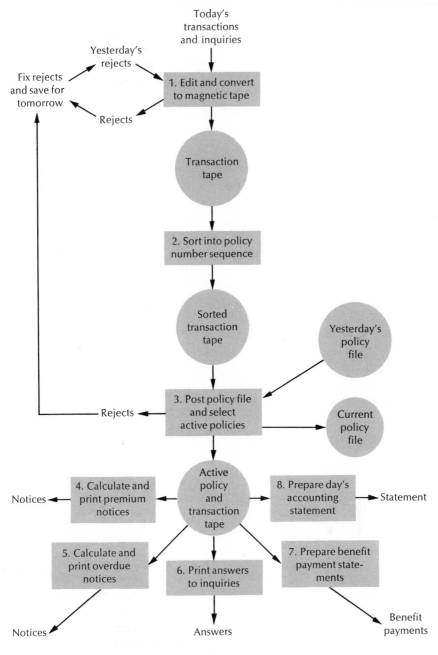

FIG. 1–1　Simplified life insurance policy processing—daily cycle.

The second of the computer's programs takes the transaction tape prepared during the first run, and sorts (reorders) the transactions into the same policy number sequence as the master file of policy records. This is done so that all of the references that will have to be made to the policy file can be made in one complete pass through it, rather than by "jumping around" in the file, which would take much longer.

In the third computer program, the day's batch of transactions, edited and sorted by the previous runs, are compared with the master policy file. Premium payments are credited to the accounts, as each payment record is matched with the proper policy record; new policy records are inserted in the right account number sequence; closed policies and those for which benefits have been paid are removed. The resulting new policy records, and the unchanged old ones, are recorded on a fresh reel of tape as the new version of the policy file. This will form the input to the next day's posting run.

There are a number of policies requiring some kind of action each day. These are policies for which premium notices must be prepared, both regular and overdue; those under which benefits have been claimed; those about which inquiries have been received; and the like. The policy records for each policy requiring action are copied on another reel of magnetic tape. It would be possible to perform the processing for these policies at the same time that the policy file is being posted with the day's payments. However, the computer's working storage is only large enough to hold the program required for one type of action at a time. As a result, it is necessary to copy the records of policies requiring further processing on the active policy tape, which forms the input to a series of subsequent processing programs in the cycle. The transactions corresponding to each active policy are recorded along with them.

During this process, additional rejects are found (e.g., transactions calling for cancelled policy numbers, benefit claims that do not match the policy amount, etc.). These are printed as before for human correction and reentry.

Runs 4 through 8 perform the processing of each type of policy requiring one of the daily standard actions, such as preparing premium notices, preparing overdue notices, and the like. The active policy tape is the input to each of them. The programmers believed that there were five classes of daily processing that would account for 95% or more of the types of transactions encountered. The other 5% they decided were special and unusual situations for which they found it uneconomical to try to prepare computer programs. These transactions they simply directed the machine to print for further processing by clerks or managers, as necessary, during the reject correction process.

They were wrong. It turned out that almost 20% of the transactions were rejected by the system at first, requiring so much clerical work that the expected savings could not be obtained. They then set to work on an emergency basis to prepare more programs for active policy processing, and were unable to reduce rejects adequately until they had increased the number of active policy processing runs from the initial five to fourteen.

It took the insurance company and its programmers nearly two years to perfect this set of programs, and to reduce the day's processing of transactions to an orderly routine free from unanticipated difficulties. They finally succeeded, however, and now the insurance company finds that it is processing three times the volume of transactions that it handled in 1964, with a total work force 10% less than that of 1964. The insurance company management feels that the installation of the computer was a far more difficult and painful process than they had anticipated, but they are satisfied with the final results and feel that they could not possibly compete with larger insurance companies if they had to incur the kind of processing cost for transactions that is to be expected with manual clerical work, especially at current cost levels. ▶

This ability of the computer to perform routine data handling operations at high speed has been of even more significance to science than it has been to business. The space program, the design of jet airplanes, and many areas of theoretical physics have for years involved experiments that produce such volumes of data that no reasonable number of human clerks and investigators could possibly deal with it.

CASE 1C

◀ A single experiment in nuclear physics that involves a high energy particle accelerator and a piece of detection apparatus (such as a spark chamber that records the paths of nuclear by-products resulting from the accelerator's output particles hitting a target) may take several weeks or even months to set up and may run continuously for equal lengths of time. The accelerators themselves are very costly (several tens of millions of dollars) and they are expensive to keep in operation (several million dollars per year). The detection equipment is also quite expensive (a spark chamber may cost several hundred thousand dollars). Clearly, there is an economic motive to provide data analysis systems that facilitate efficient use of such expensive equipment, making it possible to terminate experiments as soon as useful results are obtained or as soon as it becomes evident that they will not be obtained. Since a typical spark chamber experiment conducted over a few weeks will generate 500,000 to 700,000 stereo photographs of events taking place in the spark chamber, the data analysis system must operate at very high speed. Because of this need, devices have been developed which will scan the photographs of the particle tracks made visible in the spark chambers, and convert the tracks into series of numbers showing the locations of the tracks in the photographs. Computer programs can then process these numbers, first relating each track to a fixed set of coordinates so that its actual geometry can be determined, then performing an examination of the geometry of the track and comparing the results with pre-established criteria to identify "interesting" events. The computer then prints the identification of photographs containing these events, thereby directing the attention of the researcher to only those containing events in which he has previously indicated an interest. By this means, the number of spark chamber photographs the researcher must examine may be reduced by a factor of 10,000 and he may be able to participate in the conduct of the experiment, change it, terminate it, or go on to another in far less time and at far less cost than would have been required without the computer. ▶

It is apparent that the computer's ability to perform routine work without error and with great speed has been a primary reason why so many organizations have been willing to pay the high cost of the machine and to incur the great initial programming cost involved in using it.

ABILITY TO PERFORM
COMPLEX CALCULATIONS IN "REAL TIME"

The computer's speed is important in justifying the high cost of the machine. Of equal significance is the fact that it makes possible the solution of complex problems in a short time, short enough in many cases for the computer to predict the outcome of an event in time for the course of the event to be changed. For example, computers provide fresh predictions every few seconds of the impact point of every missile being test flown at missile ranges. If the predicted impact point becomes unacceptable, either the flight path is changed or the missile is destroyed. In the jargon of the business, this is "real-time" operation. The methods for making such predictions have long been known; in many areas methods of working out the correct answer or the optimum course of action exist. However, it is often laborious and time-consuming for humans to apply these methods every time the problem occurs. Or, as in the case of missile testing, the solution may be needed so soon in order to affect the outcome that the time required for human computation is too long. When the rules for solving a problem are known, they can almost invariably be expressed in the form of a computer program; then the computer with its great speed can produce the solution or optimum course of action very rapidly. This has made it possible to deal with many dynamic and rapidly changing situations more efficiently than ever before.

CASE 1D

◀ All electric utility companies of large size are investigating the use of computers to obtain (generate or purchase) electrical energy in such a way that all demands are met at the minimum cost to the utility company. Small electric utility companies can also obtain the advantages of computer controlled power distribution by pooling their facilities and supporting a single jointly owned computer scheduling center that serves a regional area.

The computer is provided with a description of the electrical distribution network in the area, showing the electrical losses in the network and therefore the cost of transmitting power between any two points. The computer is also given descriptions of the generating stations available within the network: the available capacity of each, the cost of operation, and related factors such as the desired schedule of overhaul periods. The computer is also informed of the existing connections between the utility's network and those of neighboring utilities, and kept informed on a current basis of the costs of obtaining power by purchase from the utility's neighbors.

As the demand for electricity changes—dropping in one area, rising in another—the computer is assigned the task of determining the most economical way to meet the changed demand. If total demand increases, the computer will determine whether more of the company's generators should be brought into action, or whether more power should be purchased from the neighboring utility, or a combination of both depending on the relative costs of obtaining the power and delivering it to the area in which the increased demand has occurred. If total demand has decreased, the computer determines whether it is more economical to shut down generators belonging to the utility or to decrease purchases of power from neighbors.

The rules for choosing among these courses of action have been known for a long time, but the calculations to find the answers are laborious because of the complexity of the problem, considering the many connections in the network and the many possible sources of energy. Since the utility must respond to a change of demand in a matter of minutes, there is no chance to perform the calculations manually. The computer has adequate speed, however, and it is so well suited to this application that its use for this purpose will probably become almost universal. The economic benefit can be very large, because an increase of a few percent in the efficiency of the utility's generating and distributing network can make an impressive difference in the profits of the company. The electric utility industry can apparently expect to recoup its investment in computers for control of power distribution many times over. ▶

In another class of "real-time" problem, the calculations to be performed are well understood and there is sufficient time for a human to perform them before the results are required. However, the volume of total work to be done (the number of times the problem occurs) is so great that it becomes impossibly expensive to assign an adequate number of humans to do the work perfectly each time. The result has usually been that the work is done less than perfectly, according to "rules of thumb." It is hoped that with the computer's help a more nearly perfect solution to each problem can be provided.

CASE 1E

◀ A large research hospital is experimenting with two areas in which it is hoped that the computer can assist the professional staff in simultaneously raising the average quality of medical help provided to each patient, reducing the risk of omission or failure, and at the same time lessening the work load on the staff.

The first of the two areas is computer assisted diagnosis. The examining physician or intern obtains from the patient a medical history, a statement of symptoms, and performs tests and evaluations, all designed to help him diagnose the nature of the patient's ailment. These data are fed to the computer, which uses programs prepared with the guidance of expert professionals to reach tentative diagnoses, and to recommend courses of future testing and specialist consultation in areas where doubt remains. It is not expected that the computer's diagnosis can be better than, or even as good as, that of the well-trained professional, but it is hoped that the computer will eventually be able to be of assistance in three ways:

1   The computer may reduce the risk that an erroneous diagnosis will be made because of oversight or fatigue on the part of the examining physician, or because of the unusual nature of the patient's ailment.

2   The process of diagnosis may be speeded up with the computer's help, thereby providing both a reduction in work load on the diagnosing physician and more rapid treatment for the patient.

3   Because the computer is available to act as a guide to the diagnosing physician, it is hoped that the professional level at which routine diagnosis is performed can be reduced somewhat. If the specialist or experienced physician can be spared the task of diagnosing influenza, indigestion, and other easily recognized and common ailments, presumably he will be able to concentrate more on subtle and challenging situations.

The second area of experimentation is patient monitoring. Here, the objective is to provide automatic sensing devices for each patient judged to be in critical condition, providing continuous readings of such important factors as blood pressure, respiration, pulse, and temperature. The computer will frequently or continuously monitor these readings for all the patients being monitored, and inform the staff of any changes in sensor readings which might indicate a significant change in the condition of the patient. The purpose of this experimental program is two-fold: first, to reduce the load of continuous surveillance and monitoring presently required of the staff, and second, to provide more rapid reaction to critical and sudden changes than is possible even with the present observation schedule.

Both of these experimental efforts are still in the development stage. The diagnosis area is incompletely developed because of the difficulty in communicating swiftly and completely with the computer. The patient monitoring area proceeds slowly largely because of the high cost of acquisition and installation of the sensing devices, though limited installations are already being made widely. It is hoped that as the solutions to these problems are found, such systems may be installed not only in the experimental hospitals now working with them, but by degrees in all other hospitals. ▶

Such applications as the above are obviously intended not to eliminate the human judgmental function where it is needed, but to relieve the trained human of the need to perform a great number of routine and mechanical evaluations in cases where his judgmental capability is not required. There are many other areas in which comparable development is occurring, most notably that of computer assisted instruction. The professional teacher has the same problems of high work load and a combination of routine tasks and more expert functions. This area will be discussed further later; in brief, by taking advantage of the computer's ability to perform complex procedures rapidly, it is hoped that all parties will benefit: the professional because of a reduction in work load and an increase in the level at which his talents are used, and the individual patient or student because he is guaranteed at least a minimum level of performance with a greatly reduced margin for error, and (hopefully) a higher degree of access to the talents of the professional when his case requires them. The attention of those wishing to exploit the computer fully is increasingly being directed to such areas.

ABILITY TO MANIPULATE MODELS

Unfortunately, the human's understanding of the problems or processes with which he deals rarely enables him to reduce them to mathematical equations capable of completely accurate solution by computers or any other mechanical means. No businesses, for example, can be completely described by equations when such uncontrolled variables as government tax or subsidy policy may have unpredictable effects. However, it is often possible in the

HUNT LIBRARY
CARNEGIE-MELLON UNIVERSITY

absence of full understanding to develop a mathematical model of a process or system which, while not accurate in every detail, is approximately correct. By using the imperfect model to test various possibilities, the manager can learn more about the process, and by steadily improving the model as experience accumulates, he can make it more and more useful. A great deal of the most interesting current computer development work is devoted to developing simulation models for both businesses and scientific systems, where precise relationships between cause and effect cannot be determined ahead of time but where the model's representation of the system is approximately correct. By experimenting with the model, by determining what effects various combinations of variables have on the results, and by developing and discarding hypotheses about cause and effect by trying them out within the model, the researcher has an unprecedented opportunity to experiment with the system being studied without the cost and difficulty of duplicating it in a real model. Indeed, many of the systems being studied could not possibly be physically modeled by the experimenter.

CASE 1F

◀   Astrophysicists have for many years attempted to understand the nuclear reactions and other physical events occurring in the interiors of stars. Such studies, once entirely theoretical in nature, are currently assuming a much more practical aspect because of the search for thermonuclear power generating systems. Obviously, the astrophysicist is not able to make a star in his laboratory and measure what takes place inside it. Until recently, all he could do was make telescopic observations of real stars and develop hypotheses about the events in the interior of the star that could produce the observed results. In recent years, however, astrophysicists have taken to using the computer to test possible models of stellar interiors. The computer's memory is divided into thousands of small areas, each a "cell" representing conditions in a small part of the interior of the star being modeled. The materials in each cell, the reactions taking place, and the flows of heat and radiant energy between the cells can be represented by the experimenter as expressions he provides to the computer's program.

Having set up such a hypothetical model of a star he wishes to study, the experimenter can then "start the star running." The computer calculates the results of the reactions occurring in each cell during a short time interval, then calculates the resulting effects during the next time interval in each neighboring cell. The effect of each cell on every other is calculated—a far too lengthy task for manual workers. He can allow the computer to run for as long as he wishes, with the computer in each successive time interval simulating the action of the entire star by computing the interactions in each cell and in every other cell. The outer periphery of the star will soon show the effect of these reactions (it will emit a certain intensity and spectrum of radiation; the star as a whole may expand, contract, heat up, cool down, or explode). The experimenter is then enabled to check the validity of his model against conditions observed in real stars. ▶

Using the computer as a tool for simulating interactions among elements of a system, experimenters studying either scientific problems or business organizations have a new and immensely powerful means of advancing their knowledge about systems and processes. As this understanding becomes perfected in a given case, the model becomes developed to the point of providing precise solutions and predictions. The computer can then be used to provide the accurate information required for operations control. This ability of the computer to manipulate models is not yet used nearly as fully as its ability to assist with clerical work, because of the difficulty of developing models and the programs to manipulate them. However, this ability is potentially of more fundamental importance, and many feel that in the long run users will benefit most from it. Its influence on individuals and organizations will be discussed in later chapters.

ABILITY TO CONTROL OTHER MACHINES

In every computer system, the central computer must be attached to other machines which it controls for accepting input from the outside world (punched card readers), for producing results in a form acceptable to its human masters (printers), and for storing files of information needed for subsequent reuse. Because of the cost and speed of the computer, great efforts have been made over the years to increase the speed and reliability of these "peripheral" devices to a level such that the computer would not have to waste time by stopping and waiting for them to operate. As a result of these efforts, computer peripheral devices have become so fast and capable that many computer applications have been developed which take more advantage of the capability of the peripheral devices than they do the capability of the computer itself. When used in such applications, the computer functions primarily as a control device.

CASE 1G
◀ Department stores have always made an effort to check the credit rating of a customer before permitting him to charge a purchase. Ideally, such a rating should include completely current information about the store's own experience with the customer, that of all other stores with which he has dealt, and pertinent information from other sources, such as records of bankruptcy courts

and the like. Furthermore, this information should be checked and reported in summary form in a matter of seconds, so that the customer and the sales person are not required to wait. It is obviously impossible to do all this, so stores have had to make do with less information and therefore take greater risks.

In a number of cities, centralized credit reference services have been set up that provide greatly improved service by using the computer's capability to store massive files of information and retrieve any given item in fractions of seconds. These firms (run for profit) attempt to collect all applicable credit information about every customer in a metropolitan area, and make it available to every subscribing firm by telephone in a matter of seconds. For example, one such organization now operating in Los Angeles obtains credit information from more than 3000 subscribing firms, as well as from other sources, and maintains credit records of more than nine million individuals. Each subscribing store has access to the file from any of the telephones in the store, and is guaranteed a complete report within a maximum of 90 seconds. As time goes on and the technology improves, this response time should be reduced further.* ▶

There is a great variety of applications in which the computer's ability to store massive files, and update and retrieve individual records rapidly, is of sufficient importance to justify purchase of a computer system. Some major ones are airline reservations, stock quotations, and (in some firms) inventory records. Also, there are many instances in which the computer's ability to control other kinds of peripheral devices has justified its use. For example, computers are used to control teletype switching centers, high speed document sorters, and devices that compose type for subsequent printing operations. As the variety and capability of the peripheral devices improves, presumably the computer's ability to control them will justify its use in still wider varieties of application areas.

In performing information handling operations, the computer is connected to peripheral devices that print documents, store files, and the like. The computer can also be connected through electrical controls to many other kinds of machinery, so it is possible for the computer to control industrial processes as well as simply to process information. This has made it possible to apply the computer's ability to repeat itself rapidly and precisely directly to production operations.

CASE 1H

◀ A large bakery of cakes and pastries had difficulty keeping its quality high as its volume of production increased. They had difficulty with variability in

---

* *Datamation,* October 1966.

the skill and motivation of the increasing number of laborers in the production operation. If the formulas the workers were to use called for only the necessary quantity of ingredients, spillage and the workers' errors would often result in shortages and inferior quality. If a sufficient margin for error in the formulas was introduced, the quality could be improved despite the errors. However, management was naturally anxious to operate economically, and not waste costly butter, sugar, and other expensive ingredients. After considerable study, the management decided to install a computer-controlled ingredient monitoring and mixing system in a new bakery they were building. The computer monitored and controlled the condition of each machine, and under control of its programs released precisely measured amounts of ingredients at the right times. The cost of the computer, its programs, the wiring, and the control instruments nearly doubled the capital cost of the new bakery. However, once the new bakery came into operation, management found that their hopes were realized; the automated bakery could produce consistent quality with a percentage of wastage sharply lower than any human production force had been able to achieve before. Because the cost of the new bakery was so high, they found that they would not realize an overall financial saving for many years, but the virtual disappearance of the quality problem was a great relief. ▶

In other cases computer control of production has resulted in more dramatic economies. For example, one of the major steel companies reports that when a computer was applied to controlling the repetitive operations involved in a hot strip rolling mill:

> Total production increased by 2%

> The percentage of product having acceptable thickness after one rolling operation increased from between 72% and 85% to 95%,

> Scrap was reduced by from 25% to 50% in comparison with earlier methods.*

SUMMARY

If the computer's only ability were that of repeating itself precisely, it would be well justified and widely used in clerical operations. It would, then, have significant value to organizations and individuals involved in clerical work. However, it also has much more fundamental strengths in its abilities to manipulate models, to control external devices, and to improve operational control of rapidly occurring events. Since the computer has been used mostly

---

* *Datamation,* August 1967.

for clerical work to date, its observed effects on organizations and individuals will prove to have derived mostly from its performance of clerical work—with surprisingly widespread ramifications. The computer's other strengths, when exploited more widely, will in the future prove to have a much more fundamental impact on individuals and organizations. As examples in later chapters will show, applications of these strengths are already widespread enough to give clues as to the possible outcomes, and to guide those making decisions about the computer's use.

CHAPTER 2

COMPENSATING FOR
THE COMPUTER'S WEAKNESSES

". . . Losses for the fiscal year were due to the installation
of a digital computer which hopelessly confused the affairs of the company."

Few companies are willing to be as candid as the Australian company reported to have included the above phrase in its annual report, but a great many have had unexpected and painful difficulty in attempting to make computers do their work. Indeed, in some areas where it had been hoped that the computer would be of great service, the computer has not only proved of little use but appears unlikely to ever be of use. The computer has weaknesses, drawbacks, and limitations which prevent its being the panacea for harassed businesses or "amplifier of man's intellect" that some proponents have claimed it to be. In this chapter the weaknesses of the computer will be explored, part of the necessary basis for efforts to understand the computer's impact on organizations and individuals, and important guidance for those anxious to exploit it effectively.

INABILITY TO PERCEIVE RELATIONSHIPS

A computer's memory is precise and infallible, while that of the human is imperfect. The human memory will record specific quantities (e.g., telephone numbers) only when they are laboriously memorized. A computer cannot fail to remember every item ever stored in it. However, a human can easily remember a face composed of hundreds of details, differing only in small ways from hundreds of other faces he remembers, each of them composed of hundreds of details. The human cannot tell how he does this, but presumably

---

* *Electronic News,* December 6, 1967.

he remembers not the details of an acquaintance's facial structure but a relationship between these details such that an "impression" associated with the face is uniquely associated with the identity of the person remembered. The human perceives faces not as patterns of discrete and measurable details, but as a relationship of them all. He perceives situations in the same way. He knows that he has time to enter the traffic flow of a highway because his experience in evaluating visual relationships tells him that his car can accelerate to the speed of the traffic before the nearest on-coming car has reached him. The human does not "solve" this problem; he does not calculate the relationships among the distances, speeds, and accelerations and produce a numerical result. The human would require much more than the available time while the computer, properly programmed, can perform such computations almost instantaneously. In this respect the computer is incomparably superior to humans. On the other hand, the computer is incomparably inferior in its ability to perceive relationships. The ability to distinguish faces is innate in the human and is practiced by him as early as two weeks of age. A corresponding ability to differentiate faces is entirely lacking in the computer, however, not only because impossible quantities of computer memory and computing time would be required to manipulate the mass of numeric measurements needed to describe a large number of faces, but also because no computer program has been developed which would enable the computer to differentiate. This and many other simple tasks easily performed by humans seem irritatingly out of reach of computers, no matter how much work goes into trying to "teach" them.

The area of optical character recognition has been the focus of much expense and effort devoted to trying to make the computer perceive relationships. The human can read letters and numbers in various forms; typewritten and machine printed, block printed by hand, and handwritten in long hand. The human does this by perceiving the characteristics of the shape he sees, and relating them to those that his memory tells him uniquely identify this shape as a letter or digit: he relates the characteristics to each other, and to those he remembers. He also considers relationships to the context in which the letter or digit appears, particularly in his reading of handwriting. The identity and meaning of the other letters in the word, and of the other words in the sentence and paragraph, are all applied to identifying the letter being read.

Optical character recognition is of great economic importance because, at present, information in media used by humans must be manually transformed into media suitable for unambiguous conversion into computer language. This manual transcription, usually the preparing of punched cards containing the content of business documents, is time-consuming and expensive. There are at least 500,000 keypunch machines at use in the United

States, each with an operator. The direct cost of each operator-machine combination is at least $6000 per year, so at least $3 billion per year are spent in the U.S. for the transcription of documents to punched cards. The economic incentive for developing satisfactory optical character reading devices is obviously very great, and machine manufacturers have for more than a decade been investing their resources in attempts to develop such machines. An examination of why they have not been completely successful, despite their great research and development efforts, is instructive in illustrating the computer's inability to perceive relationships.

CASE 2A

◀ A manufacturer of business machines decided to develop an optical character reading device. Market research convinced him that ample sales opportunities existed for machines having only a numeric capability, so he decided to omit the more complex alphabetic characters for the time being. However, he decided to include a capability to read digits block printed in pencil by humans as well as typewritten digits, because he found a large market for the capability of reading hand-printed digits: many sales slips, inventory and requisition forms, and the like are most conveniently filled out by hand. His engineers felt that the perception of relationships required to read block printing would be no more difficult than in reading typewritten characters.

Inspection of sample documents showed that it would be necessary to accept digits varying widely in size, in position on the paper, and in overall shape. The manufacturer's engineers were not daunted by these requirements, however, because of the simple observation that any human could distinguish the digits in the sample documents. They saw no reason why they could not develop a machine which could use the same relationships between the characteristics of the digits' shapes that humans use. They proceeded to exhaustively analyze large samples of both printed and hand written digits, finding by tests using typical human clerks which variations of the digits were legible. They expected the machine to be able to perform digit recognition at the same level of skill as the human clerks. From these studies they inferred the characteristics the humans used in their discrimination, and designed electronic logic circuits to apply the same rules to the digits on the documents being fed into the machine. In all, there were fourteen such rules. Each of the fourteen was applied to each digit read, identifying the presence of such characteristics as one or two closed loops, concavity to right or left, or horizontal "tails" to right or left.

Machines were built and installed that accurately applied the fourteen rules, and their performance was observed. The results are summarized in Fig. 2–1, with typical digits successfully read shown in the left-hand column and

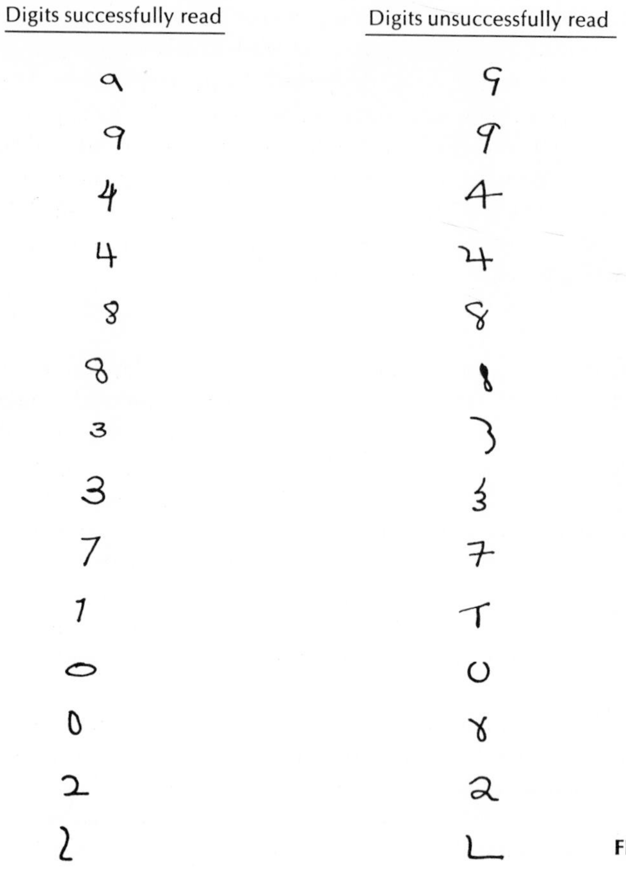

Digits successfully read	Digits unsuccessfully read
9	9
9	9
4	4
4	4
8	8
8	1
3	3
3	3
7	7
1	T
0	U
0	8
2	2
2	L

FIGURE 2–1

typical digits misread shown in the right-hand column. To the casual glance the misread digits appear little worse than the acceptable ones, and human clerks can read almost all the digits in both columns. The machine's blind application of the fourteen rules, then, provided results quite different from and inferior to those achieved by humans. Even though the fourteen rules apparently duplicated all the discrimination processes applied by humans, it became clear that the human's perception of relationships operates at a higher level that escaped the machine's designers (and still does).

The machine's users were able to obtain satisfactory results by establishing strict rules for the printing of digits to be fed to the machine (e.g., all fours should be open at the top and show a "tail" in the middle to the right of the vertical; no twos should have loops at the bottom left, etc.). The product was therefore not a failure. However, the original attempt to duplicate mechanically the relationships humans perceive in discriminating between digits un-questionably failed.   ▶

It would be desirable for computers to work in many areas involving relationships: analysis and recognition of fingerprints, interpretation of elec-trocardiogram tracings, identification of faces in group photographs, spotting potential enemy installations in aerial reconnaissance photographs, and de-termining the location of possible oil-bearing strata from seismograph traces. Sometimes partially successful "screening" operations can be performed by the computer, as in cases where a computer reduces the number of spark chamber photographs the investigator must review. In no case, though, do the machines equal the ability of trained humans. It is apparent that the com-puter's inability to perceive relationships, to perform a function innate to the human brain, virtually precludes its use in a large number of potentially useful and economically important information handling applications. Potential computer users must be sure that, if any relationships are to be perceived by the computer, explicit instructions for doing so have been incorporated in its programs.

INABILITY TO HANDLE HUMAN LANGUAGES

Human languages reflect human minds—ambiguous, emotional, colorful, de-pending heavily on shared experience, connotations, and context. Human languages are useless for communicating with computers, because the com-puter cannot apply any of these factors to language comprehension. The human, on the other hand, cannot help applying them to his comprehension. The computer is equally unable to produce human language. It can be equipped with devices which enable it to emit audible sounds, so it can be programmed to report the results of its calculations as audible sounds rather than printed digits. The sounds emitted are only syllables or words selected by the program, though, so this is not the use of language in any real sense. The computer's audio output device is simply playing back one of a limited, preestablished group of responses.

This language limitation of computers is not obvious, because computers can deal with a relatively large vocabulary of what appear to be words in human language. Computer programs can be developed that recognize any number of symbols, and these symbols may have corresponding meanings to humans. It is perfectly possible to so program a computer that it has a "vocabulary" of 10,000 words or more, both for recognizing input material and for generating output material. However, the nature of this vocabulary will be such that each word provided to the computer causes only a limited response, exactly identical every time the same word is supplied. Similarly, the words provided by the computer as part of its output material will be precisely predetermined by the program based on the results of the computation, and will always be identical if the results of the computations are identical. The untrained observer, seeing a large variety of words in human language being fed to the computer and being emitted by it assumes that it is, in fact, using language as a human does. He is not aware that these words are being used simply as symbols with no more meaning than the plus and minus signs of mathematical expressions.

CASE 2B

◀ It is difficult and expensive to prepare computer programs, because the individual instruction the computer can execute accomplishes only a tiny quantity of work. In order to complete a task of any complexity, hundreds or thousands of individual computer instructions have to be strung together in a sequence which accomplishes the required job. Within such long sequences of instructions, there are always subsequences or groups of instructions which occur many times over, each performing a simple operation such as comparing one quantity to another or ordering a group of quantities into a pre-established sequence. Years ago it was observed that if programmers could be relieved of the necessity of rewriting the groups of instructions every time the repetitive functions had to be performed, the labor of writing programs would be reduced. The programmer would be provided with a set of symbols, each symbol corresponding to a group of machine instructions that performs a frequently needed function. In preparing his program, the programmer need only include one of the symbols at the point in the program where the function is to be performed. Then the machine, recognizing the symbol, would substitute for it the group of machine instructions previously stored in the machine and associated with the symbol. Other ideas such as describing items of data by symbols were developed, all with the objective of simplifying programming by permitting the programmer to use symbols corresponding to sizable groups of machine instructions instead of writing them all out.

Efforts starting with these ideas led by many stages of evolution to today's powerful "compiler" programs. They enable the programmer to express his wishes in a vocabulary of symbols to a compiler program. It recognizes the symbols and converts them into sets of machine instructions which, compiled together, constitute the program required to carry out the task. The programmer's job is greatly reduced, because instead of writing thousands of individual instructions, he may need to write only a few score in the language of symbols acceptable to the compiler.

The designers of compilers intended to be used for business and clerical problems naturally turned to the English language as a source of symbols.

After all, if one wishes to instruct a program to "stop," what more convenient symbol for this function could there be than the word "stop"? A series of developments of English language compilers took place, culminating in today's very powerful COBOL (Common Business Oriented Language) compiler. Using it, a programmer can develop a set of statements describing a task he wishes the machine to perform that read almost like English text, thereby giving the nontrained person the impression that the programmer is communicating with the machine in English.

This is, of course, not true; the programmer is using only symbols of highly precise and identically repetitive meaning, not the original English word. To illustrate the distinction, the following list is presented. The left-hand column includes symbols acceptable to the standard COBOL compiler, together with a definition of the function of each. In the right-hand column, for comparison purposes, is presented a condensation of the Webster's Dictionary definition of the word used. It is immediately apparent from the comparison of the two columns that the words have a far more restrictive and rigidly defined meaning when used with the COBOL compiler, and that they are in only a very limited way equivalent to the same words used by the human in speaking English. In the case of MOVE, for example, if the computer interpreted the word according to its definition in human speech, the result would be wrong most of the time.

COBOL Symbol

MOVE (always used in the form MOVE[Data-name-1] TO [Data-name-2]). Meaning: relocate the information in a previously defined computer storage location to another previously defined computer storage location.

Condensed Dictionary Definition*

MOVE (as verb): to go continuously from one point to another; to start away from some point or place; to change position; to show marked activity; to propose formally in a deliberative assembly. (As noun): the turn of a player to move; a step taken to gain an objective. Synonyms: actuate, drive, impel.

PERFORM (always followed by a procedure name). Meaning: execute the procedure, or set of statements, associated with the given procedure name.

PERFORM: to adhere to the terms of; to carry out; to do in a formal manner or according to a prescribed ritual; to give a performance. Synonyms: execute, discharge, accomplish, achieve, effect, fulfill.

---

* *Webster's Seventh New Collegiate Dictionary*, G.&C. Merriam Company, Springfield, Massachusetts, 1967.

ACCEPT (always used in the form ACCEPT[Data-name] FROM[Device-name]). Meaning: actuate the input device associated with the given device name, and store one unit of information in the computer's storage. Both the unit of information and the location in computer storage are specified by the data name, which has been described previously.

ACCEPT: to receive with consent; to endure without protest; to regard as normal, proper or inevitable; to make a favorable response; to assume an obligation to pay.

▶

Mathematicians centuries ago developed a completely specific language of mathematical notation. Unlike words, mathematical symbols define rigidly identical and completely specified procedures, so mathematical symbols can readily be converted to computer programs. Because of this, the development of compilers for mathematical work was much easier than the development of compilers using terms from everyday language. Compiler languages for the use of mathematicians are therefore both more satisfactory and more advanced than those available for business data processing, so the use of computers in mathematical applications is (relatively) more fully developed.

One of the areas in which the language barrier between humans and computers has been particularly frustrating is in the application of computers to information retrieval. All scientists and engineers (indeed, almost every person engaging in organized activities in which others are also engaged) must maintain an awareness of published and previously recorded material. In most fields, not only is there a mass of material produced in past years of which the worker must be aware before he can hope to add anything new to the structure, but also there is such a volume of current material being published that it is almost impossible to remain continuously aware of it. Because of this, an investigator may duplicate work recently done by others because the publication in which the results appeared did not happen to come to his attention. More common and perhaps more serious, an investigator's direction of interest or attention might become obsolete because he is unaware of all the work being done by others in his field. Because computers can search through large files of information at great speed, from the very first appearance of computers it was hoped that the machines could be powerful aids in storing and retrieving information. For fifteen years or more efforts have been made to develop files and computer programs that would enable computers to identify and reproduce information related to inquirers' questions. The Federal Government, educational institutions, and private organizations have all been active in this field, but to the disappointment of the early workers and enthusiasts in the field only a few really effective computer-based information retrieval systems now exist. Furthermore, those that do exist impose a severe burden of strict and limited use of terminology on the user.

CASE 2C

◀ In developing new drugs and medicines it is vital to both public health officials and researchers that they be continually aware of both past and current experience with drugs under investigation or on the market, so that information about difficulties or unexpected drawbacks connected with particular drugs can lead to early termination of their use or further investigation. It is a responsibility of the Federal Government to determine that all drugs on the market, for human and animal use, are both safe and efficacious. This is a difficult responsibility to exercise, because powerful and effective drugs are also likely to be dangerous ones, even when used by experienced physicians. No matter how thorough or extensive the period of trial before a drug is put on the market, it is possible that unusual side effects may occur: sometimes in conjunction with other drugs, or with combinations of ailments of the patient, or with his physical condition, which were not experienced during the trials. If these side effects are sufficiently severe, they may justify the removal of the drug from the market, and the abandonment of efforts to develop similar drugs. The problem of evaluating such side effects is complex, because they usually take the form of ailments that could have been caused by other factors (e.g., deformed babies, low blood pressure, or allergic reactions).

In order to help discharge its responsibility, the government undertook more than five years ago to set up a computer-based system for storing and retrieving reports of possible adverse reactions to drugs. These reports were to be collected from the entire scientific community, and the services of the system were to be available to all. Because the volume of reports of possible adverse reactions is large and the searches for suspected combinations of conditions are complex, the use of a computer to store them, search through them, and reproduce them in response to investigators' questions was essential. A computer program was therefore designed which could search through the records of reported adverse reactions, each coded in accordance with many criteria such as the age, weight, sex, medical history, and ailments of the patient, other drugs the patient had been taking or exposed to, and the like. The computer program was also provided with records of the ingredients of drugs in use, so that an investigator seeking information about the effect of a particular substance used in a family of drugs could ask for appearances of the substance in suspected adverse reactions, instead of having to specify the name of each drug that contained the substance.

Early experiments with this program indicated clearly that it would not be possible to allow investigators to ask questions of the computer in their own language, even though the language used was a precise set of scientific terms. The words used by the human abstractors who assigned terms to each of the reports filed in the system, and the terms used by the investigators asking questions of the system, could not automatically be assumed to be used with identical meanings. For example, a team of abstractors might use the medical term "pyrexia" if the reaction was an elevation of the patient's body temperature, while an investigator might ask a question including the term "fever." Any human trained in the field would automatically regard the terms as synonymous, but the computer would reject all appearances of "pyrexia" while looking for "fever." To prevent problems of this kind, special dictionaries of terms were developed to be used by both the abstractors and the investigators, so that if the accepted lists were used by both parties, each investigator would be provided with all information relevant to his question and with no irrelevant information.

In attempting to provide a dictionary of terms that would cover all possible descriptions of conditions associated with an adverse drug reaction, and that would also include all terms likely to be used by investigators in asking their questions, the developers of the system found that they would have to incorporate as many as 100,000 terms. Though most of the terms had simple, single meanings, unfortunately the definitions had to be so precise that investigators were required to check all terms in the dictionary before submitting questions, in order to make sure that they were correctly used. This imposed a clerical task on the investigators so time-consuming and unwelcome that it became necessary to assign clerks to the investigators for the specific job of helping them formulate their questions. This increased the cost of the system and decreased its responsiveness. Also, the original concept of the investigator "conversing" with the machine was lost. More seriously, the abstractors of the adverse reaction reports, despite their constant familiarity with the dictionary, nevertheless found it very difficult to abstract each incoming report in a completely uniform manner, using the same terms consistently day after day. Words with similar meanings, or nearly interchangeable codings, would "creep in" to the abstracting of reports which should have been filed under identical terms, thereby weakening the system's power to respond completely and consistently.

The system worked as originally designed, but at so much higher cost than anticipated and with so much less responsiveness and utility to the investigators that operation of the system was discontinued, pending further research into improved systems. ▶

As this case indicates, the language barrier between humans and computers makes it difficult to use them for information retrieval purposes. However, the need is so great that work continues to make them more effective and responsive. While this work has not led to any solution to communication problems between man and machine, some techniques have been developed to the point that fully useful systems appear possible in some areas. One such technique involves using the computer to help the investigator formulate his question.

CASE 2D

◀ An agency developing military command and control systems was assigned the task of designing a computer-based information retrieval system to reproduce information about defensive forces available for assignment. The designers, recognizing the problems of terminology, sought ways of relieving the human questioners of the burdens of remembering the terms the machine's programs and files were designed to deal with. They developed an approach in which the computer would offer terms for the inspection and selection of the questioner. By a sequence of selections, he could formulate a question having the meaning he intended, but made up entirely of terms already existing within the machine's vocabulary. There was no chance that unacceptable or ambiguous terms could be used, since no terms could be used other than those presented by the machine to the questioner.

The mechanism used was a cathode-ray tube display similar to a television screen, and a "light pen" which enabled a questioner to point at terms on the screen and select them. Figure 2–2 shows a simplified representation of the display with which the questioner would be confronted at the beginning of his effort to formulate a question. This "tree" of terms includes all the possible types of questions the questioner is allowed to ask of the system, and terms corresponding to lists of specific names among which the questioner

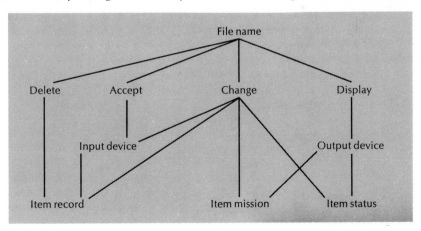

FIG. 2–2 Computer-displayed "tree" for formulation of information requests.

can make a choice. For example, the term "file name" on the first line, when selected by the light pen, will result in the display of a table of the names of the computer's files for the questioner. When he selects a file name with the light pen, the original tree is displayed again and the machine awaits his selection of a term on the second line which will instruct it what to do with the file whose name has just been selected. In general, paths down the left side of the tree are for adding or deleting items in the file, paths down the center are for changing the current status of the item, and paths down the right are for inspecting or reporting current status. The questioner proceeds to select specific terms down the branch of the tree corresponding to the function he wants the machine to perform, and at the end he has developed a command to the machine which is guaranteed acceptable to it because only terms offered by the machine have been used in making up the command. ▶

Information retrieval systems allowing man to communicate with the machine by methods such as these offer promise, because the machine's terminology is used while the system is still responsive and rapid from the point of view of the human questioner. Such methods suffer from the inherent difficulty that the number of terms offered to the questioner is limited, and that the terms he would naturally use may not be in the machine's vocabulary at all. The investigators therefore struggle to develop computer programs that will deal with terms of ever-increasing degree of generalization, as well as programs containing larger and larger dictionaries of acceptable terms. Such efforts may succeed to the point where computer-based information retrieval systems are useful for many purposes. However, such success would arise not because investigators have solved the problems posed by the computer's inability to handle human language, but because the investigators had found a convenient and acceptable way for the human to adapt himself to the machine's precise symbology. Those interested in using computers must be prepared to make this adaptation; unfortunately it is up to the human user to compensate for this weakness of the computer.

The computer's inability to handle human languages is also a limitation to the development of computer-assisted instruction. A combination of the population explosion and the technological explosion have imposed unprecedented pressures on educational resources. These pressures are felt wherever education or training must be performed: in public schools, in public and private colleges and universities, in industry, in Government and the Armed Forces. Unprecedented numbers of students must be taught subjects of ever-increasing complexity, and the demand for qualified teachers far outstrips the supply. This is true not only because of an absolute shortage in numbers of teachers, but also because many of the subjects being taught are so new that there has not been time to develop teacher-training curricula and a body of qualified educators. (This is nowhere more true, incidentally, than in the computer field itself. The great volume of computers being installed requires a corresponding volume of systems analysts and programmers to put them to use, and the shortage is severe. The ability of organized education to meet the need is inadequate because the field is too new.)

The computer's speed, its ability to perform complex calculations rapidly, and its ability to select among many paths through a program in response to varied inputs make it seem an attractive possibility to assist in the educational process. If any significant part of the educational load could be shifted from humans to machines, a significant reduction in today's critical pressures might be accomplished.

Unfortunately, in the broadest sense the educational process is one in which human language must be used in its broadest form. The communication of ideas, of comprehension, of understanding of concepts, requires a dialogue in which the teacher is as responsible as the student for sensitive comprehension. The student's replies to the teacher's questions and suggestions must be sensitively analyzed to determine the student's true level of comprehension. The teacher must adapt to the student by organizing his stimuli in such a way that the student's comprehension is furthered, and each successive response displays the greater comprehension for which the teacher is striving.

As we have already seen, the computer is ill-suited to such an adaptive and interactive conversational process. While its programs can be complex and can incorporate a theoretically unlimited number of responses to specific inputs, the computer remains a machine in which a given input always produces an identical response. Instructional programs can expose the student to a program of successive stimuli, each of which evokes one of a few pre-established responses in the form of multiple choice selections between possible answers. Each of the choices leads through another pre-established sequence in the program: the main sequence of further development if the answer was the correct one, a sequence of corrective material if the answer was wrong, and at worst a repetition of material previously covered. Such methods of presentation are most suited to the so-called "drill and practice" subjects, where the student is acquiring rote learning or specific skills rather than higher levels of abstract comprehension. Existing programs, for example, can successfully teach the student how to use the acceptable terms of the COBOL compiler language and to construct acceptable programs using them. However, the underlying ability to analyze problems and define them in such a form that computer programs can be written for their solution cannot as yet be taught by means of such programs. Similarly, a student in a foreign language can be introduced to basic vocabulary and grammatical rules by such programs, but comprehension and appreciation of the literature in the language lies beyond their present scope.

Because most such programs of instruction involve the student's choosing between alternative pages for his next stimulus they can be presented quite adequately in the form of books, without any machine needed. The computer is used in today's instructional programs primarily where it is useful to present a complex display, or where a program has so many branches that it would be impractical or inconvenient to incorporate them in a printed book. In principle, however, the art of computer-assisted instruction today is at such a level that the computer is not required to support it.

This will not always be true. As with information retrieval, the complexity of the program and the number of alternative terms with which it can deal can be expanded to such a point that a semblance of true language comprehension can be achieved. Furthermore, even if computer-assisted instruction is always restricted to vocational or "drill and practice" subjects, they constitute such a large proportion of required education that the impact of the computer would still be great. Probably, even with its language limitations, the computer can be significant in alleviating the educational crisis. If its programmers are sufficiently capable, it can probably reach well out into subject areas skeptics would assign permanently to the realm of the human teacher. The evolution of instructional programs should probably continue for at least two or three decades before a critic should presume to confidently predict the limits of computer-aided instruction. This assertion is borne out by the following series of quotes, all taken from a survey article attempting to depict the present status of computer-assisted instruction.*

Mr. Robert Callan, General Electric Company: "Computers should compute, teachers should teach, and kids should turn their own pages."

Mr. Harold B. Gores, President, Ford Foundation Educational Facilities Laboratory: "From now on, *things* should be taught by machine . . . the teacher is raised to the level of *meaning. Things* from machines, *values* from people."

Dr. Patrick C. Suppes, Stanford University: "We are on the edge of some very new stuff, very deep. With this technology we may be able to give each kid the personal services of a tutor as well informed and as responsible as Aristotle."

It is apparent that the experts are in disagreement; only time will determine who is right. In any case, it is clear that the computer's success in instructing students will be dependent on the abilities of the programmers to push back

---

* Enoch Hays, *CAI: A Commencement. Business Automation,* November 1967.

the language barrier by increasing the cleverness and adaptability of their programs. The computer's inability to handle human language will not be eliminated in the process, but only made less apparent.

A final annoying aspect of the computer's inability to handle human language is its difficulty in dealing with graphic or pictorial material. That this is the main form of human communication and comprehension is evidenced by the fact that a simple telephone number requires memorization, while the association of a face with an individual personality requires no conscious effort. This results, of course, in the human using graphic media and pictorial material widely in his work: the map, the photograph, the chart. The computer, having been constructed solely to deal with numeric, digital quantities, must be forced at considerable inconvenience to deal with graphic material at all.

CASE 2E

◄ A computer manufacturer became aware that an unmet market need existed for pictorial and graphic output from computers, and he learned that suitable devices existed for forming the images. In particular, he was attracted by a television-type device that could form a picture of very high quality. It was able to divide its screen from top to bottom into 2000 separately "painted" lines, so that a typical document ten inches high could be produced with 200 lines per inch; this would give a solid appearance to the eye. Each line was made up of 2000 spots from the left end to the right end; even more per inch. Finally, each spot could be set at any of seven levels of gray ranging from white to black. The manufacturer became convinced that this device would do an excellent job of reproducing all images (as long as color was not required), so he considered using it as a standard item in his product line for producing pictorial outputs.

When the manufacturer's programmers investigated the computing requirements required by the device, however, they made an unfortunate discovery. The device required an instruction for every point on its display; 2000 spots per line times 2000 lines, or 4,000,000 instructions in all. Each instruction had to tell the device which of the seven levels of gray was required for the spot, considering the image required and the shades of gray in the adjacent spots. The most efficient program the programmers could develop required about one thousandth of a second to compute each instruction, using the computer the manufacturer intended to associate with the image-forming device. The total time required to develop a picture, then, would be 4000 seconds or well over an hour. Since the computer and image-forming device were expensive, this was far too slow to be economically acceptable and the manufacturer had to abandon the idea of his "universal" pictorial output device.

Since many of his customers needed only a capability for producing line drawings or graphs, the manufacturer turned to an automatic graph plotter as an alternative. This device could move an inked pen over a paper in small steps in response to electrical signals. It, too, required an instruction for each step, but had the advantage that a straight line of any length required only a single instruction, giving the direction and number of steps in the line. Graphs consisting only of straight lines required relatively few instructions, and curved lines could be represented by a series of short straight lines (just as a child connects numbered dots with short straight lines to form a figure with curved outlines). The programmers found that fairly complex graphs containing both straight and curved lines could be drawn by giving the plotter from 2000 to 4000 instructions. The resulting graphs had no shades of gray, and the curved lines were clearly broken lines rather than continuous curves. However, the plotter was relatively inexpensive and could run independently of the computer once the instructions had been computed and stored on magnetic tape or punched cards. The process was economically feasible and useful for some of the computer manufacturer's customers, so he added the plotter to his product line and abandoned further efforts to develop pictorial output devices. ▶

The computer is not completely unable to deal with pictorial material, as this case shows; however, complex programs and large quantities of computer time are required. Presumably as programs improve and as computers become less expensive, the human's demand for pictorial and graphic material will be more nearly met by the computer, but always by forcing it to perform a function that it is not naturally capable of.

LACK OF PERSONALITY

The computer is purely literal; it has no emotions; it has no experience or cultural frame of reference; therefore, it has no personality. This is one of the greatest of the computer's inherent weaknesses relative to humans, because the entire body of the human's experience is in dealing with agencies that have personalities, namely, other humans. Whenever he is forced to deal with an impersonal agency, whether a bureaucracy or a machine, the human becomes defensive and hostile. He loses his "influence"; his ability to "sell" the other party; the possibility of using his personality rather than purely factual data and logic to gain an end. The human, forced to deal with an impersonal agency, feels reduced to an impersonal agent himself. He loses the grounds he has for feeling superior to other humans, and objects to being forced into the position of being the same as all others. It is hardly necessary to cite examples to prove this point because almost certainly every reader (as well as the author) has felt some of this hostility himself in dealing with bureaucracy. The following case is interesting, however, not only because it is a classic of its kind, but also because (ironically) it illustrates the drawbacks of a case cited in Chapter 1 as a success of the computer; namely, its application in the Internal Revenue Service.

CASE 2F

◀ The following item is reproduced in its entirety as it appeared in the Congressional Record.*

"IMPERSONAL, COMPUTERIZED TAX COLLECTION

"Mr. Long of Missouri. Mr. President, we get more and more, newer and newer gadgets all the time, but how many of them add one iota to human happiness?

"One of the newest gadgets of which the U.S. Government seems to be proudest is its automated, computerized tax-collecting machine.

"Somewhere in West Virginia is a monster computer that is attempting —and I stress 'attempting'—to digest the Federal tax problems of 200 million Americans. According to the Commissioner of Internal Revenue, it is the greatest innovation since sliced bread.

"I wonder.

"In the first place, the monster computer appears to make an incredible number of errors; and once they are made, it seems incapable of correcting these errors.

"Second, have you ever tried corresponding with an IBM machine? It cannot be done.

"Last, but not least, Mr. President, have you ever tried to decipher one of the computer print-outs that IRS sends to all of us? If we knew every section of the Internal Revenue Code by heart, have an engineering degree from MIT, have spent 4 years in the Army decoding section, we might have a chance.

"To illustrate the human side of this inhuman machine, I ask unanimous consent to have printed in the RECORD a letter to the editor of the Portland, Maine, Press Herald.

"There being no objection, the letter was ordered to be printed in the RECORD, as follows:

'PENSIONER COMPLAINS OF IRS HARASSMENT

'EDITOR OF THE PRESS HERALD: The Constitution on which our country is founded promises that all men are free and equal and en-

---

* *Congressional Record,* September 12, 1967.

titled to the pursuit of happiness. Today we may ask what freedom, what happiness? We are living under a dictatorship as cruel as any in history.

'Here is one small example: The writer is 78 years of age, seriously ill, and barely existing on a small pension to which she contributed during her working years. At the proper time and with a real effort she filed an income tax report. No comment having been received from Internal Revenue, she assumed the report was accepted. Then several months later, like a bolt from the blue, came a bill on an IBM form billing her for a ridiculous amount of tax plus interest, with payment demanded within 20 days. Imagine the shock.

'This bill was returned to Internal Revenue with an explanation that no exemptions had been credited. There was no reply to this. A second time a bill came with more interest added. Again the writer asked that correction be made. No reply. When the third bill came the matter was taken to a lawyer who filed an amended report.

'Now comes a blast from Augusta headquarters threatening to put a lien on any and all property. That means the little home which was to provide shelter for the declining years. This amounts to persecution.

'Again we ask "what freedom, what happiness?"

'What rights have poor slobs like us?

'We want to know.

Mary S. Spear

Friendship'

"Mr. Long of Missouri. Mr. President, regardless of the merits or demerits of this particular case, I do know that there must be some better way to deal with American taxpayers than the current, depersonalized, implacable computer system being devised by the Internal Revenue Service.

"It may make work for the tax collectors a bit easier, but it surely is hard on 200 million Americans."   ▶

It is apparent that the IRS was at fault in this case; probably the early attention of a human agent could have resolved the matter without resorting to such extremes. The interesting point, however, is that both Miss Spear and Senator Long complained of the computer and the depersonalized inhuman agency it represents. The failure, as they could probably have guessed, is actually one of the management of the local District Office of the IRS. This example could easily be supported by a hundred others that have appeared in the press, but we are all familiar with them. It is evident that the computer's lack of personality evokes very general hostility.

It is not the fault of the computer that it has no personality; it is not supposed to have, and its strengths would likely be severely compromised if it had. The fault lies in humans for attributing to the machine the faults of the organizations that use it. It is apparent, however, that humans will always object in principle to being forced to deal with impersonal agencies and the computer will always be the epitome of such agencies. It is, therefore, possible to conclude that the computer's lack of personality will always be one of its drawbacks in relation to human society, and that its users will have to compensate by providing the necessary personal element themselves.

COST

It is expensive to use computers and it always will be. This flat assertion can be made in the face of the tremendous potential that exists for reduction in the cost of building computers, because the cost of using the computer has a number of components, of which only a few are affected by reductions in equipment cost.

Cost of system elements

The cost of the electronic circuits required to perform the computer's functions has dropped by more than a factor of ten during the last decade, and may drop by another factor of ten in the next decade. However, the computer must always be equipped with peripheral devices by which it communicates with its users. These peripheral devices are always partly mechanical whether the device be a keyboard, a punch card reader, a printer, a graph plotter, or something else. The mechanical peripheral devices associated with computers have declined in cost by at most a factor of two during the last ten years, and are unlikely to do as well in the next ten years because the mechanical manufacturing technology involved seems to be relatively mature. Since these peripheral devices already constitute more than half the manufacturing cost of most computer systems, it is apparent that reducing the cost of the electronics will have only a limited effect.

Even the expected electronic cost reductions may not produce much saving, because computer systems needed for the pressing new classes of problems are much more complex than earlier computers. For example, a computer which is to provide rapid service to a remote user over a communications link requires electronic devices of considerable complexity to interconnect the computer and the communications network. The computer must also include significant extra internal storage and computing capability to handle the clerical problems of keeping each user's work from becoming confused with that of the others. Also, modern computer systems are likely to be vitally important to the organizations using them. The computer storing reservation information for an airline is a typical example. Such a computer must not be out of action for extended periods; even outages of as long as a minute or two are poor public relations, because every customer dealing with an agent who queries the computer during that period will be inconvenienced and the airline's reputation will suffer. To keep such computer systems in virtually continuous operation with low risk of failure, it has been necessary in most cases to provide duplicate facilities so that if one should fail, the other can take over the work. This is not necessary with conventional systems that do not respond in real time to remote inquiries; with them, a delay of an hour or two in finishing a given job is rarely painful. Overall, the equipment required for the modern real-time computer system involves two or three times as much electronics as a system of an earlier day that could handle the same total quantity of work. This increase in complexity will largely offset any reduction that will occur in electronics manufacturing costs.

Cost of data preparation

Case 2A exemplified the difficulty of designing optical reading devices which will read business documents as well as a human does. It also noted the economic desirability of such devices because of the cost being incurred today by computer users in keypunching their data. If it is true that no easy solution to the problem of computer input preparation is likely to be found, this cost of using the machines will remain high indefinitely.

Cost of programming

At least 100,000 programmers and systems analysts are employed in the United States today to prepare programs for computer solution.* Considering that the total salary cost of these people is well over one billion dollars per year, it is apparent that the community is paying a high price for computer programming. So far, virtually every user has had to make his own investment in programming, through people on his own payroll or through contractors, to prepare computer programs useful in the user's particular operations.

A number of alternatives have been found that reduce the cost of programming somewhat for some users. Sometimes it is possible to develop programs that will serve a group of users having similar problems. For example, the processing of life insurance policy premiums (billing, collecting, and accounting for loans) is in certain basic ways similar among all life insurance companies (see Case IB). For those companies willing to process their policies in

---

* *The State of the Information Processing Industry,* American Federation of Information Processing Societies, 1966.

a simple manner, a single "package" of computer programs will serve for all of them. Several major computer manufacturers make available life insurance programs to help sell their equipment, and some small life insurance companies have saved a great deal of money they would otherwise have been forced to invest in program development by using the manufacturer's "packaged" programs. Another palliative has been the general improvement in capability and usefulness of compiler languages, both for business data processing and mathematical applications. As compilers improve, the cost of preparing all programs is reduced. However, as has been explained, compilers are useful only in the part of the programming process where actual machine instructions are being prepared. The earlier functions (often taking more time and effort) include problem definition, flow charting, and the establishment of error controls and exception handling procedures. These functions must always be performed before machine instructions are prepared, so at best compilers could affect no more than half the total cost of programming.

Apparently, then, the problem of preparing computer programs will always be a significant one, though future improvements may reduce it significantly. In particular, programming costs may be reduced because in time virtually every graduate of the higher educational system is likely to have some capability as a computer programmer. If he has not specifically been preparing computer programs as a student of the subject, he will have been doing so indirectly during his schooling as he deals with computer-assisted instruction devices. The effects of this will be explored in more detail later. For present purposes, it is sufficient to note that with virtually every college graduate a partially qualified computer programmer, the expenditure for specialist services will surely be lower.

In sum, it does not appear to be reasonable to expect the costs of computer usage to decline much. In fact, the opposite seems to happen: the organizations having the most experience in using computers keep increasing their annual investment in them, obtaining in the process more and more useful results. The per unit costs of equipment drop, but this is more than offset by the increased number and size of computers acquired. The competence of the programming staff increases, so that simple jobs become more economical to program, but this is more than offset by the attempt to program increasingly difficult and advanced applications. In effect, the more results the computer and programmers turn out, the more they are asked to do.

CASE 2G

◀ The small insurance company described in Case IB acquired a computer to help them with policy premium billing and accounting. Relying heavily on manufacturer-supplied general purpose programs for the insurance industry, they found that they required a programming staff of only six people, with an annual salary cost of $70,000. Their annual payments for their rented computer system were $84,000, so the total annual cost was $154,000. At this cost level they were able to satisfactorily perform their policy premium accounting with the computer using traditional methods, and were eventually completely satisfied that they had made the correct decision in acquiring the computer.

After they had used the computer for several years, they became aware that competitive insurance companies were using computers in more advanced ways. The first additional application area that came to their attention was the computation of actuarial statistics. They observed that their competitors were using computers for more advanced statistical studies than they were able to make by the traditional manual methods, and they decided to investigate this area for themselves. Accordingly, they hired two additional mathematically trained programmers, increasing their total to eight, who worked with their actuaries in developing programs to support this work. After a year this project became sufficiently successful that the insurance company management again agreed that they had proceeded wisely. No new equipment was required for this work, but the total annual cost had risen to $178,000.

At about the time this project was completed, the programming staff of the organization observed that other insurance companies were using more advanced computer equipment for "real-time inquiry systems," which made it possible for the insurance company's salesmen, actuaries, and managers alike to instantly obtain up-to-date information about policy status, claims, and the like through input-output devices attached to a computer with a random access file storage device. The company's ability to respond to inquiries and to make decisions would be enhanced by such a system, they thought, and a practical financial benefit would result from the quicker collection and processing of premium payments and loan repayments. After some study, the company decided to replace their present computer system with a new computer system capable of handling random inquiries from remote points, and the existing programming staff turned their efforts to redesigning the set of programs in such a way that this real-time operation could be supported. No new programmers were needed for this, because the original programming staff had sufficient time available to develop the new programming system in a period of approximately two years. More expensive equipment was required, however. A new machine was installed at a price of $13,000 per month, increasing the total annual expense to $250,000. An extensive period of "shaking down" was required not only because the entire computer system was different, but because the company's operational procedures were changed as a result of the new methods. The shake down period took about a year and a half after the new computer system was officially operational, so its total development and installation time was 3½ years.

At this point the insurance company had been in the process of developing computer applications for a total of 6½ years. During this time their programming staff had grown from an original six men to eight, and their total cost had grown from $154,000 per year to $250,000 per year. The company's management was willing to admit (somewhat ruefully) that they had had no intention of embarking on such a continuous development program when they first considered the use of a computer. However, they also asserted that they were very glad they had, not only because the company had become much more responsive and operationally efficient, but also because they had come to feel that, considering the comparable improvements made by their competitors, it had become impossible to compete effectively without such computer support. They anticipate that future developments will probably also occur, but they view this prospect with mixed emotions. They would be just as happy if they could spend at least two or three years getting used to their current system, and fully absorbing its effects on operations. ▶

Privately supported surveys consistently show that this case is typical; that organizations professing themselves to be happy with their computer systems typically spend more for them than organizations claiming only marginal satisfaction or dissatisfaction. This very interesting result indicates that most computer users should not look for decreases in the cost of computing, but rather for increased performance and satisfaction at the same or increasing cost. If this is even approximately true, it also indicates that the cost of using computers will indefinitely remain one of the drawbacks to their use, and that potential users must be willing to pay the price.

SUMMARY

In summary, four weaknesses of the computer have been discussed: its inability to perceive relationships, its inability to handle human languages, its lack of personality, and its cost. In each case, work is underway to reduce the difficulty and to push back the barrier to computer use. However, all four of these weaknesses seem inherent to the machine, fundamental to its concept and design. Though clever designers, programmers, and users can and will undoubtedly improve the situation steadily in all of these four areas as time goes by, it appears that no complete solution to any of these problems is likely to be found. We can expect, then, that any effects on organizations and individuals that result from the computer's weaknesses will continue to be felt for many years to come. We can also expect that any successful user of the computer will have considered these weaknesses in his planning, and arranged to compensate for them by human effort.

CHAPTER 3

MANAGING COMPUTER-CAUSED CHANGES

During the fifteen years that computers have existed in significant numbers, the society using them has been undergoing changes unparalleled in breadth and rapidity. Organizations have revolutionized their products, their structures, and their methods of doing business. They have been forced (whether they wished to or not) to adapt to increased government controls, to demographic changes, and to changes in the value systems of their employees and customers. Individuals in society have been changing, too, responding to changes in moral values, different patterns of living, and altered definitions of individuals' rights and entitlements vis-à-vis government. It is debatable whether all of these changes and their effects are beneficial, but it is not appropriate here to make value judgments; the relevant point is that these changes undeniably exist and profoundly influence the employment of computers.

Both organizations and individuals are experimenting with and being affected by many new tools made available by advancing technology. The computer is only one of these, and not necessarily the most influential. Organizations have responded to new tools such as inexpensive voice and wire communications, office copiers, microfilm systems, and jet-age air travel. In many cases their organizational structures and methods of doing business have been transformed as they took advantage of these tools; successful organizations today function in ways that would have been impossible a generation ago. Individuals' lives have also been changed greatly by this recent technology as they have responded to television, to inexpensive communications and travel, to increased leisure time, and to the accompanying host of new technologically based products for occupying it. Evidently the computer is only one of a family of technological innovations affecting the behavior of organizations and individuals, so its effect cannot be entirely isolated.

A continuing "climate of change" has developed because of this flow of innovation. The effects of the computer can be assessed only within this continuing climate of change, and along with the effects of other parallel influences. In studying the effects of the computer on organizations and individuals, then, it is necessary to consider the process of change which accompanies it. This chapter is devoted to the management of this process of change in procedural areas where the computer is likely to be used, how it takes place, and the constraints upon it.

LIMITS ON THE RATE OF CHANGE

No enthusiast could be disappointed with the rate at which organizations have taken to using computers. More than 60,000 have been installed in the United States, far more than the most optimistic forecasters of a few years ago foresaw. This would seem to indicate that organizations can adapt to the computer with great rapidity, and that the constraints on their ability to change in order to make use of it must be few. This is more apparent than real, however, because most computers are performing the kind of work done by human clerks for centuries, using methods at least a generation old.

CASE 3A

◀ The data processing manager of a medium sized manufacturing company asserts that his present computers, the most advanced on the market, are processing his company's payroll using methods developed 50 years ago for human clerks; he refers to the computers as "electronic quill pens." He explains this statement as follows.

The basic accounting structure of his company's payroll was developed before 1920, on the assumption that clerks would prepare the payroll manually. In 1947, the company installed punched card machines to process the payroll, but because of the machines' limitations they found it necessary to retain the existing calendar schedule, chart of accounts, and manual accuracy controls. When computers of reasonable reliability and cost became available, the company decided to acquire one; it was installed in 1961. The major objectives were to obtain greater efficiency and reduce inventories in the manufacturing area, so the programmers concentrated on developing new approaches to those problems. The payroll job was programmed for the computer, but to save time, no restudy was made of the reasons underlying the payroll methods; the computer was simply programmed to perform the same functions as the punched card machines. The computer simulated the actions of the punched card machines, only integrating the punch card runs into more extensive computer ones and reducing the number of personnel required. In 1967 a new "third generation" computer with random access file storage devices was installed with the objective of obtaining faster response to customer inquiries, and again the programming staff were preoccupied with the immediate objective. Because the new computer was able to run the programs for the old one without change, though at somewhat reduced efficiency, no attention was given to the payroll program at all; the programs for the first machine were run on the new one unchanged.

Therefore, says the data processing manager, the payroll procedure now being performed by the company's advanced computers is the one originally designed for performance by clerks without machine assistance. Beyond reducing the clerical force required, the computer has not been exploited to improve any aspect of the procedure. He asserts that faster response times, simpler accounting, and more individually designed compensation plans are among the benefits the computer could have been providing.

The company intends in time to study the fundamental nature of its payroll requirements in connection with its overall accounting structure and employee benefits plan, but for some years to come other problems appear to be more pressing and this study has been postponed indefinitely. ▶

This case, while perhaps a bit extreme, is typical of the majority of computer users. While they have found computers immensely useful in doing work faster and in processing ever-increasing volumes of work without corresponding increases in costs, the work being performed is basically unchanged even though the computer is a fundamentally new tool. It is clear, then, that significant constraints must exist on the ability of organizations to make major changes to take advantage of the computer. The major ones are discussed below.

Habit and suspicion of innovation

When a procedure is familiar and works, there is a natural reluctance to abandon it. Individuals become comfortable with the familiar. They know what they must do at each stage; they can estimate how long the work will take them; it requires less effort to follow a familiar and established path (even though the new path may be well marked, and the instructions for following it explicit and clear). Furthermore, there is likely to be initial suspicion of a new technique, even though others' experience with it can be shown to be successful and however much its use may be recommended. Even when the individual comes to believe that the replacement technique is better, there is likely to be some doubt that the new technique will work smoothly and that all problems with it have been anticipated. The user may fear that there will be a process of "working out the bugs" in the new technique, a process which has been completed for the familiar technique.

CASE 3B

◀ When civil engineers design dams for water retention and flood control, the highest priority is given to safety: to ensuring that the dam will not leak or break under any conceivable combination of circumstances. Many years of experience have provided civil engineers with rules of thumb for dam design, which have been recorded in design manuals. If the civil engineer follows the design manual, he can be virtually assured that the design of the resulting dam will be sound.

A disadvantage of following the design manual is that the resulting dam may be oversafe, that its construction may be heavier and more expensive than is actually necessary in the particular case. This occurs because the rules in the design manual were developed for general cases. They must allow for unfavorable possibilities in the rock formations underlying the dam, and in the water flow and storm conditions that might occur, which may not apply to a particular case. It is generally felt by civil engineers that this is a price worth paying to have a high degree of assurance that dam designs will be sound. Also, the process of designing each dam in detail (from fundamental information about the conditions it will meet, the strength of its materials, and so on) is time-consuming and laborious. For smaller dams of moderate cost, it has been economically unjustified to spend the engineering time required to develop a brand new design each time.

With the advent of the computer, the picture changed. Programs were developed for assisting the civil engineer in designing dams, and the time and cost of performing a detailed design in each case was sharply reduced. It therefore became possible to abandon the design guides, and to prepare new designs based on the information describing the individual case. The programs' designers felt (and experience subsequently proved) that using the computer-aided dam design process in each case, rather than the design manual, would usually lead to more economical designs calling for smaller quantities of materials without compromising safety.

The management of a large contracting firm endorsed the use of the computer-based technique for dam design and the firm's programmers proceeded to introduce the new technique to the civil engineers employed by the firm. They listened attentively, practiced the technique until it was clear that they understood it, and then to the surprise and disappointment of both the programmers and management, returned to designing dams the old way. When asked why they refused to use the new technique, the engineers returned a number of rather self-conscious answers such as "you can't teach an old dog new tricks," that they judged a particular case to be unsuited to the computer technique, and the like. It became clear that the engineers retained a degree of suspicion of the new technique even though the firm's management had become convinced that it was satisfactory. Furthermore, their work habits in using the design guides were so well-established that they found it far more difficult to use the computer-aided design technique, even though in principle it was no more complex. The only engineers who took to the new technique with enthusiasm and ease were newly hired ones, whose orientation in college had introduced them to computer-aided techniques, and who had little prior association with the design guides. The management of the contracting firm finally concluded that it would be necessary to wait for a complete turnover in the staff of dam design engineers before the use of the computer-aided technique could be expected to become general. ▶

Requirement for proof of feasibility

Complex computer systems perform myriads of detailed functions, and must respond to a wide variety of situations. Few programmers are so adept and meticulous as to anticipate all of these in their initial program designs, so managers and users alike often demand that a new system be demonstrated feasible in full-scale operation before they will depend on it. This means that the new system must be designed, implemented, and operated for a considerable period before going into full use. This process may take five years or more in the case of complex data processing systems, particularly if (as is highly likely) flaws do appear when test operations commence, and additional time must be allowed for their correction.

CASE 3C

◀ One of the armed services decided more than ten years ago to investigate the use of computers in tactical operations. The computer was to perform logistic functions (keeping track of fuel, ammunition, and supplies) and combine this information with military data to assist tactical commanders. It was decided to design and procure specially built computers for this purpose, because the mobility and reliability requirements could not be met by general purpose machines, and because the particular capability of the computer system required was slightly different from that of general purpose computers.

After the first specially built computer had been delivered and the programs developed, it turned out that the initial design of the programs had been too simple; that the combinations of conditions encountered in practice were more numerous and complex than the programs' design had allowed for. As the programs were changed and expanded to meet these unexpected needs, they began to exceed both the memory capacity and computational speed of the machine; it was no longer able to perform its work in the required time. The project managers were forced to conclude that they had specified an inadequate machine, so they returned to the initial design phase. At this point, approximately four years had passed since the start of the project.

The designers now discovered that the state of the art in general purpose computer design had advanced to a point where both their reliability and capabilities appeared satisfactory. They therefore decided to use general purpose computers, differing from those supplied to civilian users only in special van mountings, power supplies, and the like. By following this course, the designers assured themselves that larger compatible machines would be available if necessary, and that a wide range of peripheral equipment other than that initially specified could be supplied if their initial design objectives turned out to be inadequate again. This proved to be a wise course, because it did develop that the computer system configuration had to be changed as the programs were developed and tested. After this was done, field testing was commenced. In order to adequately represent all of the conditions the data processing system was expected to meet, the field test was extensive and required more than two years for its completion. Only at the end of this time could it be concluded with confidence that the data processing system would be effective.

This project was conducted about as fast as the project managers felt they could, but nevertheless the total time to operation of the system was nine years: four years for the first unsuccessful attempt, three years to develop the programs for the second attempt, and two years for field testing. ▶

Inertia and lead time

Even when an innovation in methods is proven and accepted by all parties as worthwhile, it may take considerable time to fully implement because of the lead times involved. These include the allocation of funds to acquire the equipment, the training of operating personnel in the new procedures, lead time while waiting for delivery of equipment, site preparation, and many other factors. The total lead time for a typical data processing installation, from the study of its feasibility to full operation of the finished system, is rarely less than two years and may be many years. Extreme examples occur when a great many systems are involved and a major capital investment is required. The Bell System, for example, is pursuing a program of installing electronic telephone line switching centers (similar to computer systems in many respects) to replace the electrical switches now in general use. Obviously the replacement of all the present telephone switching centers in the United States is a formidable task; the Bell System anticipates that it will take more than 30 years. Managers must be realistic in estimating these lead times.

Limited resources to affect changes

Installation of a new computer-based data processing system is always a complex and sensitive process involving much management planning. Few organizations have significant numbers of capable managers who can easily be freed from everyday duties. Implementing a complex new system may require many man-years of managers' time, however, so even with reasonable additions to staff, the process of change may have to be stretched out over several years. The professionals involved, too—systems analysts and programmers—are unlikely to be present in numbers so large that they can simultaneously undertake every project the organization would like to pursue. It is usually necessary to arrange their assignments in some kind of priority, and a number of years may elapse before projects relatively low on the priority list are reached. Even if the organization is willing to invest in acquiring the management and professional people needed to accelerate the process, they may find insuperable limitations in acquiring and absorbing large numbers of such people. Sometimes limitations in personnel resources may lead to abandonment of a promising data processing system plan even though the financial resources required may be available.

CASE 3D

◀ A manufacturer of cotton textiles was faced with declining profits and shrinking markets, because of a combination of rising costs and new competition from synthetic materials. The company's management decided to attempt to revolutionize the company by moving into synthetic fabrics, by reorganizing, by closing obsolete facilities, by acquiring automated production equipment, and by in every way transforming the company to a dynamic and modern one. One of the areas in which they wished to innovate was in the use of data processing. They hoped that computers would not only perform routine functions such as accounting and payroll, but also support a management information system such that the company's management would be able to run the organization more efficiently, with better use of resources and faster responses, than had been possible before.

The company employed a consulting firm to design a computer-based management information system. After considerable study, a design was developed which promised to be as effective as the company's management hoped. A number of new techniques in inventory management, customer order processing, and management reporting were put together in a system that promised both higher efficiency and greater management responsiveness and control. Not only did the system seem attractive on paper, but a number of the more complex techniques had already been demonstrated in small scale. The proposed inventory control method, for example, had been programmed for a computer and demonstrated to produce significant savings.

The consultants informed the textile company's management that implementation of the management information system would require several years and a total investment of between two and three million dollars. Furthermore, to develop the many individual computer programs involved in a reasonable time a staff of thirty systems analysts and programmers would be required. The company's management decided that these high costs and staff levels would be justified by the results they expected from the new management information system, so they adopted the recommended system plan and turned their attention to actions required to execute it.

Among the initial steps management had to take was acquisition of the required thirty systems analysts and programmers. Since there were no computer professionals in the company at the time, they had no knowledge of the availability of trained people nor of the salaries they commanded. Management soon became aware of a severe shortage of properly qualified specialists, and discovered to their dismay that the salaries required to attract such people were far out of line with their existing management salary structure. It appeared that the senior systems analysts would have to be paid more than a number of the company's vice presidents managing mills and plants.

After a good deal of agonized discussion and exploration of alternatives, the textile company's management decided that this problem of professional personnel was insuperable, that it would never be possible to hire the required staff and fit it comfortably into the company's organization. They therefore reluctantly abandoned the plan for the management information system, and decided to pursue a more moderate course by implementing some of the individual applications (such as inventory control) that had been designed as part of the total system. They were therefore enabled to get by with a staff of eight systems analysts and programmers of relatively lower salaries and still obtain the benefit of the computer in a number of useful application areas.

Years later the management of the textile company were confident that they had done the right thing. They had obtained satisfactory benefits from computers in several applications, and they had managed the process of change in an orderly manner that had not adversely affected the company's progress in other areas. However, they still regretted abandoning the management information system. They still felt that had their resources permitted them to implement the system, they would have been a far more efficient and responsive organization. ▶

Clearly there are constraints on the ability of organizations to change, whether it be to employ computers or any other kind of new techniques or tools. This explains the observation that although great numbers of computers have been installed, most of them are performing the kind of work that was done before they appeared. Evidently, organizations can install computers and use them to "soup-up" existing procedures much faster than they can adapt and change themselves to take full advantage of the computer's novel capabilities. They should not overestimate their ability to change rapidly.

THE PARTIES INVOLVED

A change in ways of doing things may force many individuals to adjust their behavior. Many of them will not be enthusiastic; they will have to overcome ignorance, suspicion, and inertia. A consideration of the parties involved with the changes computers bring about will further explore the limits of the rate of change, will illuminate some of the reasons for failures of computer systems, and will explain some of the effects of computers on both organizations and individuals.

The parties involved in changes caused by computers may be grouped into five classes.

The system designers

System designers are people who are trained to develop new systems and ways of doing things, and are rewarded according to their success in doing so. System designers are found in many fields, of course: design engineers, office methods analysts, architects designing both homes and industrial buildings and many others. In the computer field they are programmers, systems analysts, machine designers, compiler system designers, and their managers. System designers are specialists in their machines and techniques rather than in psychology or politics, so their comprehension of the problems, motivations, and limitations of their systems' users is haphazard—sometimes good, sometimes bad. Their plans may (and often do) contain serious flaws resulting from their lack of comprehension of the organization or individuals affected, but it is difficult for the nontechnical managers reviewing their plans to identify these flaws because of an inability to understand the designers' technical language.

Because the system designer may press for change where change is either unnecessary or premature, because previous changes may have left a residue of unsolved problems and adjustments which must be dealt with before further change can be initiated, and because of managers' reluctance based on lack of comprehension, most system designers' proposals for change are disapproved. However, a system designer's personal advancement and satisfaction depends not on leaving systems alone but on installing new and better ones. The result is that the system designer is often a frustrated individual because his "brain children" are usually not given a chance. He spends more time defending his system plans, explaining them over and over again to others who seem intentionally unwilling to understand them, and "fighting fires" resulting from problems of adjustment to earlier system changes, than he does in designing and implementing the new systems he would like to be working with.

CASE 3E

◀ In 1958, a company manufacturing complex military equipment decided to start using computers to control its business operations. The products were complex and profit margins were narrow, so cost and manufacturing control was of critical importance. Also, adaptability and ability to respond quickly often meant the difference between success or failure in obtaining a contract. Management felt that the use of computers in their business systems could improve the company's control and responsiveness, so heavy investments were made in program development. The result was a comprehensive series of computer programs (nearly 400 in all) covering virtually every aspect of the company's business. A series of files stored on magnetic tape contained all product, inventory, and financial information, and successive programs would perform the sequence of operations needed to incorporate new data and produce the necessary information for the company's material and financial management. After nearly eight years of programming, testing, and evolution, and the installation of two sets of computers, the company felt it had a highly effective and useful data processing system. However, the computer's adaptability to change was a continuing problem; since each new contract involved some product changes and procedures that had never been encountered before, the set of programs was undergoing continual revision. Also, there were continuing difficulties and complaints from operating management when unexpected conditions produced imperfect results from the computer's processing.

Despite these continuing minor problems, the personnel who directed and operated the data processing department were very highly thought of by the company's management. Considering other companies' experience, management felt they were very fortunate in their staff of system designers and in the results they had produced. The system designers were regarded as a valuable asset, and as trustworthy and dedicated employees.

In 1965, the system designers discovered from their professional associations with their counterparts in other companies, and from the manufacturers of computers, that the latest computers were capable of performing novel functions. They learned about *real-time management information systems,* systems in which files could be combined in random access storage devices instead of separately stored on reels of magnetic tape, so that programs could be combined and individual transactions could be carried through all of the processing and control steps without waiting for daily or weekly cycles of processing to be performed using separate files. Such systems, they were told, are able to produce information for management that is far more timely and significant than the information earlier systems could produce. The system designers became convinced that a real-time management information system showed great promise for their company, and outlined what it should be like. They discovered that new computing equipment would be required, costing approximately 50% more than the equipment the company then had. They also discovered that they would need to hire specialists in technologies previously unfamiliar to them. They needed two or three designers of communication systems and the programs associated with their use, because the real-time system involved a network of remote input-output devices directly connected to the computer. They had not needed such a communication system before. They also needed one or two specialists in the file management programs needed with random access devices, and three or four more conventional programmers because the new system would involve a simultaneous conversion of all data processing functions into the new system, whereas earlier systems had permitted step-by-step development of one function after another over a period of years. The system designers wrote a report describing the outlines of the proposed new system, the benefits they believed would result to the company and its management, and the new requirements for equipment and personnel. They submitted this report with an enthusiastic recommendation to the company's management.

Management observed that the present data processing system had taken more than six years to evolve, and was still far from perfect. Because the requirements of new products and contracts continually caused new problems and difficulties, it seemed that the existing programming staff was needed virtually full time to solve these new problems as they arose. Guessing from experience at the number and magnitude of problems that would be associated with the new system, management instinctively recoiled from the idea of undertaking its development. Also, while management did not dispute the benefits the system designers claimed would accrue to the company from the new system, they were not entirely convinced that the benefits would be as great or clear-cut as claimed. They observed that the new system involved methods very different from those with which they were familiar; they feared there might be unexpected losses in efficiency or ability to respond because of abandoning methods developed over many years of evolution. Finally, although management had great faith in and respect for its system designers, they could not help remembering that the system designers had taken much longer to develop the existing systems than had been initially thought, that the costs and problems associated with the existing systems had been considerably greater than expected, and that more staff and computer equipment were required to support the existing systems than had been forecast. So, management was a little reluctant to accept at face value all the forecasts and claims made for the new system by its designers.

The result of these observations was a dilemma. On the one hand, management accepted in principle that the new real-time system would be appropriate for the company sooner or later, and they had great confidence in their system designers. On the other hand, all past experience with the claimed benefits of computer-based systems indicated that the change would be painful and expensive, perhaps much more so than the system designers thought.

The result of the dilemma was indecision. Months went by, conferences were held, amendments were made to the report, and tempers rose. Management was unable to conclude that the new system should be accepted. At the same time, management was unwilling to refuse the new system out of hand, both out of respect to the system designers and from an underlying feeling that sooner or later something of the kind would be appropriate. Frustration grew among the ranks of the system designers as they presented their concepts again and again, made minor changes, and developed further supporting material that in their minds changed little. The suspicion grew that their judgments were not valued or trusted nearly to the degree that management had led them to believe. ▶

The leaders of change

Because the system designers are the advocates of change, it is natural to regard them as the leaders of the change process. In actuality, they are only the planners of possible changes; the leadership of the actual change process is in the hands of those who manage the activities that are changing. Ultimately, he who controls salaries and issues day-to-day instructions controls the course of events.

When cooperation is entirely voluntary, the leadership of change is a selling or training function. For example, if a time-shared computer's service is being offered on a subscription basis to users who are unfamiliar with it, the leadership of the change process falls on the shoulders of those selling the service, and their success is in the hands of the users who can simply refuse it. The importance of the sales function is borne out by the observation that while a number of time-shared computer services have been successfully sold on a subscription basis and their number is growing, others of equal technical merit have failed for lack of subscriber interest. (Often such a service can be effectively "presold" if its advantages can be explained to educators, so that they will specify and instruct students in its use in the course of the formal education process. Many engineers, for example, are now being trained by professors who endorse and use time-sharing services during the course of study. Presumably their students, once in industry, will insist on being provided with comparable services.)

When changes are being implemented in industry, the cooperation of the employees is (in theory) not voluntary; they are compelled to do their best to use whatever systems and methods the organization specifies. In this case, the leaders of change are the managers of the affected organization. If a new production and inventory control system is being installed in a manufacturing plant, for example, it is the plant manager who is the leader of change. His employees will look to him for direction and guidance. The system designers can do their best to publicize the system and train and motivate the plant employees, but unless the plant manager himself enthusiastically supports and insists upon the use of the new method, the system designers are power-less to obtain its acceptance.

CASE 3F

◀ A new repair parts inventory control system was developed by system designers of a construction equipment manufacturer for use by the manufac-turer's sales and service agencies. Under the new system, records of repair parts stored by the dealer would be kept centrally in a computer system. The dealer would report his issues, receipts, and other inventory transactions to the central computer system, which would automatically initiate resupply orders when the program noted that supply levels were below the reorder points. This system was supposed to provide better service by helping dealers find scarce parts in other dealers' inventories, and simplify record keeping for the dealer because his personnel would no longer be required to maintain repair parts files themselves. It had been noted that such files were often kept sloppily and inaccurately, so they did not reflect the true levels of repair parts supplies. This condition often led to unnecessary ordering, and stocks of parts higher than actually required.

At one of the dealers, the personnel in charge of maintaining repair parts records were apprehensive about the new system, because they felt that it would involve a risk of running short. They feared that if (for any reason) the computer failed to receive or adequately handle their messages regarding issues of parts, it would not initiate reorders in time and they might run short of parts at inconvenient or critical times. These people felt that if that should happen, they would be the ones blamed rather than the planners who had developed the new system. This concern was shared by the dealer's service manager. While he had no right or authority to object to the new system or countermand its use, he indicated clearly to his personnel that he shared their doubts; that he was apprehensive about the effect on service operations if the new system should fail. The personnel, observing this, proceeded to maintain the old files in the old way at the same time that they followed the operating procedures of the new system. Each inventory transaction was duly reported to the center, but before transmitting it they made sure that they posted it to the private records they continued to keep. By this means, they felt they would be protected against failure of the new system because they could initiate reorders if the central system failed to do so in time.

The result of this, of course, was confusion and difficulty. For various reasons, including the time delay for transmission of messages, the records in the central computer and at the dealer came to disagree. The dealer's records usually showed smaller inventories of parts than the computer's records, because they forgot to record some receipts in the private files. As a result, the dealer's personnel would issue requisitions for parts which were regarded as unnecessary by the computer system. Since the authorities usually permitted these requisitions to be honored because of their own apprehension about the new system, the results were that inventories at the dealer grew even above what they had been before the new system was installed. The inventories carried were not lower than before as had been anticipated, but higher. Furthermore, the dealer's personnel, whose jobs had been expected to become easier because of the reduction in paper work, found themselves in a badly overworked condition because of their attempts to operate two systems at the same time. This situation was not improved until the dealer's service manager was replaced by a new one who soon learned about the duplicate record keeping. Perceiving that the results of the duplicate system were probably worse than the risks to be taken with the new one, he instructed his personnel to abandon the private record keeping, and enforced their compliance by assuming the risk himself and destroying the old records. It turned out that the new system worked quite adequately and that failures were rare. When they occurred, they could usually be corrected quickly by borrowing parts from neighboring dealers or by using emergency extra supplies of critical parts which had been permitted by the system designers in anticipation of possible failures. The personnel finally became convinced that the new system was in fact preferable to the old, and regarded their erstwhile duplicate record keeping as foolish and unnecessary. They rightly attached the blame for their mistake not to themselves but on the service manager who had been replaced. If he had been an enthusiastic and aggressive proponent of the new system, their difficulties would never have arisen. By his lack of enthusiasm, which communicated itself to his personnel, he tacitly encouraged their failure to comply and, therefore, a worsening of the very conditions the new system was developed to improve. ▶

It seems self-evident that the leaders of change are necessarily the leaders of the organizations in which the change must take place, but this point is surprisingly often overlooked. System designers often feel that support is guaranteed once the central management for whom they work has become convinced. They ignore the inevitable fact that subordinate management has a degree of freedom of action, and complete freedom in the degree of enthusiasm they give to the system designers' new ideas. The subordinate managers know that if the new system fails, the system designers are almost always the ones who will be criticized. It will not be evident to central management that the failure may have arisen from sloppy and imperfect compliance (or even outright opposition) to the new system's requirements, on the part of the personnel in the operating area who must support it. Central management must anticipate this, and be willing to play its part.

The vendor of equipment or services

The data processing industry is in a state of rapid evolution. The suppliers of equipment and service find it in their interests to attempt to continually improve their products, thereby increasing the products' importance to the users' organizations and the revenues received from the users. The desired increase in revenue will not occur, however, unless the user can be convinced that he should incorporate the new product or service in his own data processing structure; that it is in his interest to adopt the changed procedure incorporating the manufacturer's product. Therefore, the manufacturers' salesmen have become major initiators of the process of change, as they attempt to sell advanced products to their customers.

A responsible and effective computer salesman can (justifiably) become more of a consultant to his customers than a traditional salesman. However, because his income depends on his sales, he is unlikely to sell less than the customer can usefully employ, and may (in all innocence) sell more. The result has frequently been underused equipment, and sometimes outright failure. This point is too obvious to require exemplification; nevertheless, it has often been observed that a little more enlightened buyer resistance might have been in computer users' interests. The point, simply, is to view the salesman in the proper light. He plays a very useful role in initiating change, but users should not permit him to make decisions that should remain their own.

The user of the system's results

Data processing systems produce reports for managers, and they also produce instructions for operating personnel. In each case, the needs and attitudes of the users should be reflected in the system that serves them. It may be difficult for the system designers to fully appreciate these ahead of time, so several trial and error periods may be necessary before the system is fully useful. The inevitable language barrier between computer and user may, in fact, prevent its ever fully satisfying its users.

CASE 3G

◀ The management of a large chemical company was very sensitive to short-term market trends in new products. Of the many products introduced, a large proportion failed under competitive pressure or for lack of customer acceptance, and they wished to cut off investments in clearly unsuccessful ventures as soon as possible. Some products had early sales or production difficulties that required management attention; if this attention was delayed too long, loss of revenue or outright failure could result. The company's management therefore decided that a system for rapid collection and computer processing of sales data would be justified.

The computer was acquired, the programming done, and the system put into operation. Immediately a painful flaw became apparent: each of the product managers responsible for a given new product was presented each morning with a stack of paper about two inches thick—the production, sales, and consumption reports for the product for the previous day from every one of the company's dealers, salesmen, and plants. The product managers naturally found these reports impossibly long, and they also noted that 90% of the items were individually insignificant. They were interesting only in the aggregate, or if they deviated sharply from what was expected. It was apparent that some selectivity had to be applied.

The product managers conferred with the system designers and developed some rules for the elimination of unnecessary data that could be incorporated in the computer's programs. Unless the individual items deviated from preestablished expected values by more than 10%, they should be reported only in regional summaries: *management by exception* was being applied.

Unfortunately this did not have the desired effect. Most of the items differed from the expected values by more than 10%, and the morning reports were still too voluminous. The margin of deviation was then arbitrarily increased to 25% and satisfactory selectivity was obtained; the reports shrank to a few pages. It soon developed that the 25% margin was sufficiently sensitive, anyway, because all significant sales problems soon resulted in deviations this large.

This was not the end of the troubles, however, because not all the 25% deviations represented significant events. A storm keeping buyers at home, a local truckers' strike, a salesman sick in bed, and other events that did not require the product managers' attention could cause items to appear in the reports. The product managers found themselves spending hours on the telephone to no purpose. It appeared that the product managers could not specify rules for the identification of exceptions that would at the same time permit only significant items to be reported, and be simple and clear enough to be programmed.

At this point, the product managers decided to stop depending directly on computer-produced reports. They appointed a new group of staff assistants who would receive the daily exception reports and the summaries of the routine events for the previous day. These staff assistants had the responsibility of investigating the exceptional items, and also of entering the previous day's results on a set of charts which were kept in a uniform manner for every product. Then, in the late morning of each business day, the product managers would gather in the conference room where the charts were kept and each staff assistant would explain verbally the reasons for the exceptions reported for the previous day. Combining the overall trend charts (which were kept manually) with the investigated exceptions, the product managers felt that they were being advised as well as possible of events occurring, without at the same time being required to undertake investigations of events not significant enough for their consideration.

In this company, then, a series of attempts to produce useful management reports from the computer led to a decision to produce none. The attempt was not abandoned, but an interpretive human activity turned out to be justified as an interpolation between the best reports that the computer could produce and the information that management actually required to support their decisions. ▶

The reaction of the users of the system is equally important when the users are personnel who must comply with its instructions. The changes anticipated by the system designers must be easy for users to comprehend, and psychologically acceptable to them, before compliance with the new procedures can be expected. A classic example of unexpected difficulty in this area is the introduction of all-digit dialing by the telephone companies. The use of exchange names was never more than a meaningless mnemonic convenience; their abandonment and replacement with digits seemed to the telephone companies of no psychological significance and of considerable technical assistance in that it permitted more exchanges to be installed in large cities. They were quite unprepared for the psychological reaction of a segment of the using public, who had formed sentimental attachments to the meaningless exchange names and objected to substituting digits. This reluctance has been largely overcome, but it is significant to note that with all the knowledge the telephone companies have of their users' psychology and preferences in operating the telephone system, they were caught unprepared by this reaction to the introduction of all-digit dialing.

The "uninvolved"

Most of an organization's employees are not likely to be parties to the development of changes in methods, and the organization's customers rarely are. They may often be affected in indirect ways, however, sometimes only psychological, but nevertheless real. For example, in every company where a computer-produced payroll has been introduced and the employees are presented with checks and deduction reports prepared by computers, it is inevitable that the employees verify the amount shown with unusual care the first few times they see a machine-prepared document rather than one assumed to be produced by people. (In many companies this extra careful inspection has led to straightening out long-standing errors or misunderstandings in individual payroll situations.) When the customer first sees a punched card bill, a magnetic ink coded check, or other obviously machine-produced or machine-readable document, he too may be expected to instinctively take a suspicious attitude at first and wonder if his dealings with the company will suffer in any way. Some managements, apprehensive of customer reaction to the introduction of computer-based systems, have distributed small information bulletins together with the first of the machine-produced series of documents to attempt to allay the customers' fears.

In some cases, apparently uninvolved agencies or authorities must be considered when computer systems are being introduced. A company's legal staff may have to be consulted by the system designer to verify that legally acceptable records are kept by the computer system, so that in case of customer objection, law suits, or disaster, legally verifiable proof of the information contained in the computer files is available. The company's auditors have a corresponding interest; they must be assured that satisfactory and tamper-proof financial controls are incorporated in the computer system. Thus, the legal and financial authorities must often be consulted even though they are uninvolved directly with the functions being performed. Sometimes, even the presumed interest of government regulatory bodies may be a factor.

CASE 3H

◀ A communication system was designed to serve a segment of the securities trading industry. By using it, trading firms could communicate with one another expeditiously and economically to execute customers' orders to buy and sell securities. The developers of the system offered a number of advantages to subscribers—among them lower cost, better response time, and automatic maintenance of records of transactions in case confusion or disagreement should arise. The potential customers were interested in the lower cost and better response time, but specifically requested the system's designers to omit the keeping of transaction records. They conceded the advantage of such records in clarifying disagreements among themselves, but they feared that the existence of such records would attract the attention of the Securities and Exchange Commission. Most of them had nothing to hide, but they were concerned that unknown new kinds of surveillance or control over their activities might be initiated by the SEC if records were easily available of just what transactions had taken place, and at what time and price.

The SEC had indicated no interest or intention of instituting any new controls. However, anticipatory fears on the part of the systems' users caused the designers to intentionally omit one of the apparently attractive features they had conceived. ▶

SUMMARY

The brief history of the use of the computer is inextricably intertwined with a continuous process of change, both in individual life patterns and behavior, and in the nature and structure of organizations. The computer is both a force causing this change and a helpless victim of it. The computer's effect on organizations and individuals can be comprehended only as part of the process, which involves limits inherent in organizations and humans and also the interaction of all parties to the process of change. Because of the complexity of this process, it is little wonder that the effects of the computer have been slow in becoming apparent, and are difficult to identify surely. After all, when we reflect that with computer-based systems we are usually defining and instituting structured procedures and relationships for the first time where they previously grew only by accretion and slow evolution, we should not be surprised to find the process laborious. Management of change requires patience, realism, and management participation, particularly when computers are involved.

Part II | HOW THE COMPUTER
        CHANGES ORGANIZATIONS

CHAPTER 4

CHANGES IN OPERATIONS

Organizations using computers have undergone various changes that are directly attributable to the computer. These changes have occurred in the operational or routine business functions of the organizations, in their management and planning functions, and in their structures. This and the succeeding chapters will be devoted to factual analysis of the effects actually experienced, with a minimum of speculation and opinion. This chapter is devoted to the effects of the computer on the operations of organizations using it.

TYPES OF ORGANIZATIONS MOST AFFECTED

It is clear from considerations of the computer's strengths and weaknesses that it will be more useful to some types of organizations than to others. It follows that those types of organizations to which the computer is useful are the ones likely to show the greatest changes as a result of the computer.

The organization making most extensive use of the computer is likely to be one in which the volume of clerical transactions involved in daily operations is particularly heavy. As the number of transactions to be processed rises, and as the cost of clerical help to process them increases, the computer becomes almost indispensable for operational data processing. It is at its best and humans are at their worst where rigid repetition of mechanical processes is required and where myriads of repetitions are needed to handle the volume. Organizations of this kind are typical of the insurance and financial industries, where handling great numbers of transactions involving relatively small amounts of money is fundamental to the business. Certain government agencies, notably the Social Security Administration, Veterans Administration, and Internal Revenue Service, share the same characteristic. Public utilities and large retail sales organizations, although they deal in physical products rather than solely in financial transactions, must also process great numbers of individual customer records, invoices, and payments.

The operations of such organizations have been affected deeply by the computer. For example, a study* of seven life insurance companies showed that:

1   The number of employees in the functions to which the computer had been applied was reduced slightly, on the average, despite a great increase in the volume of business.

2   Most of the functions of the employees in these areas became more routinized and standardized.

3   All but one of the seven companies reported an increase in the managerial level at which decisions are made.

4   In every company the manager of data processing gained both supervisory and planning responsibility as the use of computers increased.

Another class of organizations showing significant changes caused by the computer is that in which mechanical processes of moderate complexity are repeated frequently, e.g., the machining of a part on an assembly line. The size of this class of organizations is restricted by several factors. If the process to be performed is simple, it can be built into the machine doing the work; the computer's power is not required. If the process is complex but is repeated infrequently, the cost of computer equipment and programming is not justified. Finally, if the process is extremely complex and not perfectly understood, the computer cannot be programmed to perform it. There is a middle ground, though, where the work is well-understood, routine, too complex for ordinary control systems, and repeated with great frequency.

For the first ten years of the computer's existence, it was only rarely applied to such tasks. More recently, three trends have combined to accelerate its use: rising cost and scarcity of labor, increasing complexity of products, and increasing volumes of production. These trends have combined to increase costs, particularly in the area of quality control or product inspection at the end of an assembly line. The process of inspection is heavily dependent on human labor, and today's complex assembly line products often require many times the amount of inspection time previously required.

CASE 4A

◀   A manufacturer of electronic components long ago became convinced that automated production lines were the key to profitable operation. The cost of

---

* Thomas L. Whisler, "The Impact of Information Technology on Organizational Control," in *The Impact of Computers on Management,* Charles A. Myers, Editor, M.I.T. Press, Cambridge, 1967.

materials for all types of electronic components is relatively low, so labor cost is significant. The manufacturing process is one requiring precise repetition of individually simple operations, and is therefore amenable to automation. Inspection of the finished components was for many years the manufacturer's most serious problem, because his customers required that the components delivered be guaranteed to meet the advertised specifications; they did not wish to perform exhaustive component-by-component testing themselves. For all but his least expensive components, then, the manufacturer was forced to perform 100% inspection.

For the simplest electronic components, such as resistors, it was possible to automate the inspection process without a great deal of difficulty. The individual components were guided to a testing station where it was necessary only to fit them into a groove where a single connection was made to the wire at each end of the component. Then, a single electrical stimulus applied to the component would produce an easily measurable response which immediately indicated the acceptability of the component. For years the production and inspection processes for resistors had been completely automated, and the resulting cost and quality combination was satisfactory.

In the manufacturing of transistors, which have considerably more complex characteristics, the company faced a more difficult problem. The manufacturing process itself could be automated without great difficulty, but the determination of a transistor's acceptability depended on the interaction of several performance characteristics, which required a series of tests to determine. The process was too complex to wire into a piece of production machinery, so the transistor production line used human operators for the testing function. Each transistor inspection station consisted of a jig into which the transistor's three connecting wires were inserted, plus a group of instruments that a girl could manipulate in a predetermined fashion to apply the series of tests needed to determine the transistor's condition. Upon observing the results, the girl could decide according to decision rules she had been taught whether each of the tests was individually satisfactory, and whether any combination of tests indicated a weakness in the transistor. She could then rate it as acceptable, unacceptable, or marginal.

This process was satisfactory for transistor manufacturing. The cost of manufacturing the transistor was high compared to that of simple components such as resistors, and by careful study and experience the cost of the inspection operation was reduced to an acceptable level in comparison to the manufacturing cost. Furthermore, none of the manufacturer's competitors had been able to do away with manual inspection either, so his competitive position was satisfactory.

The manufacturer recently decided to enter the field of large-scale integrated circuit manufacture, in which the functions of many components are combined into a single integrated circuit, manufactured as a unit. After some experimentation, the manufacturer found that he was able to manufacture integrated circuits automatically, but he also found that at least 5% of the circuits would be unacceptable despite his best efforts to refine the manufacturing process. This relatively high reject rate is inevitable because the circuits are so intricate that small random variations in the materials or in the manufacturing process cause unacceptable faults to appear, while the grosser transistors were not significantly affected.

It was therefore mandatory that all integrated circuits be thoroughly inspected before being shipped to customers. However, manual inspection proved to be prohibitively difficult and expensive. For one thing, the circuits were so small that the application of the familiar manual testing processes to individual parts of the circuits was virtually impossible. For another, the number of individual tests needed to completely check all functions of the circuit was far larger than the number required for a transistor. The inspectors took so long to test each integrated circuit that the cost advantage over individual transistors was largely lost, and the integrated circuit venture appeared doubtful.

The manufacturer turned to the computer to solve his problem. He was able to develop a testing jig for the integrated circuits which would make all the necessary contacts with their connecting leads. Then, he invested a sizeable sum in the development of a computer program to cause electrical instruments to apply the necessary tests to the integrated circuit one after another (for a simple circuit, 17 successive tests were required). The results of the tests were sensed by the computer, and compared both singly and in combinations to performance criteria stored in the computer's program. After considerable experimentation and the expenditure of nearly a million dollars, the computer-controlled automatic testing of integrated circuits was perfected and put into operation. At this point, the manufacturer began to realize the hoped-for economies of the integrated circuit and was able to offer them to customers at prices far lower than the corresponding prices of circuits employing individual transistors. ▶

Such processes as these are complex and repetitive enough to be time-consuming and laborious for humans, yet simple enough to be programmed. Most of the successful applications of computers directly to manufacturing processes are of this kind. However, there are also some basically simple processes that either consume large amounts of labor or are carried out in such unfavorable conditions that the computer and associated machinery can be justified.

CASE 4B

◀ A large bakery stores the cakes it produces in a large freezer warehouse, in small boxes containing individual cakes (usually a dozen to a box). Orders from wholesalers may specify many kinds of cakes, as little as one box of each. These orders must be filled by entering the freezer warehouse, picking a large number of small boxes from many stacks, and making up pallet loads that can be loaded into refrigerated trucks for shipment. Because of the necessity of working in subfreezing conditions, a large number of workers had to be employed so that they could work in short shifts, and they required premium pay. The materials handling function in the warehouse, then, was an uncommonly expensive one and the bakery was anxious to find a technique for reducing this cost.

After a careful study the bakery decided to build a completely automated computer-controlled freezer warehouse. Remotely controlled traveling cranes were to pick up boxes using vacuum lifts, putting them on pallets assigned to the individual customer orders. Because of the complexity of the whole-salers' orders, a computer was required to direct the traveling cranes in order to have accurate and efficient operation. This would pay for itself, the bakery hoped, by eliminating the very high cost of paying laborers for short shifts of work in the freezer warehouse.

The computer-controlled freezer warehouse was built, and is operating successfully. However, by the time full operation was achieved, so much money had been invested that many years of operational savings will be required to recover it. ▶

All the types of organizations discussed so far have applied the computer to operations they previously had to perform manually. The computer's speed in carrying out complex processes has also made procedures possible that would have been impossible without it, regardless of how many people were employed. This has led to the development of operational procedures that are entirely new, and that may have even greater effects on the organizations benefiting from them.

CASE 4C

◀ Navigation at sea is difficult because of the absence of fixed reference points to establish a ship's position. The only reference points available have been the celestial bodies, which have the disadvantage of apparently moving both as the earth turns and as it circles the sun. A well-trained navigator, of course, can perform celestial navigation satisfactorily according to long-estab-lished procedures. However, weather can preclude celestial navigation, deter-minations of position suffer from inaccuracies caused by the limitations of reasonably priced instruments, and trained navigators are relatively expensive and sometimes in short supply.

The United States Navy developed a system of artificial reference points which both increase the accuracy and decrease the skill required in navigation.* The *Transit* satellites are the references. Each one passes over a tracking station about every three hours, and the tracking station computes the precise trajectory of the satellite at that time (the orbits continually change very slightly). The tracking station's computer then proceeds to calculate the position relative to the earth's surface that the satellite will occupy every minute for the next twelve hours. This information is relayed by radio from the tracking station to the satellite and is there recorded in a memory unit. The satellite's transmitter, fed by the memory unit, beams a coded message every two minutes to tell listeners on earth where the satellite is.

As the satellite passes within range of a ship, a receiver on the ship tunes in on the signals. The signals tell the ship where the satellite is at the time of reception, and because the satellite is moving rapidly relative to the ship, the frequency of the signals received will be slightly higher or lower than the transmitter's frequency. A small computer on the receiving ship analyzes the frequency shift associated with each of several successive messages from the satellite. This analysis makes it possible to determine the moment when the satellite was nearest to the ship, and its distance at that time. The position of the ship relative to the satellite is then known, and the position of the satellite was already known. The Navy states that a ship's position may be determined within $\frac{1}{10}$ of a mile using the Transit system; no such accuracy could ever be obtained by celestial navigation however precise the instruments used. Furthermore, because the equipment on the ship is simple to operate and the computer is preprogrammed, untrained personnel can operate the Transit navigation system in all weather by day or night. ▶

Some applications of this novel kind are to be found in industry, such as the electric power dispatching application cited in Chapter 1, and the pointing of directional radio antennas associated with satellite communications. However, such applications are relatively few. Most businesses interface with human customers or with other organizations run by humans. They are not usually required to interface with objects or events in rapid movement, so the organizations are not required to respond to stimuli in fractions of seconds. Hours are almost always available, sometimes weeks or months. Response time alone is unlikely to justify use of computers, then, unless other factors associated with personnel or efficiency are also present.

---

* John N. Wilford, *The New York Times,* July 30, 1967.

One of the types of organization most significantly affected by the computer is the research laboratory, in which scientists employ computers in their work. In many cases, the computer has made possible experiments of greater complexity than ever before; in some cases, it even eliminates the necessity of making experiments. For many scientists, availability of the computing resource is as important as the availability of measuring instruments. The modern laboratory must not only provide the conventional apparatus for researchers but also the computing resource.

CASE 4D

◀ In the research laboratory complex of a large university, all the buildings are connected by a communication line network to a computing facility. This computing facility incorporates a battery of very large computers, which can be programmed to assist with the experiments being performed by many different scientists. The programs required are developed at the beginning of a research project, and are stored in random access file storage devices accessible to the computers so that the programs corresponding to a given project can be called into action in a matter of seconds. The battery of computers is scheduled by a smaller computer, which receives the requests for assistance from the scientists in the various buildings. According to their priorities and the urgency of their needs, the small computer assigns the processors to them. The control computer is also capable of connecting the communication lines from the laboratory buildings directly to the assigned computers. At the other end of the lines, in the laboratory buildings, the scientists can connect any measuring and controlling instruments they wish. Most of the time, the scientists send data to the computers during an experiment, and after the experiment is over use the computers to process the results. However, in an increasing number of cases the computers are being used to control the experiments while they proceed. The computers evaluate intermediate data and compute new settings of the experimental instruments that are more likely to produce useful results than the initial settings. These are transmitted over wires directly to the experimental apparatus, so the computer is in direct control of the course of the experiment.

Increasingly, scientists are using the computers to simulate experiments according to models of the processes being investigated, which the scientists develop and provide to the computer. As explained in Chapter 1, this makes possible the investigation of processes impossible to simulate experimentally. It can also sharply reduce the time and cost of experimental projects, because computer simulations can often substitute for exploratory or preliminary laboratory work, reducing the number of time-consuming and expensive experiments to those that will produce interesting results.

The university feels that its capability to perform research in many fields is being revolutionized in kind and greatly expanded in scope by this inter-connected computer facility. The facility is continually expanding and evolving as the scientists find new ways to use it, and no one in the university knows what form it will eventually take. ▶

CHANGES CAUSED BY THE COMPUTER

As one examines the "before and after" condition of companies using com-puters extensively in their operations, as Whisler did in his study of insurance companies noted above, it becomes possible to identify the effects the com-puter does and does not have.

Many managements expect, when they apply their computers to opera-tional functions, that the number of operating personnel they employ will be reduced. As is by now widely known, this generally does not happen. Among the seven insurance companies Whisler studied, three showed de-creases in numbers of operating personnel but the rest either increased or stayed approximately the same. On the surface, then, it appears in general that the computer does not accomplish the hoped-for reduction in operating personnel. This is not entirely correct, however, because in almost every case the volume of detailed work being handled with the help of the computer has grown considerably above the volume that was handled before the com-puter was installed, and the complexity of the typical transaction has usually grown as well. While few companies can state that they are employing fewer personnel than they did before the computer was installed, many of them state that they are employing no more.

CASE 4E

◀ During the last two decades, telephone companies have been making extensive efforts to reduce their operating costs by increasing the degree of automation in the process of placing telephone calls. Machinery has been installed and the telephone-using public has been educated to directly dial as many telephone calls as possible to both local and remote points. Direct dialing of telephone calls involving toll charges would not be possible with-out the aid of the computer, because the charges must be computed for each call. For each toll call the times of connect and disconnect must be recorded, and the recordings subsequently processed by computer to establish the cor-rect toll charge, and to associate this charge with the customer's bill. This data processing could not possibly be done by human clerks at anything like the present operating costs; the computer is essential.

The degree of success which the Bell System has had in reducing its numbers of operating personnel by instituting computer-assisted direct dialing of telephone calls is shown by some of its operating statistics:*

Category	1957	1965
Employees	640,868	611,931
Number of telephones	52,252,494	75,866,254
Number of local telephone calls (daily average)	180,084,000	266,165,000
Toll and long distance calls (daily average)	8,192,000	13,349,000

It is apparent from these figures that the Bell System was able to nearly double the volume of traffic handled during these eight years while reducing personnel by approximately 5%. Without the extensive introduction of direct dialing, this would have been impossible because the numbers of telephone operators required would have risen proportionately with the increase in number of calls. The decrease in number of personnel is not dramatic, but one can imagine what the increase would have been if automatic dialing (for which the computer is essential) had not been introduced. ▶

Because this type of experience is quite general, it appears clear that large-scale replacement of people by computers (the "office unemployment" feared by early prophets) has not materialized and will not. On the other hand, far fewer office employees are now at work than would be required if the computers were not available. This is just as well, because there are not nearly enough qualified workers available to handle today's volume of data processing manually. In this respect, the computer has been an unmixed blessing: helping management handle its exploding volume of paperwork without hindering the employment prospects of clerical personnel.

Another of the effects which can be observed in the operating areas of organizations using computers extensively is a tendency toward greater rigidity in the procedures imposed on operating personnel. All but one of the insurance companies in Whisler's study, for example, reported such an increase in rigidity. This rigidity takes the form of discipline in detail: requirements for personnel to fill out more forms, completely and accurately, and using codes and symbols instead of descriptive terms. Manual procedures are broadly adaptable to error and sloppiness in reporting, because human clerks handling

---

* *Annual Report,* American Telephone and Telegraph Company, 1966.

the transactions can infer, convert, or complete forms not filled out precisely according to instructions. Machines do not have this capability, and in the early days of computer use, managements using computers frequently failed to adequately appreciate the necessity for increased clerical discipline.

CASE 4F

◀ In the late 1950's a supply depot of one of the armed forces installed a computer to keep track of its inventory of supply items. The computer had one of the earliest models of random access file storage device, and with its aid the supply depot looked forward to a combination of decreased response times and increased control over inventories. Personnel at the various points where supply requisitions were received were provided with input-output terminals to communicate with the machine and its random access file. They could determine the number of the desired supply items in inventory, and change the machine's records to reflect the receipt or issue they were handling. By this means, all personnel could be kept equally up to date about the status of the supply depot's inventory levels.

Each time a reference was to be made to the computer, the stock number of the item needed was to be provided. The computer would print the inventory balance at the terminal, and the clerk would then send a changed record back to the computer, again giving the stock number, and cause the computer to record the new balance in place of the old one. The clerks were given tables relating the names of items to stock numbers, and were trained in the use of the terminals until all understood and could operate the system correctly.

The system was installed and put into operation, and errors began to occur. Subsequent analysis showed that in two or three out of every hundred transactions, the operator would make some error in specifying the stock number. Either the wrong stock number would be taken from the table, or an erroneous letter or digit would be typed. If this occurred when an inquiry was being made, the computer produced the wrong balance for the operator, the balance for something other than the item the clerk thought he had asked for. Each time this occurred when a clerk entered a transaction (either an issue or a receipt of a supply item), the wrong record was changed and thereafter the wrong balance was associated with some item.

After about five days of operation of the new system, it began to be apparent that things were going wrong. By then some items were completely out of stock, yet the computer's records still showed inventory balances. Also, the clerks were beginning to note reported inventory balances that could not possibly be correct; in some cases far more of an item was shown than the supply depot had ever had before. The depot's management soon realized what had happened and considered steps to rectify the situation. To their dismay, they found that there was no way to discover what errors had been made affecting which inventory records; there was no way of knowing which were accurate and which were inaccurate. It was necessary to perform physical recounts of all inventory items for which transactions had occurred in the five-day period, and to return to manual inventory control in order to prevent recurrence of the same problem.

Several months later the computer system was started up again, but now all inquiries from the remote points were received by personnel at the computer center rather than sent directly to the computer. These personnel would inspect each input transaction for apparent accuracy and completeness before permitting it to enter the computer. In addition, the computer was now programmed to perform a large number of accuracy and consistency checks on each input transaction before it was permitted to change any record in the inventory file. Finally, the operating personnel at the terminals were impressed much more deeply with the necessity for carefully checking the stock numbers before transmitting them to the center.

The combination of these precautions was successful, and the incidence of error was reduced to an acceptable level. The system has operated in this way ever since, but it has done so at considerably higher cost and with lower response time than was originally anticipated, because of the necessity for interposing human "checkers" and computer editing procedures between the point of transaction and the computer. ▶

Disasters of this kind are less common now, for two reasons. First, organizations have become aware of the necessity of enforcing rigid procedures for computer input preparation; they tend to take greater care in training personnel and in anticipating possible problems. Second, programmers have learned the same lesson and are more careful and less optimistic; they take more pains to incorporate editing procedures in their programs and to check the validity of input documents. The fact that there is less trouble now, however, does not indicate any change in the basic fact that computer systems impose increased operational rigidity. Managers must bear this inevitable fact in mind in planning computer applications.

While the computer has invariably produced increased rigidity in operations that produce input for the computer, somewhat paradoxically the computer has made it possible to decrease rigidity in many companies' product lines. One of the primary reasons for producing nothing but standard products on assembly lines has always been the cost and difficulty of keeping the records, and producing the individually tailored production instructions needed for products varying from the standard. The computer can reduce this cost and difficulty. It can keep records of individual products which vary from the standard, even though there may be thousands of them. It can also produce production instructions automatically that incorporate variations into the flow of the production line. Working with numerically controlled machine tools, computers can automatically direct the production of small runs of specialized parts that were not previously economical to produce. Furthermore, the computer's ability to issue thousands of individually detailed instructions in the correct sequence can be used to permit incorporation of variations in accessories, colors, and the like to a greater degree than previously possible.

CASE 4G

◀ One of the major manufacturers of automobiles has applied computers extensively to many areas of its operations.* One of them is production control, where the computer is used to issue instructions to the stations on the assembly line that perform the manufacturing operations. Each station performs a particular operation, but variations can be introduced (e.g., in color of paint applied or type of radio installed). If instructions covering the desired variations can be issued to all the stations affected in an accurate and inexpensive manner, the number of variations that can be allowed increases. Using a computer to prepare the instructions, the company has been able to increase the variations offered in its products. In 1962, this manufacturer produced 93 body style combinations compared to 160 for the 1967 model year. During the same period, trim combinations increased from 301 to 556. Because of this proliferation of accessories and variations, more than 21,000 separate items were required to build the 1967 product line. This increase in the variability of its product line has given the manufacturer a considerable competitive advantage; it would not have been obtained if the computer had not been available to perform the record-keeping and issue the instructions.

During the same period this manufacturer introduced a 50,000-mile, five-year warranty on its vehicles' power train components. This warranty was attractive to the public and became a competitive necessity. The manufacturer could not offer this warranty, regardless of the quality of the vehicles, without an ability to maintain service records for individual vehicles; only if adequate maintenance is performed does the warranty become economically possible. Another virtue of the individual record is its enhancement of the vehicle's second-hand value; buyers of used vehicles place a significant value on a guaranteed record of maintenance combined with the manufacturer's certification that the original warranty is still valid. These records cannot be main-

---

* John F. Sand, "Computers and the Automobile Industry," *Electronic Age*, Spring 1967.

tained by individual dealers because the customer must be given the freedom to deal with different dealers in different locations; the manufacturer must keep service records centrally. The manufacturer must therefore be prepared to keep service records on as many as ten million cars (the number he produced during the past five years), a virtually impossible task without the computer.

Using the computer, then, this automobile manufacturer has been able to decrease the rigidity of his product specifications and offer the public more diversity, while at the same time maintaining the advantages of mass production. Furthermore, he has been able to keep the maintenance records on every individual car which are essential to the five-year warranty. ▶

In conjunction with scheduling production, thousands of organizations have applied computers to the management of resources tied up in distribution systems and inventories. They have had great success in reducing inventories, by and large, because the computer can operate rapidly; it can relate each inventory transaction or delivery requirement to the total picture of the organization's resources and requirements, providing the required responsiveness with lower inventories than ever before. J. Stanford Smith, Vice President and Group Executive for General Electric Company's Information Systems Group, states "there are some observers who feel that one underlying reason for the unusually long and even growth of the U.S. economy in the past seven years has been the use of computers by individual businesses in inventory control."*

The Union Pacific Railroad, for example, had in January 1968 installed fifty-three computers in thirty-seven railroad yard offices.† The computers schedule the use of freight cars to meet shippers' needs with the minimum number of cars. The railroad's management reports that with the aid of the computer they can operate with 3000 fewer cars. Clearly the computer has had an important effect on the management of resources, a subject which will be explored further in the next chapter. The significant consideration here is that when the computer is used to manage a company's resources, there are effects on the company's operations. Data must be collected for the development of the relationships needed for computer decisions; usage of different items, typical response times, and delivery requirements must be known. Invariably, operating personnel are called upon to collect and record these data in addition to their regular duties. This often leads to an increase in reporting work load. Operating personnel are also asked to carry out instructions prepared by the computer system, with the inherent problems of interfacing with

---

* J. Stanford Smith, "Man and Computer: The New Partnership," *The General Electric Forum*, General Electric Company, New York. Winter 1967–1968.
† *Time*, January 26, 1968.

a machine rather than with human supervisors. They are required to report their actions more frequently and in more detailed terms than before, because the control of operations now depends on greater volumes of accurate and timely numbers than it did when control was performed on a semi-intuitive basis by human supervisors and foremen. The effects of these influences on operating personnel as individuals will be explored in a later chapter. Their effects on operational procedures are also significant.

CASE 4H

◀ Electric utility companies employ many work crews to install new facilities and to maintain and repair existing ones. Most of the work done is planned well in advance and can be prescheduled, but equipment failures, storms, and other emergencies often require rescheduling. Work crews are made up according to the type of job to be done. The number and type of personnel, the types of trucks, tools, and materials issued vary widely from one kind and size of job to another. Naturally, an electric utility company would like to keep the number of workers and its investment in tools and materials to a minimum while at the same time keeping up with scheduled work and providing reserve resources to meet emergencies. Effective scheduling of work crews is important because more effective scheduling can, in principle, reduce idle time and transportation time from one job to another, and maximize the productivity of any given level of resources.

An electric utility company decided to use a computer for work crew scheduling. The computer was provided with the routine maintenance schedule and a description of the new construction tasks planned. It was also provided with lists of the numbers and skills of personnel available, trucks, specialized tools, and materials. The computer was expected to combine the data to produce an optimum schedule for the employment of the resources to meet the needs. It was hoped that the level of resources needed would be reduced because of the better schedules. Should an emergency or equipment failure arise, the requirements for the necessary repairs were to be fed to the computer and its speed would make possible the preparation of a revised optimum schedule in a very short time. The ability to respond rapidly was as important a justification for the computer as the reduction in resources, in the minds of the company's management.

Before the computer could effectively relate resources to requirements, it had to be provided with some means of determining the requirements of each type of job. If a line of poles was to be installed, for example, the computer had to be told what materials of what kind are required in installing poles, and the average amount of time needed to install a pole. If any special conditions (such as difficult topography) apply to a particular job, these too should be fed to the computer, together with previous knowledge about the effect of such conditions on the standard work crew make up and working time requirements. The utility company's management found that despite efforts over a number of years to obtain work measurement statistics, the statistics available were not sufficiently accurate nor detailed for the computer's needs. They therefore had to institute a new work measurement program, and for the purpose provided all the work crews with forms to be filled out every day. Each form was to show in detail the number of minutes spent performing each task and the materials and tools used. Naturally idle time and transit time had to be shown as well, so that the time to actually perform the tasks would not be overstated.

The work crews took a dim view of this new work measurement program, for several reasons. For one thing, they complained that on days when they did a large number of simple tasks, they would spend almost as much time filling out the forms as they did doing the work. Second, and more significant, they objected to the implication they inferred that the company was planning to work them harder, to increase their work loads after collecting statistics to "prove" that it would be possible for them to be more productive. The workers' union filed a grievance, and lengthy negotiations ensued. Management was finally able to convince reluctant union officials that the purpose of the work measurement program was to improve scheduling rather than to speed up work, and that there were reasons why the workers themselves might benefit from the hoped-for greater efficiency. The workers' objections to the volume and detail of reporting remained, however, and management was able to satisfy the union only by reducing its requirements for amount and detail of information. They knew this would reduce the effectiveness of the computer's scheduling, but it was the only way they could obtain cooperation. The work measurement program then went into effect and the data were collected. The computer scheduling system was later instituted, and it worked satisfactorily and produced both economies and improved responsiveness. However, there remains some question in the minds of the system's designers whether the economies are as great as they might have been. They received less detail than they wanted, and they suspect that some inflating of work times occurred in the reports to cover coffee breaks and tardiness, as well as to reflect a remaining fear that the reported time would be used later to put pressure on the workers. The system designers feel that still greater efficiency might have derived from the use of the computer if really accurate work measurement statistics had been available. ▶

Another effect of the computer on operations derives from its rigidity and inability to deal with any condition for which it was not programmed. Management and the developers of new systems can easily overlook the fact that operations run by people can adapt to exceptions and special requests that are not intended to be part of the system. Sometimes management does not even find out that these adaptations exist until complaints arise because the computer is not providing them.

CASE 4 I

◀ More than ten years ago a telephone company installed its first computer to prepare customer bills. One of the functions performed by the computer, as part of the billing process, was the issuance of overdue notices and instructions for cutoff of service to people whose bills were not paid. The procedure for this was formal and long established. A series of three overdue notices would be sent out fifteen days apart, followed by an automatic work order for cutoff of service to the delinquent subscriber. The procedures were absolute and invariable, and company policy for many years had been to practice them rigidly. The policies were, of course, reflected in the computer programs, because management had no intention of changing this procedure.

Within a few weeks after the computerized billing system went into operation, complaints began to occur. The computer was issuing overdue notices and, later, work orders to cut off service, under very embarrassing conditions. Such cases as the following arose:

1   The owner of one of the town's leading businesses was on an extended pleasure trip in Europe, and had forgotten to leave any instructions for the handling of utility bills received during his absence. He returned to find his service cut off, and complained about this with some heat to his close friend, the President of the telephone company.

2   Every year the City Hall staff would set aside all non-essential clerical work for a period of six weeks, while they worked on the issuance and receipt of the annual real estate taxes. During this time other matters, such as paying routine bills, were set aside and attended to after the real estate tax load had been processed. Applying its routine procedure, the computer inexorably determined that telephone service to City Hall should be cut off and only an alert clerk forestalled the execution of the computer's work order.

It became apparent to the telephone company's management that they had never, in fact, been rigidly applying their overdue collection procedure. Special cases and exceptions had always been permitted by the clerks and supervisors in the billing department, and some of these (as in the case of City Hall) were enshrined as regular custom. Since most of these accommodations differed, and since each involved a personal managerial judgment, it was decided not to attempt incorporating them in the computer's programs. Instead, a group of people was detailed to inspect all of the overdue notices and work orders for cutoff of service before they were issued, and to specially investigate those which seemed to deviate from regular conditions. Human adaptability had proved essential, and was added to the system to ameliorate the unacceptable effect of applying the computer's decision rules literally. ▶

In all fairness to the machine, such failures are not its fault but are the fault of the managers planning the machine-based systems. Often they should allow clerical people to be retained in the system to deal with exceptions (as is now done by the telephone company). In other cases, the exceptions should be handled by the computer, and the fault is in inadequate preplanning of its programs. A large number of such failures in a given instance may mean, however, that the computer is fundamentally unsuited to the job at hand and that the attempt to use it was a mistake. Managers must be alert to such possibilities.

Changes in operating procedures have always involved cost and difficulty: acquisition of new equipment, rearrangement of people and facilities, transcription of files to new forms and media, and retraining of personnel. When computers are involved in operating procedures, the cost of changing them has almost invariably increased. In addition to the difficulties just mentioned, the computer-using organization wanting to improve or change a clerical procedure must reprepare the computer programs, often reorganize the files of data stored in the computer system, and perhaps change computing equipment. An example of this was presented in Case 1B, where a small insurance company was shown evolving its data processing procedures through several "generations," each requiring a substantial investment in new programs, programming personnel, and equipment. As the resulting systems become more complex, the cost and difficulty of changing them increases proportionately.

Managements have sometimes found (to their dismay) that it is virtually impossible to change an existing procedure. The detailed operations of a computer's programs are familiar only to the individuals who prepared the programs. They should always, of course, prepare a completely detailed record of everything the program does and how it does it. However, such complete records are arduous and uninteresting to prepare, and programmers are often under pressure to proceed to other programming work, so the records are frequently imperfect. This is not a serious problem so long as the programmers remain available. Changes required in programs they worked on can be assigned to them, and they can remember enough about the original programs to make the changes. However, as time passes this becomes less possible. The programmers forget the details of work done years earlier, and frequently they are lost to the organization through resignation or retirement. In such cases, if the documentation of a program to be changed was inadequate, it is necessary for the programmer assigned to make the changes to analyze how it works by a process of deduction before he is able to make changes. If the program is complex (and programs for modern systems performing advanced work are increasingly so), this analysis can be almost prohibitively difficult. Most programmers would rather start from scratch and prepare a new program. Thus the cost of changing a program becomes the cost of scrapping it and doing it over again, incorporating whatever changes are desired. This is a far higher cost than management expects or has a right to expect.

This problem often arises when the programs in use are the products of the computer manufacturer or another outside organization. As noted earlier, some applications (for example, demand deposit accounting in banks) lend themselves to standardized programs which can be programmed once and then applied in many organizations. A user will naturally take advantage of such programs, thereby decreasing the programming investment required of his own staff. However, no one in the user's organization will be familiar with all the operating details of such a program, and so the user is unable to make detailed changes in it. If the user should want to make changes and be unable to obtain the help of the original programmers, he is likely to find that he must invest the money that he saved by using the standard program in either studying it or starting over.

It is possible that this general increase in the cost of changing operating procedures may become a rigidifying influence on methods throughout industry. A "hardening of the arteries" may develop, with organizations reluctant or unable to tamper with existing computer-based systems because of the cost and risk of error involved in the change. Fortunately, the newer programming languages often provide comprehensible records of processing details as an automatic by-product of the programming process. Some other aids have also been developed, such as programs which prepare flow charts. They trace the operations of functional programs and note points at which decisions are made leading to alternative paths through the program. The result of this trace is a computer-prepared flow chart of a program, which will be of considerable help to a programmer attempting to analyze the operation of an unfamiliar program. Such tools as these should be of considerable help in the task of analyzing and understanding programs prepared earlier by others. Such help will be increasingly important, if things continue as they are, because computer users are in danger of being buried under a pile of computer programs they no longer understand well enough to change, of being constrained from changing by the "dead hand" of a past generation of programmers.

CHANGES IN THE ORGANIZATION OF OPERATIONS

Because the computer makes it possible for organizations to operate in new ways, it inevitably follows that the organization of the units performing the operations will change too. The following kinds of changes can be widely observed in organizations using computers extensively in their operations.

Many organizations have found it advisable to reduce the number of organizational units dealing with the scheduling and planning of production, or with inventory control and distribution planning. The physical location of facilities such as plants and warehouses is often determined by the time and cost needed to move goods. The computer, of course, has made little or no change in this area, so the location of physical facilities is relatively little affected. However, because of the availability of information, it used to be necessary to have a scheduling or assignment activity at every physical facility. With the use of data communications and computer scheduling, this is no longer necessary.

CASE 4J

◀ The company manufacturing construction machinery cited in Case 3F has a network of more than fifty dealerships in the United States and Canada, each of which stocks repair parts that the dealers feel will frequently be needed. In order to supply the dealers' needs, the company supports five parts depots, in which larger numbers of ordinary parts are stocked as well as many rarely needed parts that the dealers do not stock themselves. Finally, the company's twelve manufacturing plants maintain inventories of specialized and obsolete parts associated with their particular product types and also stand ready when necessary to perform emergency production runs of parts that have become scarce in both the dealers' and company's stocks. In all, then, there are more than seventy locations at which part inventories were kept. At each location files were required to record inventory levels and reorder points, and clerks were employed to keep track of transactions and see to it that inventories were kept at a satisfactory level.

While the system worked satisfactorily, there was a significant incidence of failures to supply customer needs, and a great deal of capital was tied up in parts inventories. The company installed a computer-based inventory control and scheduling system for the repair parts, in order to both improve responsiveness and reduce inventory levels. The computer's job was to keep records of the inventories on hand at each of the dealerships, and at each of the five parts depots. (It would also identify the obsolete parts for which the individual plants were responsible, but would make no effort to maintain accurate inventory balances for them. This was regarded as economical, because in many cases an order for an obsolete part could be met by making one more economically than by keeping it in stock. Many of the obsolete parts are very rarely needed.) The computer was connected to a data communication system linking all the dealers, depots, and plants. All inventory issues and receipts throughout the system were reported to the computer, which would post them to the appropriate records and produce the necessary accounting documents. Whenever an emergency request was received it was then possible for the computer to search all its files and muster the resources of all of the seventy parts locations to meet emergency needs—a capability that had never been possible before.

Each dealer and depot remained responsible for the physical handling of its inventories, and for an occasional count to verify the accuracy of the computer's records. However, the clerical functions of preparing and handling documents, of initiating reorders, and of communicating among dealers and depots were eliminated. Both dealers and depots found that they could simplify their organizational structures by combining the clerical functions associated with repair parts into those performing routine accounting, usually reducing the staff by one or two people in the process. The result was the elimination of nearly seventy organizational units devoted to clerical processing of inventory transactions, although the number of physical facilities in the system remained essentially unchanged. ▶

It might be assumed that this consolidation of clerical organizational units leads to a reduction in the number of people involved with scheduling and distribution processes, and therefore in the supervisory positions available as promotional opportunities. This is not true; in fact, the opposite is the case. For example, the Chairman of the Chase Manhattan Bank says, "Ten years ago we had one officer for every 15 staff members. Today, we have one officer for every 10 staff members, and within the next decade we expect the ratio to be about 1 for every 5."* He attributes this change in ratio to the increasing use of computers in the bank, noting that the number of clerical personnel employed has grown far more slowly than the number of supervisory positions. With the computer, the supervision of operations does not diminish, but shifts in nature from the supervision of people performing rou-

---

* George Champion, *Automation, Capital and Economic Growth,* Chase Manhattan Bank, 1967.

tine tasks to the supervision of a system requiring continual monitoring, error control, and evolutionary improvement. The supervisors of operations move physically from small dispersed organizational units to the center from which the computer-based operations control function is conducted (see Chapter 7). The skills required of them change from those involved in supervising personnel to more technical, computer-oriented ones. All this change can lead to significant displacement, because clerical supervisors are not necessarily adept at computer operations planning or supervising. Furthermore, the geographic dislocations involved are painful to many. However, as noted in the above example, the total number of supervisory positions is unlikely to decrease; relative to the number of clerical positions, it will usually increase sharply.

In situations where computers provide instructions to operating personnel, it is no longer necessary for foremen or supervisors to do so. In some highly automated plants, one can see the production workers on a factory floor receiving machine-produced instructions, with only a relatively few people in the computer room associated with the routine production of these instructions. In such plants, a class of personnel has been largely eliminated: the experienced foreman, who applies years of knowledge of the operation on an intuitive basis to developing instructions for his subordinates. Substituted for him is the computer programmer, an individual who is rarely seen on the factory floor but who operates from a remote "head office" in ways completely mysterious to the production worker.

CASE 4K

◀ A manufacturing company specializes in high precision products for the automotive industry: speed governors for diesel engines, carburetors, fuel injection systems, and the like. They are accustomed to receiving orders for relatively small numbers of units, often with specialized custom modifications required. Therefore, their production runs are both short and complex, and it is difficult to develop a work load for each machine tool that would keep it comfortably occupied. The company obtained production machines as general purpose in nature as possible, so that each would be capable of performing many different operations and the work load could be shared more evenly. However, time-consuming setups were still required before each production run, and the workers' skills varied, so it was still necessary to schedule carefully.

The company developed a computer-based production scheduling system to attempt to improve the efficiency of its operations. Each night the computer would compare the reported work done during the day to work that had been planned, and prepare a list of unfinished work to be done. This list would be combined with the plan of new work to be undertaken the following day, to develop the next day's actual production requirement. Then the production requirement would be combined with the descriptions of the current setups of the work stations on the production floor, and a schedule would be prepared for the coming day which would involve as few changes in setup as possible. This schedule would be converted to a sequence of individual work orders to be attached to each piece of work in the production process. As the piece moved from station to station during the day for the required operations to be performed, the work order for the station to which it was being sent would be the next in sequence. If the computer's scheduling were satisfactory, each station would complete a job and send it off to the station called for by the next of its work orders just as the next job arrived with its set of work orders.

After considerable cut and try adjustment, this system worked satisfactorily, but things never went exactly as anticipated. Machines would break down; men would report sick; unexpected out-of-stock conditions would occur; customers would cancel, change, or ask for expedition of their orders. These and many other kinds of events necessitated frequent adjustments and modifications to schedules during the operating day. This, of course, was anticipated by the system's designers; in order to facilitate the adjustment of schedules, the computer's operators were installed in a booth overlooking the production floor, so that they could continually review the flow of materials and activities at the work stations and observe interruptions in the flow. Each work station was provided with a telephone connected to the operating booth, by which each worker would report completion of each task and initiation of the next to the operators. The operators would compare these reports with the anticipated schedule for the day, noting any discrepancies or slippages. When they suspected trouble, they would telephone the production stations to investigate and then initiate actions to attempt to return to schedule. If this was impossible, they would initiate a new computer scheduling run, describing the changed conditions and asking for a new schedule for the remainder of the day. (In fact, such a computer rescheduling was rarely done. When emergencies arose the operators were so busy attempting to "fight the fire" that they would rarely get around to the rather time-consuming job of preparing the input for another computer run until the working day was over.)

Before the computer system was installed, the supervision of production took place according to the chart shown in Fig. 4–1. The work stations were organized into small groups, taking their production schedules from group foremen. Each group foreman would be aware of his group's machine setups, personnel absences, and the like, and would make detailed assignments accordingly. The group foremen, in turn, would be assigned daily quantities of work to be done by a Production Scheduling Department, that was responsible

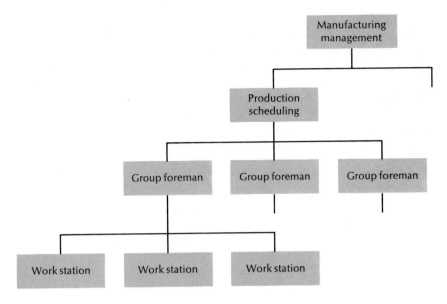

FIG. 4–1   Traditional organization of production scheduling.

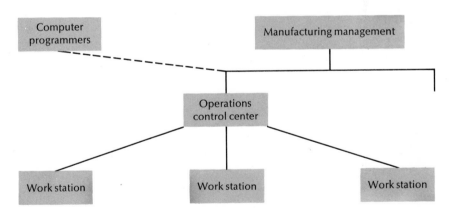

FIG. 4–2   Organization of computer-based production scheduling.

for combining new orders, work in process, and emergency conditions into the best schedule they could. They operated at a general level, assigning quantities of work to group foremen based on the overall capabilities of the group. If the quantities assigned were either too large or too small, the foremen would report the fact and negotiations involving other foremen would ensue until what appeared to be the best possible apportionment of work was arrived at.

With the computer-based system, the organization of production scheduling was as shown in Fig. 4–2. Each work station reported directly to the operations control center; the group foremen were eliminated (as schedulers, though some of them remained for training and personnel administration purposes.) The operations control center issued production schedules based not on the judgment of the operators but on the results of the computer's computations. The operators were not responsible for or knowledgeable about the computer's programs, so even they were not personally responsible for the schedules. The programmers who had prepared the scheduling programs were on the corporate staff and not permanently assigned to manufacturing; during normal operation they were not on the scene at all.

The result of this was that the workers on the production floor no longer communicated with foremen physically near them and available for consultation, but by means of computer printouts and telephones with strangers located in a booth high over their heads. They knew that not even these strangers were responsible for the way the system worked; a group of management-oriented technical specialists whom they rarely saw under any conditions had prepared the computer programs and operating procedures governing their working behavior. ▶

A later chapter will explore the impact of this kind of change in operations on the personnel involved. The focus here is organizational, and the significant point is that there has been a significant reduction in the opportunities open to the blue collar worker, and a reduction in the number of rungs on the promotional ladder he can perceive ahead of him. His operational supervision is now performed by specialists who are not members of his peer group, and usually not members of his union. The generalization made by some commentators that "a level of management has been eliminated by the computer" is much too strong, because a great many operational supervisors and foremen are still required for the necessities of personnel administration and training. Furthermore, administration of the computer-based system, troubleshooting, and improvisation remain uniquely human talents and few production processes have no need for them. However, in some organizations where operations have proved particularly amenable to computer scheduling and direction, few foremen are left.

SUMMARY

There are those who have visualized the "computer-controlled operation of the future" as something like an octopus: with a single "brain" at the center directing every minute task performed by each of the thousands of human and mechanical minions of the organization. It is apparent from this exploration of the computer's actual effects on operations that no such revolutionary reorganization or change to complete dependence on computer decision-making has taken place. Furthermore, considerations of the limitations of the computer tend to indicate that it never will take place. On the other hand, this analysis has shown that the changes actually occurring are widespread and significant, even though not so extreme. The computer has made it possible to handle volumes of existing kinds of work, flexibility in variations of work, and new kinds of work that were never possible before. It has led to a greater rigidity in procedures that must be followed by personnel of the organization, and in the organization's ability to evolve and change its systems. It has led to a very perceptible nation-wide improvement in the management of resources hitherto idled in inventories and in distribution systems. And perhaps most significant for our purposes, it has led to major shifts in the type and distribution of jobs associated with operations, and in the organizational structures of operational organizations. Every manager in a computer-using organization should be aware of these tendencies, and be prepared to help guide his organization's adaptation to them.

CHAPTER 5

CHANGES IN MANAGEMENT AND PLANNING

"The queen bee is as much a prisoner of the
*system as any other in the hive."**
JOHN W. GARDNER

Many have speculated about the effects the computer will have on the processes of managing organizations and planning their futures. Some view with alarm, some are optimistic, virtually all anticipate revolutionary changes. There is a wide divergence of opinion about what the charges will be, however, so it is particularly important that this subject be viewed dispassionately, that the demonstrated effects of the computer on the process of management be assessed without bias, and that extrapolations be made only with care. This chapter takes such a view; a manager reading it will obtain objective guidance about the computer's effect on the nature of his job.

CHANGES IN THE MANAGER

It is often forecast that managers will have to change their behavior—the way they perform their jobs—because of the computer. To most present managers this seems a theoretical possibility, of concern to them only in the distant future or perhaps only to their successors. However, most managers in computer-using organizations have already changed their behavior, though not necessarily in the ways the forecasters anticipated.

To many managers, the acquisition of a computer seems much like the acquisition of a new production tool or building. The manager assumes that he may participate to a degree in the planning process, but once the plan is made he expects to be affected very little, unless the computer is his own responsibility. In most cases he has found that his assumption was wrong, that the computer, sooner or later, affects him regardless of his place in the organization. The five reasons for this are discussed below.

---

* Time, April 11, 1969.

Enforcement of operating discipline

Within his department, the manager will be called upon to enforce the new operating disciplines accompanying the computer. This will almost always be an unwelcome responsibility because it represents a new source of potential friction and resentment between himself and his subordinates. If he is preoccupied with other problems, he may prefer to evade his responsibility for enforcing operating discipline. The computer is almost guaranteed to expose this evasion.

CASE 5A

◀ When a telephone company installs service for a subscriber it must assign a wire to him from the "bundle" of wires in the cable running near his home or place of business, and must connect the wire to a terminal at the switching center at the end of the cable. The cables pass through junction boxes at points where they come together, so a wire in one cable can be connected to a wire in another. If all the wires in the cable nearest to a subscriber are used up, the installer must move back along the cable to a junction box containing

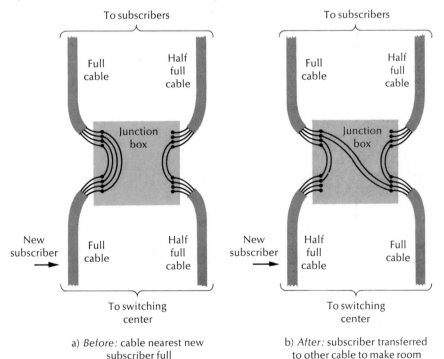

a) *Before:* cable nearest new subscriber full

b) *After:* subscriber transferred to other cable to make room

FIG. 5-1   Transfer of wire assignments in the telephone network.

another cable, transfer some of the subscribers' wires entering the loaded cable to the other one, and then attach the newly installed telephone to the wire thus freed (see Fig. 5–1). Thus, the process of installing a telephone may involve one or more transfers of other telephone connections to make room for it. Similarly, if a switching center becomes overloaded, it is necesssary to transfer some of the wires terminating there to another switching center. If the total number of subscribers in an area grows beyond the capacity of the cables and switching centers, new ones must be installed; but a telephone company will try to transfer its facilities among the subscribers so as to fill the existing equipment as much as possible before installing new equipment.

Changes in equipment assignments occur continually as existing subscribers are disconnected, new ones are added, new homes and offices are built, and new equipment is installed. Each new transfer or assignment must consider the needs of the rest of the system, and the work must be fit smoothly into the assignments of the work crews. A computer program for performing this scheduling function was developed by a telephone company and shown to do a better job than human schedulers. Other telephone companies then began to consider using computers for equipment assignment and work scheduling.

A telephone company in a mid-western city adopted such a system, and to support it instituted a new reporting system for the work crews in the field. Since an objective of the system was to maintain the records more currently and accurately than before, the work crews were required to report more completely and quickly than they had in the past. When they were rushed, they were accustomed to putting off completion of the reporting forms until the end of the week and then doing them in a batch. Sometimes they would forget to report a specific connect or disconnect of a wire, or impromptu transfers were sometimes made when unexpected conditions were found and never reported. Such sloppiness, while understandable, could not be tolerated by the new computer-based system; it could not schedule new assignments without accurate information about present ones. Firm instructions were issued to the managers of the work crews to see to it that reporting was timely and complete.

One of the area work crew managers, preoccupied with problems of equipment failure and personnel, chose not to make an issue of this reporting discipline and allowed the men to continue reporting as they had in the past. Errors soon began to appear in the computer's files associated with that area, mostly because of work crews omitting to report disconnects and transfers they had made because of unexpectedly encountering full cables. Now that the computer was being used to produce detailed work schedules, the effect of these errors was quickly noticed. A work crew instructed to assign a certain wire to a certain subscriber would find that it was already in use. A work crew instructed to transfer a group of subscribers from one cable to another in order to make room, would find that room already existed. In such cases, the work crews had to report back for additional instructions and the telephone company's management became aware that the computer's work schedules were erroneous. An investigation soon discovered the reason and the manager of the area was censured sharply for his failure to enforce the required reporting discipline. Considerable effort was required to "debug" the file for the area, to bring it back up to date; thereafter the manager took pains to see to it that a minimum of new errors crept in. ▶

In this case, as in many others, a manager who felt that the computer's operations were none of his concern found himself forced to change his behavior, the day-to-day actions he took, in order to comply with the reporting discipline that accompanied it.

Participation in system design

The manager whose function is affected by new computer-based systems finds that he must assist the system's designers in preparing the computer's programs. They will often find that some minor change in the way things are done will simplify their programming task; only the manager can tell them whether such a small change would be acceptable. Alternatively, the system designers are likely to find that some new function could be performed by the machine with little additional programming. For example, as files are being updated the computer can easily check each record for the existence of some special condition; such a check would likely have required expensive clerical labor with a manual system. The system designers will suggest such additional functions to the manager and he should be available to consider their desirability. In fact, if he has any knowledge of the computer, he should be able to suggest them himself. If the manager is not available to the system designers to discuss details, and does not participate in the design process, he exposes himself to considerable risk of disappointment.

CASE 5B

◀ The manager of the loan department of a small bank was accustomed to being informed in the middle of each week about each loan for which payments were overdue. He would authorize dunning notices individually, and they would be sent out in the mail at the end of the week. When the function of loan accounting was programmed for a computer, it occurred to the system designers that the list of overdue loans could be produced by the machine at the same time as the dunning notices were prepared. This way, a single computer run would suffice for both purposes; the old way, two different runs at different times would have been needed. They observed that according to the bank's rules a dunning notice should always be issued when a loan payment was overdue, and any adjustments could be made afterward. They also noticed that the loan manager rarely interfered with this process, anyway. Because the system designers had been discouraged from dealing with the manager of the loan department, who was inclined to think that the computer was an unnecessary extravagance on the part of bank management, they decided on their own authority to combine the two runs, and the list of overdue payments for the manager was produced at the same time that the dunning notices were issued by the computer.

The loan manager was very upset about this after the new system started operating. He was informed of the change by several irate customers who telephoned to complain about the appearance of dunning notices. It developed that, unknown to the system designers, a few customers had for months or years been proceeding according to accommodations with the loan manager to fit their payment dates into their accounting cycles. While there were few of these, they generally were important business customers whose good will the bank was anxious to retain. The loan manager angrily protested to the system designers, who accordingly went back and programmed the reporting run they had eliminated. They felt aggrieved because no one had been available to identify and explain the few exceptions to the system at the time they had made their decision, and felt unjustly blamed for what they considered was the loan manager's failure to participate in the design of a system intended to serve him.   ▶

Understanding the program's decision rules

When a computer is used to provide planning information by evaluating the effects of alternative actions, it draws conclusions from data presented to it on the basis of decision rules built into its programs. If these decision rules are inaccurate or too general, the resulting information will be misleading. The decision rules are established by complex mathematical analyses of masses of historical data, and it may be difficult for the manager to participate because of his lack of mathematical and computer knowledge. However, if he is ignorant of the decision rules of the model, he will have no choice but to apply the computer's advice literally; if he knew how the decision rules had been developed, he might be able to anticipate potential difficulty.

CASE 5C

◀   An oil company needed to install a new tank farm for the storage of petroleum products near a city the company served. They wanted sufficient capacity to handle demands for their products during the intervals between scheduled tanker deliveries. The tankers' schedules were rigid, and emergency shipments were upsetting and expensive. The computer was used to relate the records of sales of the various products (gasoline, fuel oil, etc.) during the past five years to the desired schedule of tanker deliveries. Seasonal fluctuations were considered, but within each season average demand data was used to predict the total capacity that should be allowed in the tank farm for each of the company's products. The area distribution manager, presented with the results of the computer's forecast, felt that the capacity requirements seemed a little low. However, he had provided the historical sales data and he knew it was accurate, so he assumed that the relationship between sales and storage capacity had to be accurate as well.

After the tank farm was installed, it turned out that the capacity for gasoline storage was inadequate. The system designers who had programmed the prediction program for the computer had been unaware that gasoline price wars were frequent in the area, and that they could develop and be resolved within periods of a few weeks. Sometimes (such as when new stations were being set up) the area manager found it in the company's interest to lead the price cutting; at other times (such as when stocks were low) he would find it in the company's interest to resist. The demand for gasoline would swing sharply as a result of these decisions, and sudden surges of demand lasting only a few weeks would result. The average seasonal figures did not show the effect of these fluctuations caused by price wars; the computer programmers did not have the experience to enable them to ask for data about short-term fluctuations and the area manager assumed they had been considered. The result of this oversight was a number of expensive, emergency tanker shipments plus a hurried program to add more capacity to the tank farm. ▶

New conflicts with other departments

A manager unexpectedly finds himself required to interact in new ways with his opposite numbers in other departments. This may occur simply because of competition for scarce programmers and machine time. The manager becomes increasingly dependent on the services of the computer, and as he does so he finds other managers also increasing their demands for computer assistance. Many managers come to feel that one of the most annoying constraints on their further progress is the shortage of programming help and computer time available to them for management-oriented computer applications.

Increasingly, these new conflicts between managers of hitherto separate departments are occurring because of more fundamental changes caused by the computer. As increasingly broad applications of the computer are developed to manage the company's operations, functionally separate organizational units (e.g., marketing and manufacturing) are likely to be brought together on an operating level to a degree never before experienced.

CASE 5D

◀ In a company manufacturing small electric motors, the sales department was prone to overoptimism in its forecasts. Many of the orders they told management they expected to receive never materialized, and often the orders received were delayed well beyond the forecast date. Management, used to this overoptimism, privately formed their own estimates of the actual sales volume likely to result from the sales department's forecasts.

The purchasing department of the electric motor manufacturer was motivated toward conservatism. If they overbought, they would be criticized for allowing inventories to become excessive. If they underbought, the resulting shortages and delays in orders would not affect them directly, but would be the headache of the sales department. Because the purchasing department and the sales department reported to the same management, management could perform the function of arbitration between the differing motivations of purchasing and sales, attempting to steer a course between the two extremes which would combine modest inventories with satisfactory service to customers.

A computer system was installed to manage inventories and schedule production based on the forecasts of the sales department. As soon as it went into operation, purchasing found themselves called upon to obtain larger quantities of material than ever before; they immediately questioned the computer's programs. The sales department, in turn, now saw for the first time the actual inventory levels and purchase orders outstanding and were upset at the apparent inadequacy of the company's manufacturing plans in light of the orders they expected to receive. The computer, in effect, was a "tattletale" telling each department the other's secrets; management no longer intervened as arbitrator between the two. The resulting discord between purchasing and sales took some time to clear up, and at the end of the adjustment period, sales, purchasing, and even management, found the realism of their forecasting significantly improved. ▶

Such effects are largely a result of using the machine in operational areas, and such changes in management interaction are effectively only changes in the management of operations. However, as this case shows, there are actually effects on the way managers manage and the way they interact with other managers; there is a considerably broader impact than just on day-to-day operational organization.

The heightened challenge

As observed in Chapter 3, the computer is part of a climate of continuing and accelerating change to which the manager must adapt. In most organizations, the computer is the symbol and focus of this change, the symbol of a new wave of challenge to the manager. The appearance of the computer challenges the manager to use it; to become familiar with it, with the strange people who work with it, and with the shortcomings as well as the virtues it embodies.

To the mature manager, preoccupied for many years with the details of his particular trade, this challenge may be a difficult one to accept. In many organizations, although the computer was intended to be at the service of all operating departments equally, it is in fact used only by a minority where managers have appeared who are anxious to accept and respond to the challenge embodied in the computer. The rest of the managers, temporizing for one reason or another, stay away from it. This, of course, leads to a failure to utilize the computer in the best interest of the organization and sometimes to failures to implement plans approved by top management on the assumption that subordinate managers will carry them out.

CASE 5E

◀ In the capitol of an eastern state there is large closet lined with bookshelves from floor to ceiling. These bookshelves are almost completely packed with reports of consulting organizations, committees, and study groups of many kinds, virtually all of them recommending changes and improvements in some facet of the state government procedures. A majority of these changes involve using computers in some way. At the time each was submitted, the then Governor usually accepted at least some of the recommendations in the report; such acceptance, however, was usually contingent on legislative action. The visitor, viewing this collection of reports, is informed ruefully by his guide that in the end almost none of the recommendations in any of the reports was ever implemented. In this state, it is evident that virtually every operating department has been unwilling to rise to the challenge posed by new techniques and methods, many of them implying the use of computers, and that therefore the expense for consultants and study committees over the years has been largely wasted. ▶

It is also possible for the manager to *overreact* to the challenge of the computer by attempting to institute advanced methods too quickly. This mistake has often led to the premature installation of advanced computers, underused for long periods.

This new challenge to the manager is, of course, not solely attributable to the computer. Many other changes in society, business organization, products, and ways of doing business contribute to it. Nevertheless, because the computer is frequently the physical embodiment of the challenge visible to the manager, he tends to associate the two.

Because of these five forces, the manager typically changes from an "uninvolved layman" when the computer is first installed to a participant in the planning and management of data processing in his company. As this participation spreads through the organization, attitudes toward the computer change. The computer activity is increasingly regarded by all members of management as a central service facility for the organization, a change demonstrated by the trend in many companies away from charging departments for the use of the computer and toward assuming its cost as a corporate expense, making the computer available to the departments in proportion to their needs rather than to their ability to pay. The growth of this view of the computer as a corporate resource is borne out in a recent survey* which examines the use of computers in 108 manufacturing organizations. Among other things, the study found that to an increasing degree chief executives and operating managers are participating in the planning of data processing functions.

These changes have occurred primarily because of the use of the computer in the management of operations and in clerical work. As a by-product, we have seen that the computer exerts a "backlash" effect on management. Such effects should be greatest on the lower levels of management associated most directly with operations, and decrease as the level of management rises. If the computer's only effects on management have occurred because of its use in operations, then there should be very little observable effect on top management.

This has been borne out in practice; so far, the changes in managers' behavior have been least at the top level. The future may be different, but it is undeniable that the behavior of top managers today shows little change traceable to the computer. This is understandable when one considers the primary concerns of top managers: long-range planning, including such matters as diversification and acquisition; structuring the organization for optimum results; selecting and motivating operating management. All of these involve uncertain relationships between causes and effects, the perception of broad trends and their effects in the relatively distant future, and simple intuition. Because these areas cannot be described by numerical relationships, the computer can be of little help. Overoptimistic attempts to use the computer to help management in these areas have generally come to grief. Case 3G

---

* Neal J. Dean, "The Computer Comes of Age," *Harvard Business Review*, January–February 1968.

exemplified this. It described a situation in which the management of a chemical company, forming judgments about the success of new products, attempted to use the computer to select "early warning" data most relevant to their decisions. It turned out in that case (as in virtually all similar cases) that it was necessary to provide intelligent human evaluation along with the best the computer was able to do before the managers received anything like the help they required. As that case pointed out, when an executive sees a number which is at variance with the number he expected, he asks a question; he does not take an action. Someone must answer his question, and the computer can do no more than tell him what data lies behind the number the manager sees. His question, however, has to do with understanding rather than with data.

This inability of the computer to help top management is inherent; it cannot deal with the intangibles and intuitive factors the manager must handle. However, it is also true that systems analysts and programmers have not yet developed the experience and skills to enable them to adapt the computer to assisting the manager. As time goes on, their programs will become increasingly sophisticated and the top level manager will obtain an increasing degree of assistance from the computer system. We will now explore ways in which this may happen, and results to date.

CHANGES IN THE PROCESS OF MANAGEMENT AND PLANNING

The reason for using a computer in the operations of an organization is to improve their efficiency, to manage the firm's resources better. As we have seen, in order to use a computer in operations an organization must develop quantitative measurement and reporting procedures more precise than it has ever had before. With these developed, the organization is in a position to obtain an important by-product, statistics to support improvements in operations and plans for future new ventures. The organization sometimes finds, as a pleasant surprise, that it is better able to develop detailed plans than ever before.

CASE 5F

◀ A large trucking company installed a computer to schedule its deliveries. Given information about transportation times between all warehouses and customers, times to load and unload merchandise by type and amount, and the available sizes and kinds of trucks, the computer was put to work developing optimum schedules for the company's trucks in executing each day's pickup and delivery orders. Before this could be done, a sizeable effort was made to obtain accurate data about all orders, shipments, and truck movements. With the computer system in operation, the trucking company found that it achieved cost savings ranging from 5% on days in which there was an unfavorable combination of orders, to as much as 20% on days when maximum consolidation was possible. These savings were sufficient to justify the investment in the computer, its programming, and the statistical studies that went into the scheduling system.

With the scheduling system in operation and regular statistics being collected on the movements of the trucks, management found that it had a realistic standard for evaluating operations from one year to the next, to perceive increases and decreases in efficiency. They also found that the computer could generate "simulated schedules"—schedules not for use, but for evaluating the effects of changes: possible new additions or changes in the company's truck fleet, changes in demand, or changed warehouses. For example, the company was offered warehouse space at a bargain rate in a new location in one of the cities it served. Major changes in routes would be needed to use it, so it was not clear whether this additional space would be worth even the bargain rate. The computer was instructed to develop a variety of schedules on the basis of having the new warehouse space available and their overall costs were evaluated. It became apparent that the new space would be useful as a transshipment point between large, long-haul trucks and smaller local delivery trucks, because the number of long hauls would be reduced. On the other hand, savings would not result unless there was a change in the distribution of trucks in the fleet. The number of small, short-haul trucks should be increased, and the number of large long-haul trucks should be reduced. This finding led to a number of other "simulated schedule" runs, evaluating the effects of different mixes of truck sizes in the trucking company's fleet. Finally, management accepted the new warehouse space, placed a number of orders for new, small trucks, and disposed of a number of its larger ones. The overall effect of these interconnected changes was a further increase of 10% in the efficiency and profitability of the company. Management is now enthusiastically devoted to the idea of using the computer to evaluate the effects of its possible investment decisions. Now they also use it to evaluate the desirability of new customers' business as a function of location, size of business, and type of delivery. They feel they are able to operate a more efficient trucking company than ever before, and that (for the time being, at least) they have a significant competitive advantage. ▶

Having gone through the traumatic experience of successfully installing a computer to schedule operations, then, companies such as this trucking firm find themselves with a secondary benefit that could be of even greater importance—a tool with which to test the results of alternative investment decisions and management policies. In theory, this could be of more importance than the improvement in operations itself.

Many managements, perceiving this, have undertaken to provide the computer with a capability to simulate the organization's operations so that alternative planning decisions may be evaluated. Sometimes modest investments produce effective simulations without undue difficulty.

CASE 5G

◀ American Airlines uses a computer to select optimum flight plans for its aircraft.* The computer is provided with descriptions of forecast wind and temperature conditions for about 150 geographical locations. These forecasts are revised twice daily. From these data winds and temperatures can be calculated for any given time. In addition, information on predicted atmospheric turbulence is entered into the computer and correlated with possible flight plans. When a flight plan computation is desired, the computer is given the identification of the flight, its expected payload, a list of routes to be examined, the airplane type, and a code for the criteria which will determine the "best" flight plan in this case. Criteria include flying time, schedule time, fuel burned, direct operating cost, and combinations of these factors. Most commonly, a flight plan which meets the published flying time with minimum direct operating cost is preferred. Optionally, the computer may be instructed to develop a single plan at a given altitude or route.

The computer then simulates the course of the flight over the various routes, applying the calculated weather data for each point the flight "passes." Having investigated the possibilities (up to 104 possible flight plans for the longest and most complex routes) the computer selects the three "best" plans on the basis of the criteria given it and presents them to the aircraft captain, who makes the final choice. If for some reason he dislikes them all or feels he must meet some operating constraint that they do not reflect, he can request another computer run which will provide a preferred flight plan.

In effect, the computer simulates the daily movements of the entire American Airlines fleet, providing each captain with the most economical route available. The available alternatives vary enough for significant improvements in efficiency to have proved possible. A spokesman says "the flight planning computer has made a significant contribution to economical and on-time operations of American Airlines. From a purely cost standpoint, it pays its own way and generates substantial net profit." ▶

Not all organizations are so fortunate as American Airlines. The simulation of flight plans involves factors whose interactions are well known, aircraft with predictable performance characteristics, and a moderate number of alternatives to consider. Most businesses operate in more complex and less understood environments, so a great increase in understanding will be needed

---

* Computer Selects Optimum Flight Plans," *Systems,* June 1967.

before even a gross simulation can be performed that bears any relationship to reality. The business must learn the quantitative relationships needed for the model, and often it must also establish standard methods of measuring costs and actions so that they may be related to one another in the computer. This in itself can be difficult and time-consuming.

CASE 5H

◀ A computer manufacturing firm had followed an aggressive acquisition policy, acquiring over the course of several years a number of smaller related companies operating service bureaus, doing contract programming, manufacturing peripheral equipment, and the like. It became necessary to cut budgets in order to improve profitability. Management therefore undertook to investigate the effects on total profits of various possible budget cuts within the parent organization and its subsidiaries. They were faced with two possibilities—either cut budgets across the board regardless of the individual cuts' effects, or to cut selectively, considering the effect of each budgetary item on the profitability of the whole. Because of the complexity of the organization, it was thought that across the board budget cuts might do as much harm to profits as good, while selective cutting might produce dramatic savings. The company's management decided that it would be sensible to use their own product—their own expertise in computer programming—to study the problem by constructing a cost model of the organization and simulating the effects on profits of alternative budget cutting proposals.

Within a few days after the team assigned to develop the cost model had started work, it became apparent that they were faced with severe problems. Most of the subsidiaries still accounted for their internal operations separately from the parent company; the accounting statements had to be cross related. Quantities were defined in incompatible ways, and such factors as depreciation and intercompany charges were expressed in ways which would benefit the individual subsidiary. In fact, the total claimed profits of the individual subsidiaries were almost double the actual profits of the organization as a whole! It was apparent that no cost-profit model of the organization could be developed without a major restructuring of the accounting systems of all the subsidiaries, bringing them into a common form and reflecting the true value of transactions occurring between subsidiaries.

Management was appalled to find how little meaningful information could be obtained from the existing accounting systems, and undertook to develop a new, coherent system which would permit computer simulations of cost and profit relationships. Development and implementation of the new system took more than a year, however, and by then, the short-term budget cutting had long since been done. Fortunately, intuition and experience proved sufficient to meet the immediate crisis; profits improved satisfactorily. However, management is determined never to be caught in this position of ignorance again. In the future, when budgets are established, they are insistent upon having a computer-based model of the financial relationships in the organization that will help them evaluate the effects of the alternative courses available to them. ▶

While the cost-profit structures of most organizations are probably better understood than that of the computer manufacturer with its many acquisitions, they are usually inadequate to support computer simulations that can provide accurate projections. For most organizations a revolutionary change in accounting is a major proposition, involving the installation of new reporting and information systems throughout the company's operations. The installation of computer-based simulation systems is therefore approximately as severe and difficult as the installation of computers to schedule operations, and development projects covering several years are frequently required. Because of this, few organizations today have developed comprehensive computer simulations of their cost-profit relationships. In the interim, however, it has sometimes proved valuable to perform very gross simulations of the overall numbers on the company's balance sheet, on the basis of assumed interactions. While this cannot be trusted to produce accurate projections, it may nevertheless be instructive in evaluating the kinds of effects major policy changes are likely to have.

CASE 5 I
◀   A large corporation had for many years been following a policy of leasing a large part of its production equipment. Management was reconsidering the desirability of this, and wished to evaluate the effect of changing over from leases to purchases over a period of ten years. They provided the computer with a simple model of the financial relationships among the nineteen major items on the company's balance sheet and among ten factors affecting cash flow. They then provided a projected sales and gross income growth curve for the ten-year period, and had the computer simulate the effect of the new policy on debt ratio, book value per share, and cash flow.

The results of the computer's simulation were surprising and disappointing. It developed that the return on stockholders' equity would decrease during the period rather than increase (as had been hoped) and the cash flow projections were unacceptable. The advocates of discontinuing the leasing policy challenged the validity of the simulation, because only a few gross factors had been provided for the model, and the interactions among them had been largely guessed at. However, when reruns of the simulation were performed using the attackers' own estimates of the correct values and assumptions, the results still turned out unfavorable.

All parties to the experiment ended up feeling that, while the numbers produced by the simulation were of doubtful validity, they had all learned a great deal about the capital structure of their company and the effects of various possible changes in it. Few people defended the value of the simulation's numeric results, but all agreed that the process of performing it had been well worthwhile as an educational experience. ▶

Such gross simulations can therefore be useful in the short term, even though they are based only on gross factors and guesses about the interactions between them. They may produce valid results—or they may not. However, as a first step toward reliable, more complex simulation procedures, as an introduction to a method for studying the complex financial interactions of a large corporation; simple simulations are valuable. Few managements who have undertaken such projects have been sorry that they did so, or have felt that the effort was wasted.

It appears that in time computer simulations and projections of the financial effects of alternative policy and investment decisions will become a profound influence on the process of management and planning. Because of the effort needed to discover the relationships between the factors in sufficient detail for the computer to be able to use them, and the concomitant effort of developing and installing new financial reporting systems to provide the detailed data, the state of the art is developing only slowly; few fully developed examples of this kind of computer simulation can be found today.

If it does develop (as now appears likely) that a management equipped with satisfactory simulation models of its cost and profit relationships will be in a favored competitive position, it should follow that large companies, able to afford staffs of statisticians, operations research specialists, and computer programmers, should benefit. The smaller businessman, unable to afford such resources, could be expected to suffer.

This is not necessarily true. There are several reasons why the smaller business may be able to take as much advantage of computer simulation techniques as the large one. For one thing, the smaller business is probably simpler and easier to understand. This has always been a virtue of the smaller business; its simplicity and smaller scope enable a manager to comprehend it and minimize the effects of "Parkinson's law." This virtue also applies to the development of simulations. Establishing relationships for the simulation model and collecting data to support them should be more than proportionately easier for the smaller company than the larger one.

The smaller company still suffers the disadvantage that it cannot afford the technical staff of the larger company, but this too may prove a less severe problem in the future. Because of the increasing importance of simulations in business management, computer manufacturers and programming organizations are developing general purpose simulation languages and file management systems. Using such programs, the smaller business would be required only to provide its own data and information about the specific interactions of its own financial factors. The programs would then automatically perform the file maintenance and carry out the computations needed to answer questions posed by management in the simulation language. The pioneering research efforts of the large organizations to produce general purpose "simulation software" may (ironically) be as helpful to their smaller competitors as to themselves. Finally, the inability of the smaller company to provide itself with a staff of specialists may be at least partly overcome by the changing educational background of the general manager. As subsequent chapters will show, today's students of management in colleges and graduate schools are increasingly being exposed to the techniques of statistics, operations research, and computer programming. In time, few young aspirants to management positions will be ignorant of these techniques. They will probably never equal their specialist brothers in performing advanced research or developing novel applications, but in applying (by then) familiar simulation techniques to specific problems, they may be as capable. The requirement for specialists may become less severe as knowledge of the techniques involved in applying computers to simulations becomes more widespread.

The fact that junior members of management may be able—even best qualified—to evaluate a company's alternative courses of action may lead to a significant new authority structure; a "flickering authority" residing temporarily in the hands of the person best qualified to exercise it. There are some signs that "flickering authority" has already begun to emerge, but because its development lies mostly in the future, further discussion of it is deferred to later chapters.

The computer also facilitates new methods of management control. The principle of "management by exception" is an old one; the idea that an executive should spend his time reviewing only a few exceptional conditions rather than large numbers of routine ones has been attractive for many years. The problem has always been to identify the exceptions.

In the conventional organization management is often unaware of problems until after they become serious, but to superintend operations as they occur management would have to review masses of operational data. To institute management by exception, it is necessary to interpose a staff group to review the operating data and identify those items of interest to management. This adds nonproductive personnel and delay, and leads to uncertain performance because the staff group's judgment of what constitutes an exception might not agree with that of the manager being served. With the aid of the computer, quantities of operating data can be reviewed rapidly and exceptions identified according to rules supplied by management. With suitable reporting structures established and with the computer comparing reports of operations against targets and goals and calling management's attention to those results that are anomalous, management by exception has become fact in many organizations.

CASE 5J

◀ Once a year the management of an electric utility company reviews the proposed budget for the coming year with each of its operating departments. Each department requests the funds it would like to have, management decides which proposed new projects should be undertaken, and by negotiation department budgets are established. In the process of negotiation, the apportionment of budgets within departments is also planned; each distinct operating unit receives its own. (There are eighty-three operating units in total among eight departments.) Each budget is expressed in the form of a month-by-month progression through the year, so each operating unit has a monthly target for expenditures and results.

During the course of the year all personnel and materials costs are charged to one operating unit or another. Charges are submitted each week, and all costs must be accounted for by charges to a unit. The computer accumulates the charges by unit and produces monthly reports for management, comparing the performance of each unit against its planned budget. A simple report appears of the form depicted in Fig. 5–2. There is one line for each of the eighty-three operating units. On each line appears the unit identifying number and name, the budget for the month, the actual charges for the month, the variance (positive or negative), and the year-to-date budgeted, actual, and variance. In a few minutes, management can scan this report and decide which of the units have variances that require attention. On demand, the computer can produce information about the units' charges during the month, either summarized by class or in full detail. By asking the computer for further details, management can inform itself of the background behind any variances in performance without troubling the management of the unit involved. The unit managers, in turn, have the privilege of asking the computer for summaries or details at any time so that they can keep track of their performance themselves.

The management of this electric utility company is very proud of its system, feeling that they are able to manage more efficiently and with less wasted management time than ever before, at the same time exercising a greater control over operations and operating at higher efficiency. Management credits the success jointly to themselves, for developing the operating unit concept and budget preparation procedure, and to the computer which has made possible the handling of the detailed charges that establish each unit's performance. ▶

Month _____							
Unit number	Unit name	Month's performance			Year-to-date performance		
		Budget	Actual	% variance	Budget	Actual	% variance

FIG. 5–2 Budget versus performance report.

While the pride of this company's management is undoubtedly justified, it is only fair to point out that such exception reporting systems have their drawbacks as well as their advantages; such rigid and mechanistic methods of measurement invite attempts to beat the system. In this case, the managers of the units became adept at finding ways to transfer charges to other units in order to make their own performance look favorable. The result of this, of course, was distortion of the results and confusion. Furthermore, a number of the managers of the units complained that quality of work (not reported on the monthly form) was likely to suffer in the interest of meeting budgetary targets. One manager of installation crews, for example, confessed that on one occasion he skimped on a job of installing a line of poles, where the conditions encountered turned out to be different from those initially predicted. Rather than go through the process of getting the budget changed or explaining a significant variance from his performance for the month, he overlooked the unexpected situation and installed the poles as initially planned, although he believes the poles will have to be replaced relatively soon. He would have preferred to incur a higher cost and obtain longer pole life, but the system discouraged him.

In Chapter 4 it was observed that because of the computer's ability to handle variations in the basic data, manufacturing firms are able to increase the variations in their product lines. This is particularly true when the computer is combined with numerically controlled machine tools. The tools, being operated by punched paper tapes prepared by the computer, are (from one point of view) part of its peripheral equipment, because the computer is directing the details of a production process according to an overall design provided by an engineer. Obviously, such a process enables a telescoping of the time required for the conversion of a design from initial concept to actual production. Furthermore, the costs involved are reduced: detailed design, drafting, machine setups, and operator training. A company using the computer and numerically controlled tool team can respond to unexpected demand more rapidly and in a greater variety of ways than before. This is an operational matter, but it obviously has implications for management. Manufacturing companies that used to consider themselves oriented toward mass production, and which sought large orders with long lead times, now find that they can equally well handle smaller orders with shorter lead times. The efficiencies of mass production can be applied to smaller manufacturing lots with the aid of the computer, in effect, and the company's management obtains more freedom in seeking orders and handling production requirements.

The management of research laboratories has been affected by the need to provide researchers with the computing resource. In the laboratory discussed in Case 4D, the central computing resource has become fundamental to most of the research staff's work. It is apparent that the nature and amount of computer support, the programming assistance provided, and the efficient sharing of the computing resource among the researchers has become a key to the success of the research staff. As individuals, the researchers are no longer as independent as they were; they are increasingly dependent on a centrally provided resource. Few of the researchers completely understand the computer resource, either. While they are competent to program computers for their own work, they do not understand the details of time-shared "system software" and of the programs required to manage the communication systems that connect the experiments to the computers. Furthermore, they have little interest in the relative economics of alternative types of computer resources—an important consideration, since the cost of the computing facility is very high.

CASE 5K

◀ A large aerospace company has several computers for the use of its scientists and engineers, but many of the problems they wish to use computers for are small and quicker response is demanded than the centrally located computers can provide. When time-shared computer services became available from service bureaus offering to install teletypewriters connected to service bureau computers, the company immediately recognized that the bureaus could provide more responsive service for the small problems than the company's computers could. Teletypewriters connected to time-shared services were provided for the scientists and engineers, who were pleased by the results.

As usage grew, additional teletypewriters were installed, and after a time, the company found that they had installed twenty terminals connected to five different competitive time-shared service bureaus. Each of the five offered a slightly different service with a slightly different pattern of rates. The rate

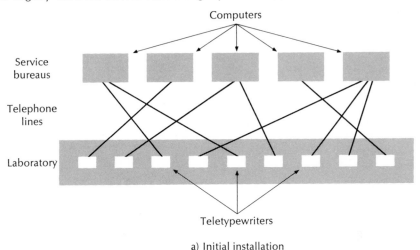

a) Initial installation

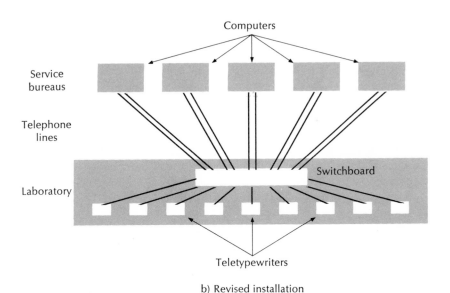

b) Revised installation

FIG. 5–3   Management assignment of time-shared computers.

schedule of one competitor favored running relatively large jobs in the service bureau's computer because the computer time rate was low; but because the teletypewriter rate was high, this service discouraged the use of the teletypewriter to handle large quantities of input and output information. Another competitor's rate favored using the teletypewriter extensively, but the cost of running programs repeatedly at the service bureau was high. It occurred to the management of the laboratory that it would be well to use one of the services for preparing programs (requiring extensive teletypewriter time and low computer time) and another for running them (with the opposite requirement). Management observed that all of the services used identical teletypewriters as their terminals, so it was possible to connect any one to a telephone line leading to any of the service bureaus. The management of the laboratory thereupon installed a special switchboard for the purpose, and instead of installing separate lines from each teletypewriter to a single service bureau, they brought the lines from the terminals to the switchboard and connected them interchangeably to the lines leading to the service bureaus (see Fig. 5–3). The switchboard operators were trained to connect the teletypewriters to the service bureaus on the basis of the descriptions given by the engineers of the kind of work they expected to do. The result of this innovation was a significant decrease in the total charges for time-shared service bureau time, with no decrease in the satisfaction of the scientist or engineer.   ▶

In respect to the computer resource, the management of the research computer facility has become an active partner of the researcher instead of simply an administrator in the background. The researcher cannot and will not make himself completely knowledgeable about all aspects of data processing, so both efficiency and adequate service imply trained assistance by the laboratory's management. This should benefit the researcher by providing him with more flexible and powerful tools without forcing him to devote time to becoming an expert in a new field. However, if management should do a poor job of providing service and of adapting the computing resource to the varying needs of the researchers, a severe handicap to their work and a high degree of unhappiness could result.

SUMMARY

The manager has usually been forced to accept the computer as a personal concern because its use has changed the methods of managing resources. The manager must adjust to new disciplines, to understanding and participating in the design of computer programs, to new forms of interaction with other members of operating management, and to the overall challenge of the wave of change focused in the computer. In some organizations, the computer has also affected the product line and the method of controlling the organization.

Responsiveness to varying demands has sometimes been improved, management by exception methods have been introduced, and in some companies simulation models have been developed which increase the efficiency of resource management and the accuracy of planning. However, most of the effects on management have derived from the computer's effects on operations; computers have not yet penetrated the functions of senior management. Some of them, such as evaluation and selection of management personnel and broad policy decisions based on intuitive perceptions of the distant future, may never be significantly affected by the computer. However, as time goes on, the use of the computer "creeps up" the management ladder; data derived from operations permit the building of increasingly useful simulation models which can assist management in evaluating the effects of ever more complex investment and procedural decisions. Young candidates for management positions are increasingly oriented toward use of these methods (Chapter 9) and as they obtain influential positions, the pace of change in management methods may accelerate. In fact, because of the emergence of "flickering authority" it may be unnecessary to wait that long. This phenomenon will be explored later.

STANDARDIZATION AND CENTRALIZATION

"Most managers in this corporation perceive the nature of the computer-induced change and the implications it has for the structure of control. They are still generally dedicated to the idea that decentralization is a positive virtue but are reluctantly becoming aware that it will be necessary to re-define in some fashion."*

Anonymous

THE COMPUTER AS A STANDARDIZING INFLUENCE

The previous chapters have shown that when an organization applies the computer to its operations, many procedures are standardized—document preparation, the use of codes and identifying numbers, and methods of measurement. This is a natural consequence of the nature of the computer. More fundamentally, it is a natural consequence of the installation of any rigidly structured way of doing things. With or without the computer, such standardization is a necessary concomitant of any attempt to formalize operations. The computer is the major single force in our time for formalizing operations, though, so without doubt more standardizing of previously informal operations has occurred because of the computer than for any other reason.

In most cases this seems to be a neutral influence. The standardized procedures are simply different ones, and no inevitable change in the organization seems to result. As this chapter shows, though, the computer also forces standardization at a higher level than that of item identification and document preparation, and at this higher level standardization has a more significant organizational influence. It also creates problems for managers, and requires their attention.

---

* Thomas L. Whisler, "The Impact on Organizational Control," in *The Impact of Computers on Management,* Charles A. Myers, Editor, M.I.T. Press, Cambridge, 1967.

When standardizing of documents, file records, and their handling procedures is to be performed, in most cases existing files must be converted to the new, standard forms. In organizations with large files this can be a most expensive and painful experience.

CASE 6A

◀ A large mail order firm sends catalogs to approximately twelve million customers four times a year. The total expense of this mailing is very high, and the company is anxious to keep on its mailing list only customers that actually produce business. But to do the necessary checking, it was necessary to institute a procedure for correlating customer orders with the names and addresses on the mailing list. With millions of orders to be matched against twelve million names and addresses, it was quickly proven that a computer was justified, both to correlate orders with mailing lists and to make the necessary changes in mailing lists and print labels for the mailings.

Before it could use a computer, the company had to convert its files of names and addresses into a standard form and store them on magnetic tapes suitable for computer processing. The mailing lists had been handled in twelve regional locations which stored them in a variety of forms. A few (unfortunately, a minority) already stored the names and addresses in punched cards that were suitable for computer input. The majority used imprinting plates designed for use with automatic mailing machines; however, several different kinds of machines and a variety of plate formats were used. To convert the names and addresses to a standard customer file, the company had to both transcribe the information from the plates to magnetic tape, and convert to standard codes and formats so that all the name and address files from the regional locations could be handled by a common computer program.

The company investigated all the automatic methods they could find for performing this conversion, including optical reading of the names and addresses printed by the plates and direct sensing of the impressions on the plates by a specially developed machine. None of these automatic methods proved feasible, so it was necessary to manually key punch the information from the addressing plate impressions into punched cards suitable for computer input. Since the company did not have nearly enough key punch operators to perform such a massive job, it negotiated with firms offering contract keypunching services. After obtaining a number of competitive bids, the company found that a bid of $6.00 per 100 name and address conversions was the best it could obtain, or a total contract price of $720,000 for the twelve million addresses. When this was reduced to take account of the fraction of the files already on punched cards, the final cost was $600,000. In addition to all the other expenses of acquiring a computer, developing its programs, and instituting new operating procedures, then, the company had to meet a very large one-time file conversion charge before it could use the computer. ▶

Files for the computer must be in standard form, and they must also be accurate. Inaccuracies creep in to manually maintained files in the best run organizations, and in most cases the organization can tolerate them because the clerks dealing with the file can recognize, adapt to, and correct errors as they are encountered. It is invariably necessary to purge such errors before converting a file to computer operation, however, because the computer has no such adaptability. This may mean such additional tasks as physical counts of inventory or comparison of file records and transaction records, adding still further to the cost of converting files. However, some organizations have been pleasantly surprised to discover offsetting savings in the process. Typically, errors in files tend to show quantities on hand lower than they actually are rather than higher. If the quantity is shown as too high, the physical goods or balance will sooner or later run out, and the error will be found. If the file record is too low, "lost" inventory representing wasted capital may exist indefinitely.

CASE 6B

◀ The telephone company of Case 5A, in instituting a computer system for maintaining the records of assignment of telephone lines to customers, had to convert its existing paper assignment files to the computer's format before it could start. This was a massive job because conversion teams had to examine the existing files for each area, compare them to field checks of the actual assignments in order to purge errors, and then have them key punched for computer input. The teams discovered a sizeable number of errors in the file resulting from installers' failures to report that facilities were freed when customers were disconnected. Failures to report the assignment of facilities when a customer was connected were self-correcting, because installers would find the lines in use when a later attempt was made to use the same line. When a line was recorded in the file as still in use when it actually was not, however, the situation would not be discovered automatically.

The conversion of assignment files was performed by specially trained conversion teams over a period of three years, at a total cost of $900,000. The company had expected this to be a part of the development cost of the computer-based assignment system, to be returned only in subsequent operating savings. However, by the time the conversion was finished, it developed that $550,000 worth of lines (at new equipment installation cost) had been "found" during the conversion process, so more than half of the conversion cost was returned as a by-product of purging the file. ▶

Usually a computer is initially put to use within one division of an organization or within one operational function, so the standardization it brings with it is confined to the division or function initially supported. Later, as additional functions affecting other divisions are programmed for the computer, a tendency to company-wide standardization of computing methods, programs, and even equipment very often develops, and standardization at this level can influence the organization in unexpected ways. This company-wide standardization results from attempts to pursue the following desirable objectives.

Reduction of programming cost

Computer programs are expensive to prepare, so it is desirable to standardize data processing procedures used in the divisions of an organization, and to use computer programs prepared by one division in others. The saving resulting from such standardization can obviously be significant; if there are four divisions each independently developing payroll programs for computers, the substitution of a single standard payroll program would save about three quarters of the total programming effort. Such standardization of data processing procedures is not always as easy as it sounds, however, because there may be good reasons for diversity of procedures between divisions; they may be overcome only with difficulty. However, once a standard program is in use, the company may find itself with a new capability to manage detailed operations on an interdivisional basis. Though this was not the original reason for standardizing programs, it may have much more important effects than a reduction in programming cost.

CASE 6C

◀   A manufacturing company's divisions were engaged in several industries: automotive, aerospace, and general metal fabricating. In each division, the primary function was the building of machine tools, transmissions, and other kinds of mechanical assemblies needed by the industry served. Each of the divisions had independently discovered that numerically controlled machine tools enabled them to respond faster and more economically to small orders, and had independently been ordering such tools for their own needs. In the process they had developed requirements for computer preparation of paper tapes for the numerically controlled tools; each had also developed accounting, payroll, and similar data processing programs for its computer. Corporate management, observing the diversity of computer efforts, decided that for economic reasons there should be a consolidation of programming effort. As much as possible, standard programs should be used by all divisions so that the company could employ a minimum number of programmers. With the divisions' more or less willing concurrence, management instituted the de-

HUNT LIBRARY
CARNEGIE-MELLON UNIVERSITY

velopment and implementation of standard, corporate-wide programs for manufacturing control and production scheduling. The managements of the divisions were willing to see this done both because they hoped for more sophisticated computer programs than their own divisional staffs were capable of producing, and because they agreed that the total corporate cost of computer programming could be reduced.

When the standard production control and scheduling programs went into effect, the detailed production resources and commitments of each division became known to corporate management. Management discovered for the first time that the divisions' numerically controlled machine tools could be used on one another's projects; unlike previous, more specialized tools, the new ones the divisions had been buying were general purpose. Since production requirements varied among the divisions and tools of one division were occasionally idle when those of another were overloaded, management started to assign the numerically controlled machine tools of all the divisions to the needs of the whole corporation rather than to the individual division's needs. Division management found with surprise and chagrin that they had lost control of part of their production facilities, as corporate management began to schedule the use of interchangeable numerically controlled tools to meet corporate needs. It had not been anticipated at the time the standard programs were developed that this would happen; neither divisional nor corporate management had realized that this centralization of operating control would take place. ▶

Standardization implies interchangeability, and when information about the availability of interchangeable resources is available at a central point, it is highly likely that central management will take advantage of the information to interchange resources in the interests of the organization's efficiency. Standardized computer programs do not necessarily cause this, but they are unquestionably an influence leading toward it. The objective of standardizing computer programs to reduce costs can, then, lead to more fundamental effects; it begins to become clear that standardization can influence the organization.

Commonality of equipment

Standard computer programs imply standard computers to run them. It is, of course, possible to prepare standard flow charts and then prepare the programs themselves for different computers. Often it is possible to prepare the programs in a compiler language (such as COBOL) which can be converted automatically by compilers into programs for different computers. However, different manufacturers' computers have different characteristics; a program written with one in mind is rarely ideal for another. If standard programs are to perform equally well in different locations, it is logical to install an identical computer in each. Identical computers can also serve as backup for one another; if one should fail, the programs and data awaiting processing can be shipped (with whatever delay is implicit) to another site. Finally, standardizing computers simplifies the evaluation of possible new equipment. Modern computer systems are so complex that many hours of study and testing are needed before a company's personnel can fully appreciate the virtues and limitations of any particular one. If a company has three or four different types of computers, and periodically replaces each with a different or more advanced model, some of the company's most expert personnel must spend practically all their time becoming familiar with different varieties of computers. If computers are standard, a company's computer staff will spend less time learning about new machines.

CASE 6D

◀ A large oil company had been formed through a series of mergers of oil companies serving regional areas. Each had developed computer systems for its own use; they used equipment of three computer manufacturers. Each division had a programming staff familiar with its particular type of equipment, and expected that any equipment replacements would involve similar machines provided by the existing supplier. As time went on, however, each of the divisions attempted to develop increasingly advanced applications and found that their ability to evaluate and select increasingly complex computers, software, and data communications systems became steadily more limited. At the same time, corporate management began to learn about the potentialities of corporate-wide operating control and reporting methods, so they became interested in standardized reporting and data processing procedures. As a result, a corporate group was established to consider standardizing the computing equipment in the divisions. Although considerable opposition was voiced by the computer personnel within the divisions, eventually a decision was made to use identical equipment from a single manufacturer and all divisions were required to transfer their existing operations to that equipment. This was done over a period of three years, and while some of the personnel in the divisions still thought nostalgically about the replaced equipment that they still believed to be more efficient and convenient, they all agreed that the corporation had achieved some benefits through the standardization. ▶

This does not imply that standardization of computing equipment is a good idea for all corporations. In many cases the computer operations within one division are entirely different from those of another, and may logically be performed by different computers indefinitely. In other cases, the technical requirements of a particular computer application may dictate the choice of a particular machine, which may not be suitable for the more conventional work done in other parts of the organization. For such reasons, many organizations will quite correctly choose to use nonstandard computing equipment indefinitely. However, it is undeniably true that many organizations, like the oil company, are standardizing computing equipment to obtain economy in programming, to minimize technical complexities, and to make mutual backup possible. The manager considering computer standardization must consider the factors applying to his individual case.

Uniform reporting to management

When divisional information systems are nonstandard, top management will almost certainly be presented with inconsistent data. The programs developed by the divisions will surely incorporate different assumptions, definitions, reporting cycles, and degrees of detail. As a result, detailed reports will differ.

These inconsistencies in detail were always present, but before the computer appeared, top management by necessity was provided only with overall financial data which could be brought into consistent format with relatively modest clerical effort. Given the computer's speed and ability to handle detail, however, many managements expect more detailed and responsive reporting from their divisions, and discover the inconsistencies that have always existed.

CASE 6E

◀   All supply depots of one of the armed forces make monthly performance reports to their management. One of the indices of performance is the number of "stock-out" conditions that occurred during the month, the number of requests for material that could not be met because of shortages. Stock-out conditions were not reported before computers came into use, because too much clerical time would have been needed to count and report the number of individual occurrences. With computers in use at the depots, however, it became possible to count the stock-out conditions as a by-product of normal transaction processing and automatically produce a report.

When the computer-produced reports of stock-out occurrences became available, it appeared that one depot had a consistently better record than another depot handling comparable items. The first reported about half the number of stock-out conditions as the second, even though they operated under the same policies. Management suspected inefficiency in the management of the poorer depot, and dispatched a team to investigate.

The team found that the difference between the two was not one of fact but of definition. In the depot with the better record, the desired delivery

date of each order was considered. The amount requested was then compared not only with the amount in stock, but also with the amount expected
to be received from new shipments before the desired delivery date. If the
sum of the amount in stock and the amount expected prior to the desired delivery date was adequate to cover the amount requested, the depot did not
charge itself with a stock-out condition. This was risky, because sometimes
expected orders were delayed, and when it came time to deliver, the expected
items were not on hand. The depot with the poorer record defined the stock-
out condition more rigorously. When an order could not be met from stock
on hand at the time the order was received, they recorded a stock-out condition. They did not consider that new shipments expected in time to meet the
order should be counted, because they could not be certain of receiving them
in time. This difference in definition, explained the investigating team, accounted for their consistently worse record.

Management was somewhat irritated to learn about this difference in
definition; they had been wasting their time on a problem that did not exist,
and felt that the difference should never have been allowed to occur. Measures were immediately taken to establish a standardized definition of the
stock-out condition. ▶

Commonality of operating procedures

In many large organizations personnel are transferred between divisions, usually encountering information systems in the new divisions that are functionally the same as systems they knew before. A payroll system in one division
will probably compare to a payroll system in another division; similarly, financial accounting, marketing, production control, and the like will have their
counterparts. However, many differences in detail can occur; if a system in
the new division differs from the corresponding one in the old, wasteful retraining of the transferred personnel may be necessary.

CASE 6F

◀ For many years each Command in the United States Army developed its
own data processing procedures to support supply, finance, and personnel
accounting. There were good reasons for delegating this authority to the
Command level; conditions in Europe differ from those in the United States
and from those in the Pacific, and the requirements of supporting Commands
are very different from those of field Commands. The data processing systems
developed by the Commands reflected these differences and, naturally, the
personnel trained to operate them became familiar only with the particular
system in use in the Command to which they were assigned.

In keeping with the standard method for describing personnel skills in the Army, those who had worked with data processing systems in functional areas had codes recorded in their personnel records corresponding to these skills (e.g., "finance data processing system operator"). It is basic to the system that a man to whom a code applies can apply his skill wherever he is assigned. For example, a radar technician should be able to go to work immediately whether the unit to which he is attached happens to be stationed in Texas or in Vietnam. The data processing skill codes were considered in personnel reassignments, and in many cases an operator of a data processing system in Europe found himself assigned to a comparable position upon returning to the United States. To the confusion of the system and the disappointment of the commanding officers, it turned out that the data processing personnel could not perform as expected. When the operator of a finance data processing system in Europe was assigned to operate a comparable one in the United States, he required weeks or even months of familiarization and study before he could do the work he had been doing satisfactorily before. The personnel planners became aware that the proliferation of different data processing systems was creating complexities in the personnel assignment system, and they complained to the authorities responsible for the control of data processing system development. For this and other reasons, these authorities proceeded to undertake a standardization of the data processing systems across the Commands. Because of the very real differences in conditions to be met, however, this standardization process was a difficult one and could only proceed slowly. ▶

Summary

The computer has caused considerable standardization in using organizations, most of all in computing activities themselves. As earlier chapters pointed out, reporting and data collection standards are necessarily imposed when the computer is used to process operational data. We now see that the standardizing influence of the computer goes beyond this, and appears in several forms. Standardization of computer programs between divisions of organizations suggests more centralized management of resources, as well as leading to reduction in overall programming effort. Top management imposes new standards in order to obtain consistent data. Standardization of computing equipment sometimes follows the program and data standards. Last but not least, standardization of operating procedures, established to permit the flexible reassignment of personnel between divisions, can influence personnel policies.

Although standardization clearly influences organizations, there is no evidence that basic changes occur because of it. The fact that procedures are more highly standardized in one organization than in another does not seem in itself to account for major differences in philosophy, style, or structure between the two; only minor consequences can be traced directly to the computer. The fundamental structure of organizations depends on factors more profound than the standardization of operating procedures or data processing methods. The scope of the individual manager's authority may change somewhat, but he need not fear a serious loss.

THE COMPUTER AND ORGANIZATIONAL CENTRALIZATION

There are a number of reasons why it is logical to think that the computer should exert a centralizing influence on organizations. After all, it may be reasoned, one of the primary reasons for decentralization of organizations has been the inability of central management to control the details of a large enterprise. Only by splitting an organization into units small enough to fall within a single manager's span of control can detailed operations be satisfactorily managed. Traditionally these small units are fitted into the whole by means of a hierarchical organization, with groups of organizational units reporting to successively higher levels in the pyramid and top management dealing with only a relatively few regional or functional managers on a regular basis. If this assumption is true, with the computer's volume handling capability and speed available, it is no longer necessary to construct large organizations in a pyramidal fashion; it now becomes possible to bring all the transactions to a central computer-equipped operations center, from which all the detailed operations of the organization can be managed on a day-by-day basis. Figure 6–1 depicts the concept of such a change in a simplified fashion, with the pyramidal human-managed organizational structure at the top, and the conceptual centralized structure below.

The concept of the operations center is attractive, because if all the organization's resources can be brought to bear on each of the individual demands, the whole should be able to operate more efficiently than if each demand is met only by the resources of one small organizational unit within a pyramidal structure. We have seen in earlier chapters that such increases in efficiency have occurred with computer management of resources; at least, in some cases.

It is now possible to test such conjectures on the basis of experience. Since many organizations have used computers for ten years or more, it should be clear from observation of them to what degree this conjecture about computer-based centralization is true. If they were going to centralize and develop operations centers based on the use of the computer, many of them should

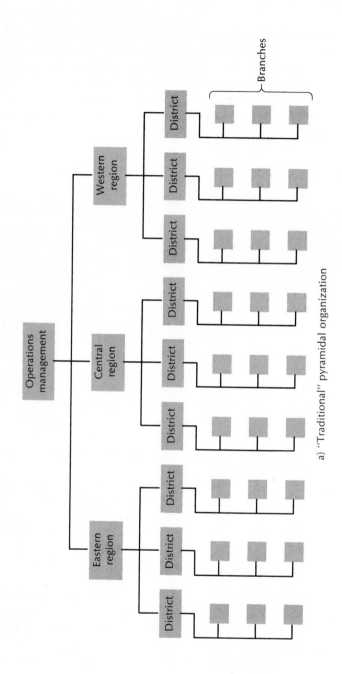

a) "Traditional" pyramidal organization

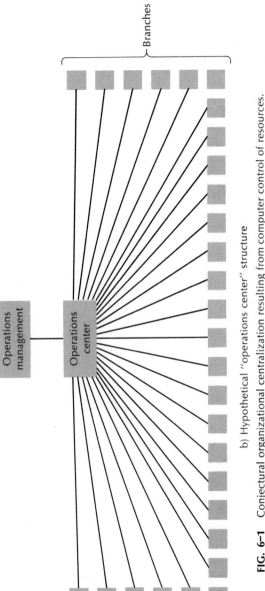

FIG. 6-1   Conjectural organizational centralization resulting from computer control of resources.

b) Hypothetical "operations center" structure

be well on their way now, and it should be possible to resolve this question once and for all.

As we have seen in previous chapters, centralization of the management of routine operations has unquestionably occurred in many organizations.

CASE 6G

◀ Twenty years ago a large insurance company with more than 300 branch offices performed its policy accounting in sixty-five locations. These locations were equipped with accounting machines operated by clerks, with individual policy records kept on ledger cards. Each of the sixty-five offices served a group of sales offices within a small geographic area, and were able to offer a high degree of responsiveness because messenger delivery and mail service was rapid over such short distances. The number of clerks employed was very large, however, so when computers became available, management turned to them in order to reduce the cost of clerical labor.

By 1958, the insurance company was performing its data processing in twelve regional centers, each equipped with a computer. The sixty-five offices had been consolidated into twelve in order to efficiently use the volume handling capability of the computers, but it was still felt necessary to have data processing centers within the regions served in order to provide satisfactory responsiveness to the sales offices. Besides, the largest computers readily available were not capable of handling much more than $\frac{1}{12}$ of the company's total transactions.

In the years following 1958, the company's experiments with data communication systems (using telephone lines to transmit batches of data from point to point) proved successful, and the lower "per transaction" cost of using the larger computers that had become available was manifest. By 1964, the company had further consolidated its data processing into three large computer centers located in the East, Mid-West, and Far West. Each was connected to the fifty or more sales offices it served by means of data communication lines, so that responsiveness was more rapid than even the manual system employing sixty-five locations had provided. At the same time, greater economies were developed because of the larger computers in use; their relatively lower costs per transaction and reductions in personnel more than offset the new data communications costs.

Since 1964, the insurance company's management has considered a further consolidation of the three regional data processing centers into one central one at headquarters. Still further economies of scale would be gained from the use of very large computers, and a small degree of further personnel reduction would occur. On the other hand, the data transmission costs for transmitting very large volumes of data over long distances would rise sharply;

there would apparently be little if any further economic gain from more consolidation. So far no decision has been made, but the question of further consolidation is frequently re-evaluated.

The company does not feel that it has centralized its operations. It has consolidated its accounting offices, and has largely eliminated the supervisory level devoted to managing groups of clerks. However, the sales offices and all the other levels of management remain, and the company prides itself on retaining a "personal touch."   ▶

Not only clerical operations have been centralized; as some of the earlier case examples have shown, the physical handling, storage, and manufacturing functions of some companies have been consolidated because of the use of the computer. Case 1H described an automated bakery which serves the entire country from a single plant. They found that the economies to be gained by automated production lines were so great that the high cost of shipment was more than offset. This is, of course, not a general rule. Manufacturing organizations dealing in products of high bulk, or having manufacturing processes of relatively low complexity, still generally find it advantageous to manufacture in dispersed plants near the markets served. However, there is no question that some manufacturing companies have centralized facilities partly because of the efficiencies to be gained by computer control and scheduling.

It is improper to attribute this centralization of operations entirely to the computer. As the case of the insurance company demonstrates, reliable and reasonably priced data communications are essential to such centralization. Regardless of the availability and economics of the computer, the centralization could not have occurred without satisfactory data communications. In physical distribution and manufacturing, a correspondingly important influence has been the improvement in transportation systems that has occurred during the period of the computer's rise. Reduced costs and higher speeds of road transportation coupled with the competitive improvements in rail, air, and water transportation have been at least as important a factor in centralization of the handling of goods as the efficiencies gained from the computer. As explained in Chapter 3, the computer has been only one of a group of evolutionary influences which together make this change possible; the computer by itself would rarely have been sufficient.

One result of such centralization of operations is a separation between the responsibility for operational data processing and that for local sales, service, and customer contact. In the case of the insurance company, for example, sixty-five regional data processing centers serving only four to six sales offices each could respond quickly and on a personal basis to the needs of individual salesmen. With only three giant data processing centers, however, located remotely from most sales offices and serving more than fifty each, there is bound to be a greater communication gap between the salesmen and the data processing function. As might be anticipated, this can lead to difficulty.

CASE 6H

◄ A large brokerage firm has thirty-five local offices where "customer's men" handle the individual investor's information needs and accounts. For many years each local office kept the account records for its customers, performed the accounting, stored the stock certificates, and handled all administrative matters. The firm felt that this was advantageous because the customer's men always had complete records at their fingertips, and should there be any difficulty or misunderstanding, they could clear it up personally with their office staffs. The firm knew that this caused high clerical costs, though, and there were sometimes inconveniences when a customer moved from one city to another and had to have his records transferred, or when an institutional account did business with the firm in more than one local office.

For many years the firm used a data communications network for execution of customers' orders. For stocks traded on the New York Stock Exchange, for example, they would transmit buy and sell orders from all thirty-five offices to the floor of the Exchange for execution. All other types of security transactions were also centrally executed, either at an exchange or at the firm's home office. As the economies of large scale computers improved and as data communications systems became more reliable and less expensive, it naturally occurred to the firm's management to share the use of the existing data network with accounting information and perform data processing centrally. Since they had to pay for the network anyway, they reasoned, why not expand its capacity a little and bring all the accounting transactions as well as the messages dealing with order execution to the central office in New York? It would then be possible to justify the use of a computer for accounting and obtain sizeable clerical savings.

Such a system was installed more than five years ago, and difficulties with it still arise. At first, the primary source of difficulty was shortcomings in programming; the computer could not satisfactorily handle all the kinds of accounting transactions that arose. The wide variation in customer accounts, ranging from small individual investors to large estates and institutions, meant that many special programs had to be prepared, and the computer programmers failed initially to anticipate many of the situations that would arise. In the first few years of operation these difficulties were ironed out, and the incidence of unexpected types of transactions that the computer could not handle dropped to a low level. At that point the growth of business volume posed a new problem, because the firm entered a period of expansion in which both the size of its customer body and the activities of the customers rose greatly. The data transmission network became overloaded, the computer became overloaded, and the clerical procedure involved in handling stock certificates and accounting documents became overloaded. The firm had encountered similar peaks of activity in earlier years, but with the accounting and handling of documents decentralized in thirty-five locations, it had been easier to deal with them by adding one or two additional clerks in each office and asking the customer's men to help with overloads in accounting. Now that the system was centralized and dependent on a single mechanized center, expansion was not nearly so easy. The company took more than a year to expand its facilities to comfortably handle the increased volume.

During most of this period the customer's men have been critical of the decision to institute centralized, automated accounting. Their customers received poorer service, and they themselves were less able to clear up difficulties than they had been with local accounting. While they appreciated that the firm had saved money, and some even conceded that with the current volume of transactions they could no longer perform the accounting locally, nevertheless they yearned for the "good old days" when they had the accounting functions as well as the trading functions under their personal control. ▶

This kind of difficulty has been widespread; many companies have suffered from the increased division between accounting and customer contact that has occurred because of centralization of data processing. Many managers having a sales and customer service orientation regard this as a serious matter, and regret the complaints and occasional lost business arising from this division. They have little choice in regard to the processing of large volumes of data, however; it is economically virtually impossible to return to the manual data handling that preceded the computer. To minimize the problem, managements often apply pressure to the data processing group to become more sales oriented, to make themselves better aware of the problems of customer contact, and to improve the variety and responsiveness of the computer's programs in the interest of improving customer service. The problem of responsiveness is often alleviated (the previous case notwithstanding) by the development of data communications and real-time computer techniques. Reestablishment of close interaction between customer representative and data processing is unquestionably one of the main reasons for the great interest in fast response computers.

This problem of customer responsiveness has been so severe that many companies have refused to centralize operations, or done so only partly, even though the economies of doing so were clear to them. They clearly fear that the rigidity and mechanical nature of an organization such as that in Fig. 6–1b would be intolerable.

CASE 6 I

◀ In a casualty insurance company the decision was consciously made to forego the advantages of computer premium accounting. The company deals largely through a network of independent agents who often represent several insurance companies in noncompeting areas, and who may sell a number of different companies' policies to the same customer. These agents feel that they must retain the customer's records, because only they are in a position to know all the coverages that the customer has from the different companies. They reason that if the casualty company were to take over the premium accounting records for its policies, they would lose much of their ability to provide service and to retain the customer's business.

The company's management became convinced that this was true, that better representation and sales would result from leaving the accounts and billing in the hands of the agents, even though it meant that they had to incur significantly higher commission costs. They had no real choice anyway, because they were anxious to retain their effective agents and the agents' implied threat to transfer their services to a competitive company was enough to win the point.

In this case, then, it does not appear that there will ever be centralized data processing in this casualty insurance company's premium accounting, even though economics clearly dictate its advisability. The agents insist that they must retain the records in order to provide service, and the company agrees with them. ▶

Centralization of operations, particularly data processing operations, is made possible by the computer and is often instituted in the interest of greater efficiency. Most organizations appear to believe, however, that other functions (such as those involving customer contacts) should not be centralized even though the computer makes it possible. They appear to feel that such centralization brings disadvantages with it, loss of flexibility, and potential for error. Divisional or regional managers have typically lost authority over routine data handling but they still retain sales, personnel, service, and all customer contact functions. As some of our cases have shown, it would have been possible for central management to take over these functions using the centralized files of information made available by the computer. This has happened sometimes, with both good and bad results. In most organizations, though, central management has intentionally avoided such a takeover. Their reasons are several:

1 Central management feels that local decisions are often better made locally, applying knowledge of the particular circumstances and conditions (e.g., the customers' habits, local labor markets, or relations with local governments).

2   Nearly the same number of decision makers is required to make a given number of decisions, regardless of where they are located. As we have seen, it is erroneous to assume that a computer makes decisions. Rather, it prepares information indicating that a particular decision is correct and then presents this to a human manager for action. This can be done on a decentralized basis as well as on a centralized one, and no personnel saving results from centralization. Managers, being familiar with the decision-making process, readily perceive this.

3   Future managers must be trained. Incumbent management usually wishes to have positions available where candidates for future management positions can obtain experience in the vagaries of the business, and acquire management skills of decision-making and personnel selection and motivation. Most managers believe that the best way to provide these positions is to "parcel out" responsibility to carefully monitored segments of the organization, and allow the potential future managers to work their way up through successively more important segments as they acquire experience and demonstrate their ability. It is evident to the manager that the opportunity to do this would be greatly reduced in a highly centralized organization.

Summary

For many reasons, then, broad organizational centralization does not seem to be occurring because of the computer. Resistance to such centralization occurs for emotional reasons as discussed in Chapters 2 and 3, for practical reasons of benefit to the organization as discussed above, and because the functions the computer is best able to perform are of value only in day-to-day operations. The hypothetical operations center of Fig. 6–1 is *not* emerging, and since there has been ample time for any trend toward it to become evident, one may venture to guess that it never will. Changes in the part of the organization devoted to data handling in support of the line functions have been more frequent, however. Figures 4–1 and 4–2 showed a typical change in the organization of production scheduling; such changes have been frequent. Also, as several cases have shown and as the next section of this chapter will discuss, centralization of data processing is very frequent. These are, however, supporting rather than line functions.

But all the time evolution continues. The computer is used for broader applications affecting increasing combinations of organizational units; the computer's files grow, and their usefulness for simulation, scheduling of operations, or evaluation of management decisions increases; and by degrees individuals' attitudes change. In a study of 108 manufacturing companies* a variety of

---

* Neal J. Dean "The Computer Comes of Age," *Harvard Business Review*, January–February 1968.

levels of use of the computer was discovered. Some used it for corporate-wide integrated applications (4%), some used it for multidepartmental applications (26%), the rest strictly within single departments (70%). However, 92% of the 108 companies agreed that the trend was toward more integrated use of the computer, toward development of applications crossing departmental and disciplinary lines, and stated that in three to five years they expected to be able to use the computer for multidepartmental or corporate applications.

Perhaps experience to date, which clearly supports the absence of computer-caused centralization, is not conclusive. Perhaps the rate of change is slow and the organizational influence of the computer will be felt over a much longer time than most prophets foresaw. Perhaps the fifteen years of experience available for study are not enough to indicate what will take place in the future. Many managers seem to feel intuitively that this is so, that most of the change is yet to come. They typically observe the increasing influence of the computer and of the quantitative management techniques it represents with a vague but distinct disquiet. The quotation at the beginning of this chapter typifies this disquiet—the attitude of men who, still devoted to the principles they have practiced for their entire careers, begin to feel that these principles are perhaps becoming obsolescent, that something unwelcome and unclear in detailed nature seems to be inevitably rising to supersede them.

Part IV of this book is devoted to an attempt to perceive the outlines of this "something" on the assumption that they are implicit in clues perceptible today. As will be shown in Part IV, the picture is by no means one of unrelieved gloom. While compromises may have to be made with what are regarded as organizational virtues today, new potentials appear to be arising, new dimensions of freedom and flexibility which were previously impossible. These considerations apply to the future, however. For the present it is clearly correct to say that while the computer has been an influence for the centralization of the supporting data handling functions of the organization, it has generally had no similar effect on the overall organization. The manager must be aware of the dynamic and ever-changing influence of the computer as its applications evolve, however; he must be prepared to change his mind.

MANAGEMENT OF THE COMPUTER

The available evidence does not show that organizations are being centralized in any overall way because of the computer, but it does indicate that portions of them are. We have seen that the scheduling and control of operations tends to become centralized. This is even clearer in the case of the data processing function itself.

CASE 6J

◀ In early 1968 a private survey was made of eight large, multi-divisional organizations. In all eight computers had been used for ten years or more, and in all eight the initial pattern of computer management was completely decentralized. In the 1964 to 1965 period each had computers and programming and system analysis groups scattered among its divisions. Each group was then entirely independent of any other, and reported only to its divisional management. Corporate-level computing resources were rare, and where they existed their sole function was to fill special data processing needs of corporate management.

Between 1964 and early 1968, the eight organizations had changed as follows:

1 Three had completely centralized system analysis and programming. All computer personnel received their assignments from corporate headquarters, though in two of the three, they were still physically located in the divisions. Computers were still dispersed through the divisions, but their procurement, operation, and management were also controlled by corporate data processing management.

2 Three of the organizations had centralized system analysis and programming of standardized interdivisional programs, but still permitted divisions to develop programs for internal use. In each, about half of the corporation's computer personnel were located in the corporate staff, and about half in the divisions. In all three corporations, as time passed, one after another of the important data processing functions were being redefined as company standards or interdivisional applications, and thus being transferred from divisional control to corporate control. However, in each corporation both divisional and corporate management believed that there would always be unique programs required by single divisions and that some programming resources would always remain in the divisions.

3 Two of the eight companies remained decentralized, with all data processing personnel distributed among the divisions and reporting to divisional management. In both, however, there was more corporate influence on divisional data processing than there had been three years earlier. Corporate data processing groups had been established to "consult with and assist" the divisional data processing groups in evaluation and acquisition of advanced equipment, in solving problems and in personnel matters. In both cases, the corporate data processing group had been asked to establish improved systems of accounting codes for uniform financial reporting throughout the divisions.

In summary, all eight of the organizations started with completely decentralized computer programming and operations. Three of the eight had become completely centralized, three others were partly centralized and becoming increasingly so, and the two that remained decentralized had established centralized "consulting" groups whose influence was increasing. ▶

As this study convincingly shows, there is a strong trend in large multidivisional organizations toward centralizing the management of the data processing resource (in smaller organizations, it would necessarily be more centralized from the start). The reasons why this is so are not difficult to perceive; they are similar to those causing the computer to be a force for standardization. There seem to be three primary ones.

Desire for standardization

As we saw earlier in this chapter, there are compelling reasons why standardized data processing procedures are advantageous to large companies. But how are standards established, and how is compliance with them enforced? No one division is in a position to consider the needs or observe the performance of other divisions equitably; it is almost mandatory that a corporate staff group perform the function. It follows, however, that the corporate staff group will meddle in the data processing procedures of the divisions and must seek authority to enforce compliance with its standardized procedures if it cannot obtain compliance voluntarily. Naturally, friction may result.

CASE 6 K

◀ An aerospace company with five geographically separated divisions had its corporate headquarters at the site of the largest division. All five divisions had installed computers at one time or another. In two divisions the computers performed both business data processing and engineering computations, while in the other three, relatively small computers performed business data processing alone.

Corporate management, as part of an attempt to revitalize the company, instituted a "profit center organization" across divisional lines to provide more responsive and explicit measurements of performance, and to increase operational flexibility. In support of this profit center organization, they developed a computer-based accounting and reporting system in which all activities and charges were reported in a uniform, detailed manner and measured against anticipated performance (like the management by exception principles discussed earlier). Management assigned the authority for development and installation of the standardized reporting system to a corporate staff group especially established for the purpose.

At the same time, management became aware of the existence of large time-shared computers that could perform both engineering computation and data manipulation for management more responsively than the relatively simple machines the divisions had installed. Management was attracted to the time-sharing concept, and wanted to study the desirability of replacing the separate divisional computers with a large, time-shared central one available through remote input-output devices to all the profit centers in all the divisions. Since this replacement of equipment would universally affect every computer and every program, management understood that the study would be a long and complex one, best performed by an objective, central group.

In view of these two considerations, management decided to assign complete authority over the corporation's data processing functions to the corporate staff group initially established to develop the new financial reporting system. The head of this group was entitled "Corporate Director of Data Processing"; he reported directly to the Executive Vice President for Operations. Some thought was given to making the post subordinate to the corporate Comptroller, but since a primary concern was with the computing support of research and engineering activities, and also since it was anticipated that computers would be used more extensively in production and industrial applications, it was judged desirable to separate the post from any one functional affiliation.

Since the corporate headquarters were at the site of the largest division with the largest programming staff, it was convenient to transfer the staff and equipment from divisional control to that of the new Director. The computers and personnel of the outlying divisions were also organizationally subordinated to the Director, but for the time being they continued to respond mostly to their divisional managers.

The first difficulty arose when the Corporate Director began to assign the most senior system analysts from the divisions to develop new corporate-wide procedures. There were objections from the divisions these system analysts had previously served that they could not be spared from pressing divisional assignments. The manager of the central division was particularly concerned, because as he pointed out, the other four remotely located divisions continued to obtain most of the services of the data processing personnel they originally had, while his central division (by accident of physical co-location with headquarters) had lost the use of its computer personnel to the new Directorate. The Director had to concede the justice of this contention, and began to make up his system development teams for corporate applications with personnel from the remote divisions as well as from the central one. He also found occasion to borrow a few people from the remote divisions to apply to an important problem of the central division, thereby demonstrating that under some circumstances they could gain as well as lose by the organizational change. Each of these borrowings was accompanied by a struggle with the affected management, though, so the Director did less borrowing than he had expected. He also postponed the planned study of a centralized, time-shared computer because he now perceived that the standardized programs for it would require years to develop.

The next difficulty arose when the standardized financial reporting system was ready for implementation and was presented to the divisional managers. To a man, they rejected it as inapplicable to their unique operations, too time-consuming and difficult to support, and requiring a change from existing methods so radical as to be impracticable. A process of negotiation ensued in which:

◄ The diplomatic ability of the Director of Data Processing was tested,

◄ The ability of his system analysts to develop a single, universally applicable coding system from a mass of divergent detailed requirements was tested,

◄ The determination of top management to persevere with the installation of the common profit center system was tested.

At the time this is written it is still not clear what the final result will be. It is clear, however, that the process of centralizing the data processing organization in the interests of standardizing procedures and equipment has brought with it a host of the kind of problems associated with the process of change (Chapter 3), and that these problems will not be solved quickly or easily. ▶

Shortage of personnel

Few organizations have as many programmers and systems analysts as they would like. For many, as they attempt increasingly ambitious computer applications the shortage grows worse rather than better. Even though new personnel are continually hired, the most experienced are likely to leave for better opportunities elsewhere. Furthermore, the increased technical demands of advanced systems (e.g., data communications technology, time-sharing computer systems, and the accompanying software) call for knowledge and experience not found among most companies' programmers. Companies tend to find that the quality and quantity of their computer-trained personnel are increasingly tight constraints. In order to use the personnel optimally, they find themselves compelled to bring the personnel under central management so that they can be assigned to the most important projects of the whole company rather than just to those of divisions.

CASE 6L

◀ A large electric utility holding company consists of many semiautonomous local electric utilities, operating under a corporate management that views its role as that of overall financial manager for the group. The individual companies have for years been installing and using computers for engineering, accounting, and customer billing functions. The corporate management appreciated that the companies were duplicating one another's data processing efforts by preparing programs many times over for such functions as customer billing, and knew that savings would result from doing them centrally. However, they felt that the healthy competition they were able to foster among the companies benefited all by improving the quality of the programs, and that, in principle, any interference in the management of the individual companies would do more harm than good.

One by one, the affiliated companies have become interested in advanced computer systems. In most cases, they are interested in time-shared computer systems with inquiry consoles in the offices where customer service and billing matters are handled. The clerks, using the inquiry consoles, can obtain complete and up-to-date information so that better service can be provided when a customer calls with a question or request for service. These time-shared computers involve more complex equipment and programs than the companies are used to. They cost more than previous computers did, and much of the experience of the companies' programmers is not applicable. Corporate management discovered to their sorrow that the price of duplication had become unreasonable, since there were no more than a handful of computer programmers and system analysts throughout the corporation who were experienced with time-shared systems.

Reluctantly, and after much study of the problem, corporate management instituted a centralized data processing authority to develop standard programs to be used throughout the company for the time-shared customer service applications, and transferred the few experts in time-shared computers to the corporate authority. As far as possible they left other applications in the hands of the affiliates, but they appreciate that once the present effort is successful, other corporate-wide time-shared computer applications will almost surely follow. Also, now that the thrust of new application development is shifted to the corporate staff, it is there that most improvement in experience and ability will occur rather than in the affiliates.

The company has instituted centralized control over their data processing, and knows it will grow, but they did not and do not want to do so. They assert that they saw no alternative, that the shortage of competent personnel forced them to standardize programs and manage the personnel resources centrally. ▶

Growth of applications complexity

This problem, associated with the shortage of personnel, derives from organizations' desires to institute steadily more complex computer applications. In the case of the electric utility holding company, the shortage of personnel would not have been so severe if the company had not become convinced that time-shared systems were desirable. Such advanced systems usually incorporate data from more than one functional part of a company, and serve more than one functional part. As the applications of computers spread across the business it becomes impossible for a functionally oriented group to deal with them, to have a balanced knowledge of the several functions, or to avoid parochial viewpoints. Only the company-wide view of corporate management is appropriate.

CASE 6M

◀ The automated bakery of Case 1H installed a computer for controlling production and for operating its freezer warehouse. After considerable effort, the production control and warehouse operations were running well, and the team of Production Department people who had developed the computer programs decided to undertake more advanced applications. They felt that the next step was to tie in their production control system with the ordering of raw materials for production, so that the inventory, management, and production scheduling could be performed as a single process.

While the Production Department's team was developing its computer applications, another team within the Comptroller's Department developed a set of financially oriented computer programs. Starting with the payroll and conventional accounting procedures, this team, too, had progressed steadily toward more sophisticated computer applications. They had successfully programmed the purchasing and accounts receivable functions of the company, and decided that their next step, too, was the management of raw materials inventories. They felt that since they were responsible for the purchasing system and for the company's financial resources, it was logical for them to control the expenditure of money for raw materials. The production people did not see it that way; they felt that the ordering and management of raw materials was a natural by-product of the physical needs of production schedules for which they were responsible.

Both parties agreed that each had to work closely with the other's programs and data, but each felt that it should be in charge of the effort because its contribution was the most important. Corporate management found this confusing, and was unable to decide in favor of either of the parties. Finally, with the advice of a team of consultants they decided to do away with both the production and the financial computer programming groups, and to merge them into a single one reporting to corporate management. This radical change was intended to eliminate the cause of the disagreement, and management hoped that the two groups would find a way to work together on the new, broader computer applications that necessarily transcended the old functional lines. ▶

Enough large organizations have completed their change to centralized data processing to make clear the general form of the new organizations. As Dean found in the survey of 108 manufacturing organizations previously cited, the trend is toward the establishment of a central data processing executive reporting directly to the top management of an organization. This executive is explicitly not placed within any of the functional departments of the organization, because the applications for which he will be responsible will transcend functional lines. The programming and system analysis resources of the company report directly to him; thus, perhaps for the first time, a significant line function is found reporting directly to the office of the president or the executive vice president. In many cases, large organizations also permit groups of programmers and system analysts to remain physically dispersed among the departments, partly because of the inconvenience of and resistance to wholesale moving, and partly because computer applications remain that affect only individual departments. These may still be permitted to be implemented entirely within the departments. However, in all cases these personnel are subject to assignment by the central authority, and if a corporate-wide project requires their services, it almost invariably takes priority over a departmental project.

Most large organizations have (so far) continued to use numerous computers located where the work is, rather than completely centralized computing equipment at corporate headquarters. In cases where the files to be used by corporate management dictate their consolidation in one place, the computers follow; but as long as the files of information pertaining to the departments, plants, and dispersed facilities are primarily updated by and used by personnel there, economics invariably indicate that the equipment should remain there, too. The reasons for this are simple: long distance data communications are expensive, there is mutual interference between large numbers of different kinds of jobs run at the same time on the same machine, and there is competition for priority of service. This does not mean, however, that the departments have any more control over the equipment than they have over the personnel. Because of standardization of programs (and often equipment), and because of the increasing difficulty of evaluating and selecting new types of equipment and programs, the specification of equipment and control of its operational use are also performed by the corporate authority. The equipment, then, is located wherever the work is; but the kind of equipment se-

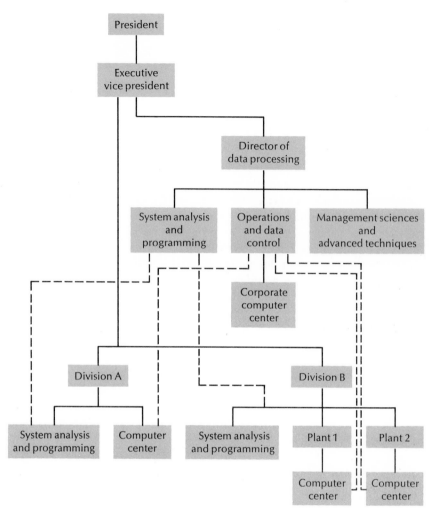

FIG. 6–2   Centralized data processing structure of multidivisional organization.

lected, the programs for it, and the way it is used are under complete central control.

Figure 6–2 depicts the approximate organizational structure that seems to emerge. Naturally, peculiarities of particular organizations cause variations from this general structure; even the personal characteristics of the managers involved may do so. However, this chart is sufficiently representative to provide useful guidance to those concerned with the structure of data processing organizations.

The corporate director of data processing reports to the executive vice president or whatever corporate executive is responsible for the organization's operations. Sometimes this is the president; sometimes it is the senior financial executive, but only in cases where the senior financial executive has broad corporate responsibility. As we will see below, the trend is away from affiliating data processing with financial management.

The system analysis and programming functions report to the director of data processing. Most system analysts and programmers are centralized and report directly to him. These people work on the organization's standard programs and those directly supporting corporate management. They also spend part of their time on programs designed to support individual divisions. If the staff is large, as it typically is in a large organization, system analysis and programming may well constitute two separate and co-equal organizational units rather than one as shown here. However, some organizations prefer to keep all system analysts and programmers in a "pool" and assign them as teams; there seems to be no clear trend one way or the other.

Operations and data control is responsible for the operation of the corporate computer center, devoted to applications benefiting corporate management. The corporate operations group is also responsible for overseeing the operations of all other computers in the corporation, seeing to it that standardized applications are always handled uniformly, that satisfactory accounting and financial control standards are applied in all computer centers, and providing advice, guidance, and training for operating personnel throughout the organization.

A third group, here called "management sciences and advanced techniques," also reports to the director of data processing. It takes many names and is sometimes more than one unit, but its functions are always more or less the same. This group is responsible for the evaluation and development of long range hypothetical and experimental data processing techniques that might be used by the organization. Usually, the operations research analysts of the company will be found in such a group, and the personnel engaged in the development of simulation models, optimizing techniques, and the like. As these applications become demonstrably feasible and can be selected for definite adoption, responsibility for their detailed planning and implementation moves over to the system analysis and programming group.

The organization may have any number of divisions; two are shown here arbitrarily, reporting through the executive vice president to the president. Because each probably has an identity, geographic location, and product line of its own, it will have data processing applications unique to it. Each is therefore permitted to retain a system analysis and programming group to be devoted to divisional programs, or to assisting the corporate group with implementation of standard programs as the relative priorities dictate. The final authority over the assignment of these people necessarily resides in the director of data processing, but he usually finds it necessary to be responsive to the desires of divisional management. This "tug of war" between the demands of the corporate group and the demands of divisional management for the services of the data processing personnel on division staffs is obviously a potential source of continuing difficulty, but most organizations seem to find this compromise arrangement preferable to either total concentration of the people in a single location or total decentralization. It is often observed that a continuing competition for resources leads to a healthy, continuing re-examination of project priorities.

As indicated above, the computers are found where their work is. Figure 6-2 shows a single computer center for division A, and for division B two computer centers located at manufacturing plants. Each of these is responsible, above all, for providing adequate service to the plant or division served. However, each is also responsible to the director for satisfactory operation of standard procedures and for maintenance of the accounting control and personnel standards established by the director. Here again is a source of friction; authority over the computer centers divided between the "customer" directly served (the plant or division) and the central directorate which establishes and monitors the methods of performing the work. Friction occurs, but again most large organizations seem to have found this divided authority preferable to either one extreme or the other, because experience tells them that both corporate and divisional requirements must be represented in the management of the computing centers, and experience also proves that with a spirit of cooperation on both sides such an arrangement can work well.

The managements of many organizations may be somewhat surprised to see this form of organization emerging. In the great majority of computer-using companies the computer activity now reports to the controller or financial vice president rather than to a central executive, and it has always been in the financial area that the responsibility for data processing has resided. If this kind of structure is becoming typical, then a general reversal must be occurring in this traditional association of data processing with financial management.

There is no question that this reversal is taking place widely. The evidence is incontrovertible; the study summarized as Case 6J provides impressive evidence, as does Dean's study of manufacturing organizations. Even more impressive, perhaps, is a survey published by the Japan Computer Usage Development Institute* which contrasts the organizational status of computer

---

* *Computer Utilization in Japan,* Japan Computer Usage Development Institute, 1967.

installations in Japan with those in the United States. During this study 157 Japanese and 250 American firms were surveyed. In 62% of the Japanese organizations, the computer operation reported directly to central management; this was true in only 6% of the American firms. By contrast, the finance or accounting department was responsible for computer operations in only 18% of the Japanese firms whereas 78% of the American firms assigned computer operations to the financial management function. These figures tend to prove conclusively that there is no intrinsic association between data processing and the financial function, that the traditional association between the two in America has arisen more from habit than from intrinsic desirability. In the United States, to a much greater degree than in any other country, the computer was preceded by less versatile data processing techniques—punched card systems, accounting machines, and the like—that were used almost exclusively for accounting and financial data processing. In most organizations these were the only data processing machines in use at the time the computer was first introduced, and it was natural to apply the experience of the personnel in the financial organization to installing and operating the new (and, initially, apparently similar) tool. It has now become apparent that the computer tends to outgrow the inevitably somewhat parochial viewpoint of finance, and associate itself with the broader viewpoint of the central management group.

Centralization of data processing at the corporate level poses new problems of allocating data processing costs. When the divisions employed their own computers and programmers they paid for them, sometimes allocating the costs to still lower levels and sometimes not, but in any case, having a clear measure of divisional data processing cost to evaluate against its effectiveness. When the major data processing cost is incurred at the corporate level, though, and most of the effort goes into standard programs to be used by all the divisions, how can the cost be divided fairly among the divisions? Since this is not a directly relevant subject, it will be dismissed with only the following observations:

1 There are many variations between one extreme where the corporate group works almost entirely on divisional assignments and the other extreme where it works entirely on central ones, so many compromises are arrived at.

2 Some residue of corporate cost always remains that cannot fairly be charged to any division, and the more applications are standardized the more they must be supported by corporate management. Apparently, standardizing the data processing function implies centralizing its financial support.

While the large organization centralizes its data processing because of the increasing complexity and breadth of applications and because of the shortage of resources, the smaller organization must look to other alternatives; there are no separate pools of programming and system analysis talent to consolidate. At best there is one relatively small group, and management may despair of the possibility that their few people will ever be able to deal competently with all the increasingly complex data processing applications they would like to attempt. The same difficulty faces the smaller research laboratory and college because, as we have seen, the researcher requires increasingly sophisticated computing facilities, and the small research establishment is likely to have difficulty obtaining and supporting the specialized technical staff needed to acquire and support it.

For the smaller organization a different kind of centralization of data processing seems to be emerging, though in a small way so far. Because the data processing services required by smaller organizations often have an element of commonality (e.g., computational time-sharing services for scientists, inventory record keeping and accounting for retail firms), outside organizations may find it feasible to offer services, using advanced computers and programs, that will provide the desired support to groups of subscribing organizations. The subscribers have, essentially, pooled their payments for data processing in order to support the single firm that serves them all. More than one-hundred large time-sharing computers* are now used by profit-making service bureaus providing computational time-shared services via remote input-output devices to engineers and scientists. More than 20,000 small business organizations† now subscribe to the services of organizations providing computers and general programs for groups of users having common needs. These data processing services are growing rapidly, and represent an important new element of the data processing industry. It appears, then, that the small organization can join the trend to centralization of data processing by sharing the support of a central service with other users having common interests.

SUMMARY

It is clear that the data processing activities that support the operating functions of organizations are being centralized more quickly and dramatically than the line functions of the organizations. Broadly speaking, data processing is a staff function rather than a line one, so this is perhaps logical; line functions

---

* Frederic G. Withington, *The Computer Industry: 1968–1973,* Arthur D. Little, Inc., Cambridge, 1968.

† Frederic G. Withington, "The Market for a Computer Utility Industry," *Computers and Communications—Toward a Computer Utility,* F. Gruenberger, Editor, Prentice-Hall, Englewood Cliffs, N.J., 1968.

traditionally demand more layers of management supervision and more disper-
sion, while staff functions, such as purchasing, contracting, and personnel, lend
themselves to central administration. It might have been anticipated that when
shortages of data processing resources (relative to management's aspirations)
began to pinch, the increased efficiency associated with centralizing a staff
function would become the dominant factor.

The fundamental question—centralization of the line functions of organizations because of the computer—seems to require the answer "not yet."
Perhaps, as was considered in Chapter 2, the assertion is correct that the management functions of line organizations are such that computers are only partially relevant and can never in themselves cause general centralization above
the operating level. However, we have seen evidence that "never" may be
too strong a word; perhaps the centralization is occurring, but more slowly
and in a different form from that anticipated. Some possibilities in this area
will be discussed in Part IV. However that may be, so far as experience to date
is concerned the answer is clear. The computer has rarely, if ever, been a
force for overall centralization of management functions. Few if any managers
need fear that it will take over their jobs—though it will surely change them.

CHAPTER 7

DR. FRANKENSTEIN'S FATE

*"As corporation after corporation finds itself virtually overwhelmed
by the task of making its computers make sense, it is incumbent upon the
producers of this hardware to help their customers avoid and overcome
drawbacks. Promises to train and guide personnel in the proper use
of the equipment must not be empty unless these managements want
to be known as the 'robber barons' of the Twentieth Century."**
BART LYTTON

Computer manufacturers attempt to obtain orders in competition with other
manufacturers by meeting the needs of their potential customers better than
the competitors do. In the process they change and adapt to better meet the
needs of the customers. The adjustments the computer manufacturers must
make to deal with the users' problems are similar to the adjustments the users
must make to deal with the same problems. It is instructive to examine the
computer manufacturers for clues to the changes using organizations are likely
to have to make, since the computer manufacturers, having the computer as
their primary preoccupation, are likely to change earlier and more completely
than the average user. The user, aware of the changes the manufacturer has
made, may then decide which of them also apply to him.

In this chapter we will review the demands the computer user makes on
the manufacturer, the conditions under which the manufacturer must operate,
and the organizational adaptations he has made in an effort to meet the user's
demands. The concentration will be on those areas where the user's influence
is felt more immediately and profoundly—marketing, product development,
and cash flow (because users and manufacturers share the investment in the
user's computer installation). It will be shown that in each of these areas the

---

* *Business Automation,* December 1967.

user has a comparable though smaller problem to that of the manufacturer. Manufacturing and other internal functions with characteristics unique to the computer business will be passed over more lightly.

THE USERS' DEMANDS

In the preceding chapters we have reviewed many cases in which computer users attempted to overcome the weaknesses of computers in order to utilize their strengths. The demands the computer user makes on his supplier are clearly implied, and require no further exemplification here. Briefly, the primary user demands are the following.

Demonstration of the product

Users are aware that delivery dates for computers and their associated software are frequently delayed, and that products once delivered frequently contain "bugs." Therefore, most potential computer buyers demand demonstrations of the product being proposed before contracting for it. In order to meet this demand, the computer manufacturer must install demonstration systems within reasonable distance of every potential user. Since the computer manufacturer offers a number of different computers, each with a wide variety of optional memory sizes, peripheral equipment, and the like, if the manufacturer is to be able to demonstrate even the major types of systems offered for sale he must invest very heavily in demonstrators.

Assistance during development of the initial programs
for a new computer

More often than not the computer user does not know how to use the machine he has ordered. He must be instructed in its use and given day-by-day assistance in preparing the initial set of programs for it. Once the first programs are running, the user will (hopefully) know enough about the machine to continue without full time assistance thereafter, but the manufacturer must be prepared to provide expert personnel full time during the initial installation phase. He must therefore employ enough customer assistance personnel to provide every customer with a satisfactory quantity of assistance. Since each computer sale involves from one-half to two man-years of assistance (depending on size), a successful sales record involves a heavy personnel commitment. Furthermore, the assistance personnel must either be based within commuting distance of every customer ordering a computer or must be temporarily moved (at high cost) to the customer's location.

Continued support for the system after its initial installation

Before ordering, the potential user will want to be satisfied that the equipment will be adequately maintained, that improvements to both the hardware and the software will be installed promptly and competently, that additional user personnel can obtain instruction in programming or operating the computer at any time, and that specialized supplies made available for the computer by its manufacturer (e.g., magnetic tape reels, disk packs, and the like) will be readily available. This means, effectively, that few orders will be obtained from users beyond commuting distance of one of the manufacturer's branch offices. Even if temporary assignments of personnel are made to help with the initial installation, the requirement for a local branch office remains because some personnel should remain within a reasonable distance indefinitely thereafter. It has developed that, if a computer manufacturer is to have a chance of obtaining orders in every significant business center in the United States, he must support on the order of 100 branch offices.

A full line of optional equipment

The user is aware that some manufacturers offer optional peripheral equipment which might some day be of use to him (e.g., optical character reading devices, random access memories, remote terminals, and the like), and even if he has no interest in these at the time he orders his initial computer, he often wishes to be assured that they will be available should he ever want them. In order to sell even simple computer systems, then, the manufacturer is obliged to develop complex peripheral equipment simply to assure the users that it will be available if needed. The same consideration applies to advanced general-purpose programs. Even if the user has no use for, say, a data transmission system control program when he first orders a computer system, he is likely to request assurance that it will be available to him if needed.

A larger compatible computer

The user may have no intention of outgrowing the computer he is about to order in the foreseeable future, but the experiences of other computer users have probably made him aware that computer capacity is often exceeded much more quickly than the user expects. Therefore, the manufacturer will be expected to demonstrate (or at least promise) the availability of a larger, faster computer that will run the programs the user is about to develop without any reprogramming. A computer manufacturer's product line should contain a computer one step larger in capacity and price than the one he hopes to sell in large numbers.

A flow of new products

The user knows that technology advances and that today's machine will be superseded by a new one tomorrow. He will wish to be assured that his supplier is as likely to introduce new models incorporating the latest in technology as any other supplier, and also that they will in some way be compatible with the machine now being selected, so that the user can change to a new, up-to-date model with a minimum penalty in reprogramming.

Competitive software

The user has talked to competing manufacturers and other users, and he knows that certain software is usually made available for systems of the type and size he is considering. He will expect to be offered compilers for several programming languages, a choice of operating systems, and various supporting programs along with the computer he is selecting; he would prefer to be offered more than competitors make available. In particular, if the computer manufacturer has developed application packages which the user can substitute for programs he would otherwise have to develop himself, they will be welcome.

A minimum commitment

Practically all computer users acquiring their first computer, and all users whose needs change frequently, are uncertain how long they will want to keep the machine they order. If they are pessimistic, they will wish to reserve the right to return the computer if it should work out badly. If they are optimistic, they will be concerned about outgrowing the machine in a short time and needing to exchange it for its larger compatible successor. This means that the overwhelming majority of computer users prefer to lease them from the manufacturer rather than purchase them. Typically, four out of five will lease rather than purchase, but when a model of computer is new and untried, practically all users will lease it initially. When IBM delivered the first models of its System 360 computers, for example, 95% of the customers leased and 5% purchased them. The manufacturer must provide the money to make the sale and prepare the customer for delivery, then manufacture, deliver, and demonstrate successful operation of the machine before the customer makes any payment. Then, on the order of two years' lease payments are required to offset the investment in the machine before any profits are generated. The implications of this to the revenue and profit position of the manufacturer will be reviewed later.

Individual using organizations with special needs or unusual attitudes will impose many other demands on the manufacturer, but these summarize the needs of most and make the implications clear. Practically every one of these user demands reflects a step in the evolution of his own data processing which he wishes the manufacturer to take along with him. The way the manufacturer organizes himself to meet the demands is therefore parallel to the way the user must organize to meet them himself. In the remainder of this chapter, we will study typical manufacturer organizations to derive guidance for the user.

MARKETING ORGANIZATION AND POLICY

In the early years of the computer business it was not clear that the computer user was going to make the demands itemized above. Most companies entering the computer manufacturing business regarded it as a relatively straightforward matter of designing a competitively attractive product, obtaining orders for it, providing some training in its use, delivering it in working condition, and then forgetting it apart from arranging for its maintenance. Fifteen years ago the marketing organization of a small computer manufacturer, reflecting this attitude, was likely to be made up of approximately 50% salesmen and 50% support personnel. The support personnel would be located half at the home office and half in the branch offices with the salesmen. Their primary function would be to prepare technical arguments the salesmen could use to sell the products against competition, to answer customer technical questions, and to teach courses.

Once the manufacturer had the good fortune to obtain a number of orders and faced the task of fulfilling them, he would learn quickly about the users' demands for assistance in preparing the initial programs. He would have to hire more technical representatives; the number of technical representatives would rise to double the number of salesmen as technical representatives were assigned for periods of six months to a year or more to individual customers to help them prepare for installation. The number of branch offices would begin to grow to meet the customers' demand for local service, and the quantity of business needed to support this larger marketing organization would begin to grow.

Later, as the business grew and a large number of computer installations existed in the vicinity of each branch office, the manufacturer would find that existing customers continued to request help as they undertook novel programs, installed new types of peripheral equipment, or became confused over the use of new software issued by the manufacturer. This ongoing demand for technical help increased the total demand for personnel; now, the typical branch office would employ four technical representatives per salesman. Roughly 25% of them would be occupied helping existing customers, 50% would be assisting users installing new equipment, and 25% would be working with the salesmen attempting to obtain new sales.

Now, to his dismay, the manufacturer would find that even with four technical representatives per salesman it was no longer possible for the branch office to provide technical support for all products. The details of complex software such as compilers or operating systems are familiar only to those who have designed or implemented them, to a few specialists who work with them full time. If a difficult question arises about a subtlety in the use of a program, or about a suspected flaw in its design or implementation, the typical technical representative in the branch office is helpless to deal with it and must call on specialists at the home office for assistance. Similarly, some of the more complex and less widely used machinery (such as very large scientific computers) are unlikely to be directly familiar to the personnel at a given branch, and again, specialists must be available to support them.

Specialization is forced on the organization not only by the increased complexity and diversity of products but also by size alone. The function of conducting training schools and teaching courses, for example, is performed as needed by any of the technical representatives of the smaller computer manufacturers. When the marketing organization and the number of students and courses grows large, the company invariably decides that it will be more efficient to establish a staff of educational specialists to teach courses on a full-time basis. Not the least of the reasons for establishing this full-time educational system is the growing need for internal retraining. The customer demands a continuing flow of new and up-to-date computers, peripheral equipment, and software. The manufacturers' salesmen and technical representatives must be trained in the new products and must receive sufficient direct experience to be able to lead the users in installing them. A moderate size computer manufacturer typically has a force of salesmen and technical representatives in excess of 1000 people and introduces from three to ten major new products every year, so his internal retraining effort must be substantial.

Every computer manufacturer, then, finds it necessary to increase specialization and to establish hierarchies of support rather than to continue expecting each branch to support all products. Even the largest of all, International Business Machines Corporation, has established such a structure. In early 1968, IBM had seventeen regional centers in the United States to support large computers and forty centers to support small computers and punched card equipment.* The function of these support centers is to back up the hundreds of IBM branch offices in handling the myriad special products, technical questions, and obsolescent types of equipment that must still be supported.

Finally, as the years pass and the variety of old and new products in use proliferates, the number of contracting arrangements must become greater

---

* *1967 Annual Report,* International Business Machines Corporation.

and greater. Some users will have purchased their machines and be paying for them on installment plans, contracting for maintenance. Other users will be leasing computers on a long-term, low-rate basis, others on a short-term basis. Some will take advantage of purchase option credits to convert lease contracts to purchases at reduced price. Some with obsolescent machines will be offered reduced purchase prices so that the manufacturer can eliminate the machines from his inventory. Some will have contracted for a variety of software and services in addition to equipment. A contracting organization must deal with all of these possibilities and the salesmen must be compensated fairly for every change his customer makes, whether it is an addition to a presently installed computer system, replacement of it by another, return of the system, or a change in type of contract. As the number of possible situations grows, so does the complexity of the sales compensation plan. The document one computer manufacturer gives to its sales representatives to explain the standard sales compensation plan contains 17,000 words and five tables.

As the computer manufacturer's marketing force proceeds through these steps of evolution, it adds specialized organizational units, hierarchical levels of structure, and increasing management complexity. All these resources are focused on the customer; they all came into existence in response to his demands. The following case typifies the way a mature computer manufacturer provides marketing support to his customers.

CASE 7A

◀ Figure 7–1 depicts the customer support functions performed by the marketing organization of a moderate size manufacturer of business computer systems, and their relations with one another and the customer. The main line of authority is sales management. The local branch is responsible for relations with the customer and reports to one of six regional offices, and the regions report to central sales management at the home office. Most branches have demonstration models of the smaller, more common computers; the regions have larger and more expensive models. Sales management is responsible for all matters affecting the customer, but the only specialized function under its direct control is that of contracting. Most contracts are standard and are handled by the branch with only review at higher levels, but the many varieties of special contracts are handled by specialists in the region or the home office. Sales management is responsible for the provision of adequate support to the customer by the various specialized support functions, but because each is a highly structured organization with its own technical supervision, branch and regional sales managers do not have technical management authority over them.

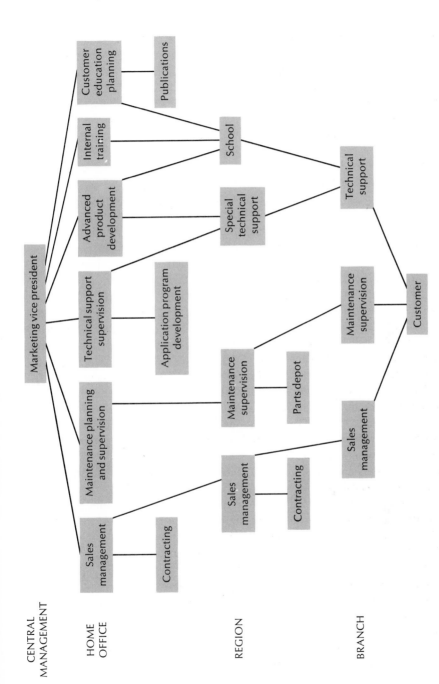

FIG. 7–1 Customer support functions of computer manufacturer's marketing organization.

The largest support function (in numbers of people) is the technical support function, each of the branches having from three to four technical support representatives for each sales representative. Most of the time they are working with the customers, providing advice and technical assistance, and supplementing customers' staffs as necessary and as committed by the salesmen in the process of obtaining orders. When highly abstruse technical questions are asked, or when new products are involved with which the branch personnel have not had experience, the technical support personnel in the branches are helped by specialized staffs at the regional offices. Certain types of questions (for example, about the details of compiler programs) are frequent enough to justify maintaining an expert in the subject in each region. Other questions, such as those having to do with new products just being introduced, come in "waves" and then die out as the branch personnel become familiar with the new products. In order to help with such questions, the regional technical support personnel are provided with lines of communication to the advanced product development group at the home office. The regional technical support groups also supervise the technical quality of the technical support personnel in the branches, and are themselves supervised by the central technical support group at the home office. This group is primarily administrative in nature, establishing personnel policies, hiring and promoting personnel, and supervising the quality of the work. However, they also direct the course of the technical support effort, helping with new product introductions and sales campaigns, and also directing the development of application programs. The technical support personnel learn from the sales organization and from their own personnel in the field what customer programs are likely candidates for generalization into application programs, to help sell computers to other customers with similar problems. They assign application program development projects to a special group reporting to home office technical support.

The advanced product development groups, responsible for both software and hardware products, are not generally involved in selling. However, they must see to it that the introduction of new products to the sales force is supported by adequate information. This means they must provide preliminary information to technical support representatives who are responsible for answering questions about advanced products, and they must also provide suitably organized and detailed information for internal training programs designed to acquaint the sales and customer support personnel in the field with the nature and use of each new product. The advanced product engineers must occasionally teach courses for the field personnel in the regional training schools—a duty they regard as a chore, but accept as necessary.

The regional schools are used for both customer training and internal training. Each region has several professional teachers on its staff, and also calls on personnel from the branches and from the home office as necessary to conduct courses. The regional schools receive their material from the internal training and customer education planning groups at the home office which provide the course outlines, the reference manuals, and usually the instructors for the first round of each new course. After a course has become a matter of routine, the staffs of the schools and the branches are expected to be able to teach it thereafter.

The provision of all reference and promotional publications is the responsibility of customer education planning. Actually, every one of the home office support groups has its own publications to issue and maintain; the publication group is responsible for more than 500 individual documents, each of which is subject to continual change and updating, and must issue between 50 and 100 new ones each year. For the sake of efficiency, the publication control function was assigned to a single group, and because most of the publications are distributed through customer training that function was selected.

Finally, the maintenance organization has its own hierarchical structure parallel to the others. There are many people in the maintenance organization; in branch territories where there is a great deal of equipment installed there may be more maintenance engineers than there are salesmen and technical support personnel combined. Each branch stocks the most frequently needed parts and is responsible for all routine maintenance of the computers installed in the branch's territory. However, each region is equipped with a much more extensive parts supply, both to keep down the quantities of routine parts in the branches and to provide a central point for less frequently needed parts (needless to say, parts inventory records are maintained on computers). In addition to the regular personnel, the region is staffed with a small group of veteran engineers who serve as troubleshooters for the personnel of the branches.

At the home office there are few practicing maintenance personnel, but a large administrative work load exists in hiring, salary administration, training, and the development of procedures (both improved procedures for existing products and new procedures). Again, the regional schools are used for most training of maintenance engineers, but it is the responsibility of home office maintenance to provide teachers and methodology. ▶

All manufacturers of computer systems must establish a marketing structure somewhat like this. If they did not, the customers' machines would not work, the questions would not receive answers, the field personnel would not understand the products, and the salesmen's commitments of product capability and customer support would not be met. Such failures would lead to loss of reputation and increasing difficulty in obtaining orders. More immediately important, the failure to meet expressed or implied commitments can lead to damaging lawsuits accompanied by the worst of publicity. Despite their best efforts, all the major computer manufacturers have faced such suits. In one well-publicized case,* International Business Machines lost such a suit brought by a Boston grocery firm. IBM's customer support and marketing administration are well known to be second to none, but the requirements of customer support are so severe that even IBM can apparently fail.

Typical computer users making routine use of smaller computers have little awareness of this "inverted pyramid" of supporting services. They need deal only with the local branch, whose personnel should be able to handle all their problems. Except for an occasional visit to a regional school or to the home office for a special demonstration, such customers have no contact with the rest of the structure. However, if the customer is an exceptional one, using the largest and newest equipment or the most advanced programs made available by the manufacturer, he will sooner or later come in contact with many of the supporting functions because his branch will not have the knowledge to help him. When this happens, the lines of organization and authority become confused. Once the customer obtains contacts at the region or at the home office which are of more value to him than the branch personnel who cannot directly provide answers, he tends to rely on these contacts and bypass the branch. This confuses both parties because the number of possible individuals the customer can call proliferates so that he may find himself frustrated in attempting to find the right one, and the possibility of his obtaining inconsistent information arises. However, the customer's desire to get the information from the "horse's mouth" is understandable.

The user's director of data processing must see to it that comparable functions are performed internally for the data processing services he offers to his customers (e.g., the financial system for accounting, the production control system for manufacturing, the marketing information system for sales). There must be maintenance and improvement of existing programs, assistance to customers, training for both customers and data processing staff, advanced product development, and publications. The nature of the functional organization the manufacturer has evolved in light of customers' needs to support the marketing of his computers is therefore similar to that of the organization

---

* *The Wall Street Journal,* March 27, 1968.

that uses the computer system. The manager concerned with the services offered by his company's computer activity should ask himself whether all of these functions are represented; they should be.

PRODUCT DEVELOPMENT ORGANIZATION AND POLICY

Fifteen years ago it appeared to computer manufacturers that each computer system was a separate product, complete in itself. Typically, the overall characteristics of the system were developed by a small executive group and then a single team of engineers skilled in all the technologies involved in the computer system commenced the design. Matters were scheduled so that the computer and its peripheral equipment would be finished at the same time, and then the designers would start thinking about the next product. This simple approach was possible because each computer system differed completely from all others, and very few variations and options were offered. In 1956, for example, the IBM 650 computer was offered in two models with only five minor options available among the peripheral devices,* and no element of the 650 system was used with any other system.

As time went on, the customers' demands for optional peripheral equipment, for larger compatible computers, and for a flow of modifications to installed systems that would bring them technically up to date became evident. It was necessary to offer more and more versions of the basic computer, and more optional accessories. For example, in 1967 the IBM 1401 computer (which replaced the model 650 referred to above) was offered in fifty-four different models with ninety-one optional features, many of them major peripheral devices of specialized nature also used with other computers.† In addition, three larger, compatible computers were available as replacements for 1401 computers.

With such a proliferation of products and a requirement for continual modernization of each type of equipment, manufacturers had to give up the idea of developing each computer system as an independent product. Each major element of the computer and each class of peripheral equipment was generalized so that all of the computers in the manufacturer's product line could use comparable (very possibly identical) components and peripheral equipment. In order to keep the product line continually up to date, per-

---

* *IBM Machine Service for U.S. Government,* International Business Machines Corporation, July 1, 1955.
† *Authorized Federal Supply Schedule Price List,* International Business Machines Corporation, July 1, 1966.

manent engineering development groups were assigned to each generalized area. Instead of developing computer systems one by one, the manufacturer was now developing a flow of components which could be assembled at will into products of a wide diversity of sizes and types.*

As this evolution was occurring in the development of computer equipment, software entered the picture. When computers that could overlap input and output and computation were introduced around 1957, systems of general-purpose software to control these simultaneous operations became necessary. As the machines became more complex, capable, and versatile, the software had to follow. Automatic programming concepts involving compilers and the like also evolved and increased in complexity. To the user, the performance of the software and the hardware merged; the combination of the two determined the total productivity of the system, not the software or hardware alone. The manufacturer's product planners had to face the fact that software and hardware required joint and co-equal development. (This concept, a foreign one to hardware-oriented engineers, was slow to be fully realized.) In addition to engineering groups continually working on the major components of computer equipment, then, the manufacturer had to establish development groups working on operating systems and automatic programming software. Whenever a new computer system was considered, the products of all these groups had to be considered in the light of sales objectives, competitors' actions, available financial resources, and the evolution of user demand. The product planning function became, in a sense, a total business planning one for the computer manufacturing organization.

CASE 7B

◀ Figure 7–2 depicts the functions involved in the product planning of the computer manufacturer whose marketing functions were shown in Fig. 7–1.

A continuously operating product planning committee is responsible for integrating all information provided by the functional elements and for final decisions. When important decisions are impending, all officers of the company are likely to join the committee's meetings. At other times the meetings include the committee staff and are devoted to preparing evaluations of pos-

---

* This kind of evolution in the engineering process seems to be typical in many mass production-oriented manufacturing organizations with diverse products. It is analogous to the large automobile manufacturer, for example, whose engineering is organized by component areas such as engines, transmissions, chassis, suspensions, and bodies. These are assembled into products of various sizes and types which appear distinct to the customer, but which employ a very high percentage of common components.

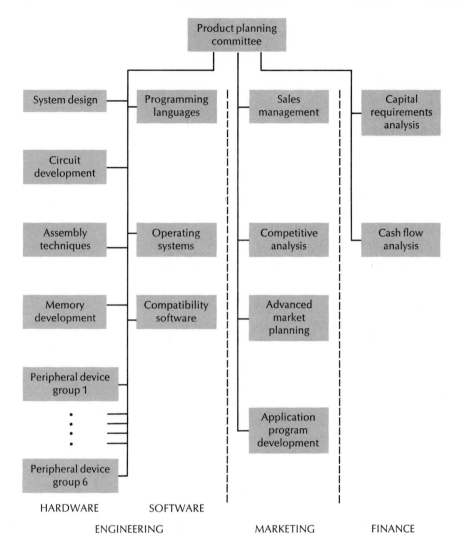

FIG. 7–2 Computer manufacturer's product planning functions.

sible products. A vice president of product planning is head of this committee, and he receives a flow of reports and forecasts from the development groups.

As might be expected, the engineering department contributes the largest number of reports. There are ten continuously functioning engineering groups responsible for various elements of the computer systems: one developing new system design concepts, another working on new circuit modules, another developing packaging and assembly techniques, and a fourth designing new internal memories. Six other groups deal with classes of peripheral equipment (e.g., high speed printers, punch card equipment, magnetic disk files), each continually attempting to develop newer and better products in its area. Each of these ten groups reports regularly to the product planning committee on its accomplishments and on the characteristics of new products or techniques it could introduce at certain dates.

This manufacturer has chosen to combine his software and hardware development groups in the engineering department, on the grounds that the two are equally basic to the development of new computer systems. There are three software groups, one responsible for the development of new programming languages and compilers, another responsible for operating systems, and a third responsible for providing simulator programs that maintain the compatibility of new computers with those already installed by customers (recognizing the customer's demand for a minimum amount of reprogramming when he trades in one product for another).

The marketing department contains four groups that provide regular reports to the product planning committee. The sales management group presents its views of events occurring in the field, and three home office staff groups present the results of their studies. One of these is responsible for analysis of competitors' products and their probable effect on the company's; another (mentioned in the description of marketing functions) is responsible for identifying possibilities for the development of applications programs; and the third attempts to predict what the customers will be wanting two to five years ahead because most of the possible new products could not be delivered until then.

Last but far from least, the finance department is continuously participating in product planning. Not only does finance advise the committee on the amount of money available to put into the development of products (the capital requirements analysis group), it also considers the impact of a proposed product on the revenue being produced from the machines already installed (the cash flow analysis group). Since most of the manufacturers' computers are leased to the customers, a product which is a direct replacement for an existing one may cut off as much revenue as it generates. On the other hand, the customers must be provided with up-to-date equipment lest they switch to the competition. A continual compromise must be made, then, between the desirability of preserving present lease revenues and the desirability of introducing more advanced products. The cash flow analysis group studies these issues and the committee considers their results together with all others in arriving at its decisions. ▶

Some of the implications of this to the manufacturer are obvious. For one thing, the requirement that he maintain all these continuously functioning groups means that his product development function will be very expensive; he must maintain a breadth of product line and volume of sales sufficient to support it (as well as to meet the even greater cost of maintaining the minimum marketing organization). Another implication is that maintaining common interface standards and common standards of compatibility among all existing and proposed products is perhaps the single most difficult problem the manufacturer faces. He must somehow stay abreast of competitive and technological progress in a dozen areas while developing products that will work together with existing ones interchangeably.

The significance of this product planning organization to computer users is comparable to that of marketing. The computer user must continually review possible changes to his information systems: new programming techniques and improved equipment are continually becoming available. He must evaluate new equipment and software for usefulness to him (the engineering functions), he must consider what other users are doing and what other manufacturers are offering (the marketing functions), and he must consider both the capital investment required for a change and the undepreciated value of existing investments (the financial functions). While few users will need as many separate functional groups as the manufacturer does, each must nevertheless consider most of the same areas from time to time.

INVESTMENTS AND CASH FLOW

Computer manufacturers have been surprised and displeased at the complexity of the marketing and product planning organizations they have had to develop in order to meet user demands. They have been even more surprised by the financial requirements that have emerged.

Most computer users lease the machines from the manufacturers, and pay nothing until their machine is installed and operating satisfactorily. This means that before he can obtain any revenue the manufacturer must:

1   Invest in development of the machine,

2   Invest in development of the programs for it,

3   Invest the sales effort needed to obtain the order,

4   Provide the support needed to prepare the customer for installation of the machine,

5   Pay the manufacturing cost of the machine,

6   Install the machine on the customer's premises, put it into working order, and demonstrate it.

In addition, the manufacturer must make the related investments we have noted earlier. These include investments in demonstration machines to be installed in branch offices and in development of specialized peripheral equipment and larger, compatible successor machines. These investment implications were imperfectly appreciated by most manufacturers when the industry was young.

CASE 7C

◀ In 1955 an electronics company introduced a small computer system for scientific applications. It was inexpensive, its peripheral equipment was modest, and (at that time) no great investment in software was required. The electronics company knew it would have to lease the machines in order to meet the demands of most customers, but felt that the total investment in development, initial marketing, and manufacturing of machines would be no more than one million dollars. Their hoped-for financial development is traced in curve A of Fig. 7–3, which shows cumulative cash flows over a period of seven years. Each year's net cash income or outgo is added to the total to date; a net cash investment during a year drives the curve down further while a net return turns it upward. When the total cash invested in the project is repaid, the curve crosses the axis and climbs to the plus side of the axis. As curve A shows, the manufacturer expected lease revenues from the computers to offset additional investments during the second year and start the curve turning up. By the end of the third year, the manufacturer hoped to have recouped his investment and to be making a net profit on the enterprise at a rate of about $2 million per year.

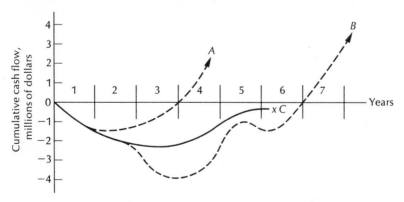

FIG. 7–3   Cumulative cash flow curves for computer manufacturer.

By the end of the second year the manufacturer's management observed that they were not proceeding according to plan. The curve was continuing to drop, and investment had almost reached $2 million. At this point they hired a management consulting firm to advise them on the causes of and cures for this deviation from plan.

The management consulting firm found that the primary cause of the deviation from plan was inability of the marketing organization to produce the anticipated sales rate per dollar of cost. The average salesman was producing only two orders a year instead of the anticipated four, and the cost of support (customer assistance personnel, demonstrator machines, and the like) was significantly greater than had initially been planned. The total number of orders was satisfactory, which obscured this fact, but only because a series of small expansions of the sales force had been made. The solution to the problem, then, was presumably an increase in the effectiveness of marketing. However, the consultants found that this could be obtained only at an increase in cost. More sales training was recommended, more demonstrator machines and support personnel per salesman, more peripheral equipment options to suit more users, and more programs for specific customer applications. All of these would drive the curve still further down during the third year, and then (to make matters worse) if these measures produced the anticipated upturn in sales, still more cash would be required to manufacture the machines to fill the orders obtained. Thus, the cumulative cash flow curve would reach a bottom of nearly $4 million during the fourth year before starting to turn up. At this point it would rise sharply, but then the consultants found that still another major investment would be needed. In order to obtain sufficient orders in the third and fourth years to cause the required increase in revenue, the manufacturer would have to promise his customers a larger successor machine for delivery at least as soon as the sixth year. During the fifth year, then, just at the time the cumulative cash flow curve was rising satisfactorily, the consultants felt it would be necessary to invest in development, marketing, and then manufacturing of the new machine, which would cause the curve to dip again. Finally, at the end of the sixth year the two machines together would both be producing significant revenues and the cash flow curve would rise very sharply; during the seventh year, indeed, the net positive cash flow would be on the order of $4 million rather than the $2 million per year that the electronics company had initially forecast for the fourth year.

This was completely unacceptable to the management of the company. They had no intention of investing $4 million in their computer activity, and were unable to wait six years for its return. They understood the consultants' recommendations about more effective marketing, a successor machine, and the other costly items that would be involved in following curve *B*, but they hoped that a business of more modest size could be obtained without these investments. So, instead of investing more money in marketing, they cut it back, eliminating the unproductive salesmen and keeping only those who had proved productive. They invested only minimal additional money in peripheral equipment and software development, and made no plans for a successor machine. The cumulative investment curve immediately stopped dropping and began to rise during the latter part of the third and the fourth year, but then (as the consultants had predicted) it developed that the incoming flow of orders was too small to add many new installations, and the revenues from the cumulative installations were insufficient to support even the modest cost of the existing marketing and product development organizations. The result was that curve C actually developed, the cumulative cash flow remained negative, and there was no sign that it would ever turn positive.

During the fifth year the management of the electronics company realized that their strategy was "too little and too late," and that by then it was impossible to improve matters without essentially starting over, developing a new marketing organization and a new product line. They therefore proceeded to seek potential buyers for their computer operation, and succeeded in selling it during the middle of the sixth year for a price only a little greater than the remaining cumulative investment. They agreed that the consultants' advice had been essentially correct, and that the only way to remain alive in the business would have been to invest at least at the level recommended. However, then as before, they felt that it would have been entirely beyond their means to do so, and wished only that they had known at the start what they were getting into. ▶

The computer manufacturers, then, have been forced by the demands of their users to invest heavily in the organizations required to meet them, and even more in the products whose manufacturing costs will be repaid only slowly by the users' lease payments. This problem, bad enough in itself, was worsened by the pace of technological progress.

The so-called second generation of computers incorporating transistors and magnetic core memories was introduced to the market during the period 1957 to 1961. Most of the manufacturers hoped to see these products produce lease revenue for at least six to eight years, so that their cost could be repaid and a satisfactory profit generated before they were replaced by newer machines. However, the pace of technology and competition forced the manufacturers as a group to introduce their third generation products during the period 1963 to 1966, so in many cases they replaced customers' machines with newer, more economical ones before the earlier machines had produced anything like the planned revenue. This depressed the cumulative cash flow curves for several more years and increased the manufacturers' investments to amounts far larger than were anticipated. Those manufacturers interested in full line business computer systems, wiser because of the earlier experiences of such companies as the electronics company cited above, generally planned initial investments in the business ranging from $20 to $50 million but uniformly found that figures in excess of $100 million ended up more realistic.

Technological progress is a curse from the financial point of view of the manufacturer, because it requires him to supersede his existing products before they have adequately paid for themselves. On the other hand, it has been a blessing from the point of view of his growth. As technological progress has made computer systems progressively more powerful and effective per dollar of cost, the market for them has expanded tremendously. The manufacturers have benefited accordingly, and found that although it took much longer to become profitable than had been planned and much more investment was required, they grew more sharply than they had expected to. This can be exemplified by the history of the computer manufacturer whose marketing and product development organizations were depicted in Cases 7A and 7B.

CASE 7D

◀ This manufacturer decided in 1956 to enter the business computer industry and undertook to build both a product line and an organization to support the effort. First deliveries were made in 1958, and between 1958 and 1962 four different computer systems in different price ranges were introduced. These machines enjoyed satisfactory success and by 1963 the manufacturer could see that at the end of that year there would be more than 200 computer systems of all kinds installed. The cumulative investment would reach the originally planned maximum of $40 million in that year. According to projections, the 200 computers would produce revenues sufficient to cover expenses in 1964 and, with additional installations thereafter, would keep the business profitable on a current basis from then on. During 1963, however, the manufacturer's engineers perceived that many changes were occurring in computer technology, particularly in the areas of electronic circuits and software. They convinced management that it would not be possible to follow the financial plans that already existed; instead, in order to maintain and increase their existing position in the industry it would be necessary to invest immediately in the development of an entire new family of computers which would supersede the present ones; the additional development investment would be at least $15 million. The Board of Directors authorized this, and the new computers were developed and announced for sale during 1964 and 1965.

They were successful, and volume deliveries occurred during the years 1965 to 1967. During this entire period the computer manufacturer's investment continued to grow (i.e., he operated at a loss) first, because of the $15 million development cost of the new computer family; second, because of retraining and expanding marketing; and third, and most important, because of the manufacturing costs incurred in meeting the large volume of initial orders the marketing organization was successful in obtaining. By the end of 1966 the total investment had reached $120 million, three times the original commitment the company's directors had authorized back in 1956. However, the income from this investment was by now really substantial. Most of the 200 second generation machines that had been installed prior to 1964 were still in place and still returning revenues. By now the machines were depreciated, and these revenues were a source of substantial profit. Furthermore, more than 1000 of the third generation computers were now producing revenue; the current total income was well above that needed to support the product development and marketing organizations of the company. It was now possible to show the Board of Directors that the cumulative cash flow curve had turned up, and in 1968 it was possible to show a substantial corporate profit. ▶

The data processing investments of the computer user are closely analogous to those of the computer manufacturer. When a computer user decides to implement a new information system, he must invest in system design, programming, file conversion, training, parallel operations, and (more often than not) in new equipment required for the new information system. Presumably it is anticipated that this development investment will be repaid in some way—by direct operating savings, improved corporate responsiveness, management control, or in the form of some other benefit. If the development investment is to be fully repaid, the operating benefits must be accumulated over a period of time. If a new information system superseding the old one is developed before the initial investment is repaid, the cumulative investment increases. The computer user then finds himself in a position similar to that of the manufacturer. In order to take advantage of newly evolved techniques and equipment he may find himself replacing existing systems by new ones repeatedly, long before the cumulative investment in earlier systems is repaid. While this may be wise in many cases, it nevertheless means that over a period of years the user probably ends up investing far more in his data processing equipment and personnel than he had anticipated when he started his first development.

Few computer users have kept records of their total data processing expenditures in detail (indeed, they are often difficult to separate from other expenditures) and few can accurately measure the resulting benefits. Thus, few can say what their cumulative data processing investment or cash flow curve is. Most are uncomfortably aware that they have invested much more than they initially intended, however, and though most will also say they feel they have obtained their money's worth, they (like the manufacturers) wish they had known what they were getting into.

DATA PROCESSING SERVICES

In reviewing the list of demands the computer user makes on the manufacturer, one is struck by the fact that many of them would be better met if the computer user did not have to buy (or lease) the machine at all. The user's desire for a minimum ownership commitment, his wish to be able to choose freely among optional peripheral equipment and larger compatible computers, and his desire to be continually supplied with both hardware and software as good as anything available from competitive suppliers, all imply that the user would be better off if he never installed equipment of his own, but only temporarily obtained the services of machines owned by others. He could then use only the amount of computer time he needed for as long as he needed it, and whenever something better or more suitable appeared on the market he could switch freely. A firm in the business of supplying such services, being a specialist and being able to spread his costs among many customers, would be in a better position than any one of them to keep abreast of the latest technology and to acquire and offer improvements to its existing equipment. While it is true that the user's freedom to use a data processing service instead of his own equipment is restricted because the characteristics of the computer system he uses must be well suited to his own problems, nevertheless many computer applications require similar equipment, so the use of such services is practical for many.

In recognition of this fact, a sizeable computer service industry has arisen. According to one study made in 1968* this service industry grossed $650 million in 1967 and is forecast to grow to between $1500 and $2500 million by 1972. These services are of many kinds, some offering retrieval of particular kinds of information (e.g., stock quotation services), others offering convenient immediately accessible facilities for developing and running scientific programs (time-sharing services), others offering complete data processing services to businesses, and still others offering just computer time with users providing their own programs. The firms competing in this industry are an interesting study in themselves, being aggressive, adaptable organizations oriented toward conceiving and exploiting service opportunities that have never existed before. The most successful of them offer numerous different services, and often manufacture some of the equipment required to support

---

* *The Computer Industry: 1968–1973*, Arthur D. Little, Inc., Cambridge 1968.

them. The computer manufacturers themselves, aware of the opportunities in this area, usually compete in the data processing service business. However, the computer manufacturers do not dominate the service business and many smaller firms are prospering in it.

The user, of course, benefits from having a greater choice of ways of getting his work done. In the past, all he could do was acquire the equipment which seemed best for his purposes at the time and then attempt to do all of his work on it, even though the machine might be unsuited to some parts of his work. Now, with a multitude of different data processing services available, he can easily use several for different purposes, perhaps greatly reducing his investment in equipment acquired from a manufacturer.

Some users of data processing equipment see a new business opportunity for themselves in the growth of the services business, having computers with unused time and (sometimes) programmers who are not continually busy. Banks in particular have been prone to enter the data processing services business, because they not only perceive an opportunity to establish a profitable business but a means of establishing relationships with potential customers for banking services. A study conducted by the American Bankers Association in 1966* asked each of 544 banks to report the percentage of its gross income accruing from data processing services in that year, and to forecast what the percentage was likely to be for 1970. The results were as follows:

Percentage of Gross Income Derived from Data Processing Services	Percentage of Banks Reporting	
	1966	1970 (expected)
More than 10%	—	33%
6 to 10%	8%	23%
1 to 5%	29%	35%
Less than 1%	55%	8%

It is apparent that financial institutions will be among the largest forces in the data processing services business; these and other companies not heretofore considered to be part of the data processing industry (notably communications companies) will be competing with existing suppliers.

SUMMARY

Many computer users, frustrated and unhappy because of incomplete or imperfectly skilled support from the manufacturers, tend to feel exploited. The quotation at the beginning of the chapter reflects this feeling. As this chapter

---

* *Datamation,* June 1967.

has shown, however, the computer manufacturer has received at least as many shocks and unpleasant surprises as the user. He has found that the complexity and cost of the organization he must maintain to attempt to meet user needs are far greater than he had expected. He has also found that his capital investment has become much larger than projected at the time he entered the business. The harassed user may take some comfort in this observation, because the monster has treated him no worse than it has its creator.

More relevant to the present subject, it is clear that the manufacturers' struggles to cope with the computer business provide many lessons for the computer user, and enable us to reach further conclusions about the effects of the computer on organizations. Both manufacturer and user have learned that they must treat the computer not as a piece of equipment to be acquired and then ignored, but as one aspect of a continuously changing process. To the degree that the organization itself is dynamic and changing, its data processing equipment, programs, and personnel are also. Most computer-using organizations must therefore view the data processing function as a continually changing arm of the business with continuing design, evaluation, and acquisition functions—and continuing investment requirements. The function must be managed accordingly; new programs and equipment must be evaluated in terms of their adequacy in meeting user needs, their initial investment, their operating cost, and their effect on systems already installed. Each new investment should be planned in consideration of previous investments so that the cumulative effect of all the organization's investments in and benefits from data processing is positive. In this sense, managers in computer using organizations should view data processing as a business just as much as the computer manufacturers do.

Part III | HOW THE COMPUTER
CHANGES INDIVIDUALS

CHAPTER 8

THE PRIESTHOOD OF THE MACHINE

*"If I were a crook, I'd work through computers."**
PROFESSOR ROBERT FANO

Since it takes time and specialized knowledge to apply computers to the problems of organizations deciding to use them, staffs of specialized personnel (systems analysts and programmers) always accompany the computer. The day-to-day use of the computer involves still other personnel for data preparation, operating the equipment, scheduling its use, and performing clerical tasks. Since the number of these people is often substantial (from ten or fifteen in a small computer installation to hundreds in a very large one), appropriate levels of supervisory and managerial positions must also be created and filled.

This chapter is devoted to these people—their nature and attitudes, how these differ from the attitudes of other personnel, and the influence of the "computer people" on the organization as the computer's influence and importance increases. In a sense it is these people, not the computer, who cause the changes we are exploring—the machine is useless and therefore a neutral influence until they program it as they see fit. The manager seeking to exploit the computer can do so only through these people.

SYSTEM ANALYSTS AND PROGRAMMERS

System analysts and programmers are employed to prepare applications for the computer. Because they work primarily with the machine, they are often viewed as highly specialized technicians having little relevance to or need for information about other functions of the organization. In fact, in order to understand the applications they are studying and to evaluate the desirability

---

* *The Wall Street Journal*, April 5, 1968.

of changing the way an organization performs its functions, it has developed that they must be equipped with much more than just knowledge of their tools.

CASE 8A

◀ A large business which has employed computers for years has evolved job descriptions for the personnel it employes in data processing. The job description for the position of system analyst reads (in part) as follows:

The system analyst will:

1 Analyze existing systems to determine their functions and identify weaknesses.

2 Design new systems incorporating advanced technology to improve the functioning of existing systems and/or to perform new ones.

3 Estimate development and operating costs of new systems, compare them with costs of existing systems, and present the comparisons in a form suitable for management decision.

4 Develop supporting and conversion procedures for new systems.

5 Supervise project teams made up of junior analysts, programmers, and user personnel performing such work.

6 Coordinate his work with user representatives to assure accuracy and completeness of system designs, supporting, and conversion procedures.

7 Study new data processing methods to determine their usefulness and applicability.

Job descriptions for programmers and for personnel associated with operating the machine speak more of skills uniquely associated with computers and less of such creative capabilities as these. However, job descriptions for data processing managerial personnel refer almost entirely to management capabilities, and make almost no reference to knowledge and skill associated specifically with the computer. Clearly, above the level of routine work the company has found that the technical skills associated with computers are only a minor part of the story. ▶

The more creative and responsible computer people must be able to communicate with other personnel in the company very readily if they are to perform such functions as these. However, it is usually observed that they tend to confine their associations with other company personnel primarily to those involved in computer work. The social associations of computer people are largely with other members of their own group, or with computer people employed by other organizations. The reasons for this are easy to identify. First, they share a common interest in the technology, in computer hardware and software; much of the dissemination of information about this rapidly developing technology takes place by word of mouth among computer people. Second, the combination of age, background, and salary found among computer people is usually quite different from that found among other personnel employed by most organizations, and this naturally leads to differences in viewpoints. Computer people are relatively young for the simple reason that the field itself is still young; the greatest demand for computer people has only developed in recent years, so only a few data processing careers are longer than ten years. Computer people differ in background and values from their colleagues in other parts of the organization. They have not depended for advancement on years of experience so much as on specialized education and a talent for programming work for which they can quickly obtain recognition. Finally, computer people tend to be paid considerably more than others of the same age level simply because of the workings of supply and demand. An authoritative report prepared in 1966* estimated that there were some 60,000 system analysts practicing in 1965, and that the number would approach 200,000 by 1970. It also estimated that there were from 60,000 to 120,000 programmers in 1965 and that their number would grow to between 200,000 and 650,000 by 1970. This kind of growth in demand has naturally led to escalation of salaries, and it is not uncommon in 1968 for a highly valued system analyst to receive $18,000 to $20,000 per year even though he may be less than 35 years old. Because of high turnover reflecting pressures from competitors for proven programmers and system analysts, all employers are forced to join this escalation. The author, for example, experienced a fourfold increase in salary during his first twelve years in data processing.

Because computer people preferentially associate with one another rather than with other members of the organization, communications difficulties arise. The computer people, recognizing that they are specialists employed to provide services to generalists, appreciate that it is their responsibility to be able to communicate in terms comprehensible to the rest of the organization. They try to remove specialized computer jargon from their reports and conversations. However, they still have difficulties because terms derived from the sciences or mathematics are sometimes used so frequently in their circles that the computer people are unaware that laymen are unfamiliar with the terms. Thus, a computer system analyst making a presentation to management is likely to use terms such as "parameter," "real-time," "on-line," "update,"

---

* *The State of the Information Processing Industry,* American Federation of Information Processing Societies, 1966.

"simulate," "throughput," all of which he considers normal vocabulary but which many managers are not familiar with.

Computer people tend to regard themselves as professionals, hired by an organization to work in its interests but not affiliated with it in any fundamental way. This attitude develops for several reasons: their preferential association with one another rather than with other employees of the organization prevents their becoming part of its basic life; their frequent reassignment from one project to another in different parts of the organization prevents the development of loyalty to any given part of it; the demonstrated fact that the excess of demand over supply makes it easy for them to change employers. In fact, many computer people develop the attitude that advancement should ordinarily be expected to involve a change in employer. This detachment leads to the development of attitudes often associated with consultants (indeed, many computer people become consultants and much computer work is done by consulting firms).

Successful computer people attach a high value to the professional quality of their work, looking more to their peers in the data processing organization for evaluation of it than to general management or to the user, because only their professional peers will appreciate the nuances of the work.

They are trained to be objective, because they must obtain information about present methods and the potential of future ones from users whose attitudes are colored by years of association with present methods, and who have organizational status that might be threatened by a change to new ways of doing things. They therefore become trained investigators, skilled in separating the facts of a situation from the emotional attitudes surrounding it.

They become skilled in operating as teams, because most computer application development projects require the efforts of closely cooperating groups ranging from two or three to scores of people. Like other professionals, they tend to discount prior accomplishments or prestige of position when working in such groups; it is the ability of the individual to contribute to the objective at hand that determines his position of leadership and his importance to the group. In an application development team one may find a senior system analyst in his forties working under the direction of a junior analyst in his twenties who is paid no more than half as much, because the younger is trained in a new aspect of technology or new method in which the older is less skilled. Such a situation does not seem unusual or strange to either party, and they could (and do) reverse their roles in approaching some other aspect of the work. Often personnel from the user organization are assigned to work as members of such teams, and their reactions to this kind of team structure vary. Many find it impossible to overlook differences in age, seniority, or position and become hostile or defensive. On the other hand, some managers of user organizations enjoy the "vacation from position" that such a team effort affords them, and find the emphasis on knowledge of the situation and creativeness refreshing.

Many young women are able to work well in such groups. The graduate of a women's college with a bent toward mathematics or the sciences often had difficulty in the past obtaining a satisfactory job without graduate education. Now, many such women do well in computer work; the shortage of personnel is alleviated, and a welcome new career opportunity is available.

As the great majority of cases has proved, despite these inevitable differences in attitude between computer people and others in the organization, a spirit of cooperation and mutual concentration on the common goal prevents serious frictions from arising. However, the differences are sometimes magnified into barriers that seriously impede the work.

CASE 8B

◀ In 1960 a large electric utility company acquired a computer for several purposes. It was to serve the financial functions (primarily customer billing and accounting) and the engineering functions of planning operations and designing additions to the company's generation and distribution system. The computer was a large one, because many customers were to be billed and because the engineers planned to run complex programs on the computer. The new computer replaced a smaller one which the company had used for three years, and which had been supported by a staff consisting of six programmers and a manager. The six programmers were expanded to twenty-five in order to provide enough personnel for implementing the new applications planned for the large computer, and the same manager was continued in charge.

The data processing manager, unaccustomed to dealing with computer programs of the size and complexity of those to be developed for the new computer, made some overoptimistic commitments to users about both the content and completion time of programs the users had requested. Once the teams of system analysts and programmers started to work, the manager discovered by degrees that more time and effort were going to be required for most of them than he had estimated. The delays were aggravated by the fact that since most of the computer personnel were newly hired and inexperienced, they made many mistakes and wasted considerable time.

The data processing manager, trying to avoid criticism by management and the users, did not report his growing awareness that his commitments had been unrealistic. Instead, he asked for more staff hoping that by increasing the size of his teams he could accelerate the work. He was granted the additional people. By now, however, the average amount of experience with the company's problems that individual systems analysts and programmers had was diluted to practically nothing; few had been employed by the company more than two years. They had difficulty understanding their assignments, particularly since the accelerated time schedule now imposed upon them allowed virtually no learning time. User personnel were dismayed to find how little the system analysts and programmers understood about the areas they were assigned to work on, and the computer people (reacting defensively) tended to blame the user personnel for misunderstandings about methods and requirements.

As the initially promised completion dates began to pass unmet, these feelings of hostility grew. The user personnel were now convinced (and so reported to their managers) that the computer people were inept, cocky, and unwilling to take the time to understand the subtleties of their problems. The computer people felt that the user people were unreasonable and that the data processing manager had imposed impossible deadlines upon them. The customer billing department, in particular, complained with such effect that virtually the entire force of computer people was assigned to completing their work. The billing finally did get done, but because of the pressure the programs were initially inefficient and error-ridden, so little reduction in the hostility accompanied their completion. The engineers, now receiving little help from the computer people, hired some of their own and turned to a service bureau for their computing, thus incurring an expense that had not initially been forecast: this particularly irritated management.

The result of it all was that the computer was inefficiently and belatedly performing only a part of the work for which it had been acquired. The computer people, the customer billing people, the engineers, and management were all unhappy, and no one was satisfied with the performance of the data processing manager.

Management, appreciating that a serious impasse (a sort of "credibility gap") had developed, tried to decide what steps to take to correct it. They found this more difficult than most of their problem-solving decisions because of their lack of knowledge of the technicalities involved. The data processing manager excused his failure by describing technical difficulties and shortcomings of the computer manufacturer to management. They were unable to evaluate the justice of these claims, so they found it difficult to decide whether he was primarily to blame. The issue was finally resolved after management hired a team of data processing consultants to analyze the situation. Their primary assignment (though not the advertised one) was to report on the validity of the data processing manager's technical arguments and on his apparent competence. The consultants reported that these were low; the data processing manager was replaced, and by degrees the situation was corrected. ▶

THE MANAGEMENT OF THE FUTURE?

Many competent young people who aspire to future management positions enter the data processing profession. They believe that in data processing they will learn more quickly about the companies that employ them, that they will have more influential positions sooner, and that they will have more opportunity to observe and come to the attention of management than in any other area open to them. There are also the more mundane considerations of the relatively higher early salaries associated with data processing and the prestige associated with it; it is an "in" thing to do. It is likely, therefore, that management should look to the ranks of data processing specialists for some of its candidates for future management positions. Furthermore, as the data processing functions in the organization become more important, more centralized, and more associated with management activities, top computer people necessarily rise in influence, status, and salary. They must develop management skills within their own discipline. As the number of personnel and the structure of the data processing function grows, the more successful data processing professionals must learn to fill the management positions created. It is highly likely, then, that in many large organizations competent young people starting in data processing will grow into management positions of steadily increasing authority within data processing. Then, the best qualified may transfer into general management with not only their innate talent but also their knowledge of the organization developed during their data processing activities equipping them for broader responsibility.

This will unquestionably prove true, and examples can be cited. For example, in one manufacturing company the assistant to the president, the comptroller, and the director of corporate planning are all former managers of data processing. However, there are also examples to the contrary; examples indicating that data processing experience is not necessarily equivalent to experience and practice in the skills of management. The data processing professional, having advanced rapidly in his own field and having directed many important projects on behalf of his company, may not believe this; he may well come to feel that he could "fill the shoes" of most of the managers he has met. While he may be entirely correct in thinking this so far as the functions of information systems are concerned, there are many other things associated with line management with which data processing managers may be wholly unacquainted. The data processing professional may lose sight of the fact that he is not intrinsically different from any other management candidate and that it will probably take him as long to learn the interpersonal and line management skills required of a functional manager as it does any non-data-processing candidate.

CASE 8C

◀ A large aerospace company established computer centers in most of its divisions during the early years of computer development, and as time passed, they grew. In addition to being used for engineering, they were used more and more for financial and business management applications. Finally, as with most other large organizations using computers to an advanced degree, the company decided to integrate its data processing centers both to economize on resources and to make possible the development of advanced, management-oriented information systems designed to improve every aspect of the company's operations and planning.

One of the data processing facilities managers had already distinguished himself. He had directed the organizing and building of the largest and most economically managed computer facility in the corporation and he had achieved an excellent reputation for being able to deal with the managers of the functional organizations he served. He was highly thought of by his data processing peers in other divisions as well as by his customers, and it was natural for the corporate management to select him to head the company's new integrated data processing development effort. He was made a vice president, promoted to the corporate staff, and given authority over all the divisional data processing centers.

The charter given to the new vice president of information systems was a very broad one; he was told to revamp and restructure the management information system of the corporation. To him, the term "management information system" was virtually synonymous with "management system," because he subscribed to the doctrine that information is synonymous with decision and control. He therefore felt (though he admitted this only privately) that he was (in effect) structuring a new version of the corporation which would inevitably have himself as president, and he proceeded to set about attaining this objective.

Conceivably he might have attained his objective in time; in similar corporations such men have attained such objectives. However, in this case he proved himself unequal to the task. He found himself dealing with senior corporate vice presidents instead of the division functional managers he was accustomed to, and he became involved in a far higher level of abstraction and intuitive management than that to which he was accustomed. The corporate vice presidents did their honest best to help him devise information systems which would improve their ability to do their jobs, but the best efforts of both parties could discover no really significant improvements that could further the vice president of information system's plans. Frustrated, he came to the conclusion that the inability of his systems to help the corporate vice presidents was evidence that they were doing their jobs improperly. (It did not occur to him that there might be aspects of their jobs of which he was ignorant.)

At this point he began to suggest to the executive vice president and president of the corporation that unless he was given the authority to perform certain of the corporate vice presidents' jobs, his management information system plan could never be a success. The corporate vice presidents, of course, rose to this political challenge and once battle was joined it became evident that in political combat the vice president of information systems was inexperienced. The corporate vice presidents were able to convince the president that he was out of his depth, that he was attempting to deal with issues for which he had neither the experience nor the innate talent, and that his recommended course of action would lead to nothing but chaos.

The president reluctantly agreed and the vice president of information systems was courteously fired. A replacement from within the company was appointed, but his charter was far more restricted than that of his predecessor. He was to be concerned only with management of the data processing function itself, and with such integrated information systems as the corporate vice presidents chose to request him to undertake. The president felt that he had learned a lesson about too rapid promotion of promising young professionals, and strongly regretted that the corporation had lost a man who had been an exceptionally able division data processing manager. ▶

Without question, many future top managers will come from the ranks of the present data processing community, partly because many of the most able young people are entering this community and partly because (as will be discussed in the next section) the techniques associated with data processing are becoming more widespread in general business management. But cases such as the above seem to indicate that there is no short cut to management capability necessarily found in the data processing profession, and that it will take as long for data processing professionals to become qualified as top managers as it does managers in some entirely different line. Managers working with computer people should remember this and not assume that they understand management's needs.

In universities and research laboratories another class of "priesthood of the machine" has emerged. The scientists and educators, as we have seen in earlier chapters, need increasingly sophisticated computing assistance. The hardware and software required to provide this assistance has become so sophisticated that only specialists are competent to select, install, and implement new computer systems. These specialists are (in a strict sense) part of the administrative staff, because their job is to provide facilities to support the academic and research staff. However, the knowledge and skill they must have is so great that they are the professional peers of many of the research staff. Furthermore, in many universities and research laboratories there is an interest in experimenting with computers and attempting to improve them. The researchers wish not only to use computers as tools to support work in other areas, but they are interested in working with the computers themselves to learn more about data processing methods and techniques and to contribute to their development. The computing administrators are often involved in and direct aspects of this computer research, so they have become a hybrid of administrative and academic staff member.

CASE 8D

◀   At a large Eastern university, interest in computers began to develop almost twenty years ago. It first appeared in the engineering department where the electrical engineers had already been accustomed for some time to using analog computers for network analyses. Then, when the programs for digital computers became a subject of interest, the mathematics department took up computers not only as tools for performing numerical analysis but also as a new, abstract mathematical subject—the study of theoretical logical and mathematical mechanisms. When it became apparent that computers could help in the substantial administrative work of the university, the business office became interested in data processing. About the same time (somewhat belatedly compared to some other universities) researchers in linguistics and library science discovered the potential of the computer for assisting them in their work. Because they were primarily interested in data handling facilities of the kind that the administrators also needed, they combined their efforts with those of the university's administrative staff.

The engineering departments cooperatively bought a single, relatively small computer, acquired a supervisor for it and a small staff of operators, and permitted users to program and run it themselves. The relatively few users who emerged in the first few years were able to occupy almost all of the computer's relatively modest capability, so this casual arrangement worked smoothly. The mathematics department used a small amount of the engineering computer's time for their numerical analysis work, and had little need for quantities of computer time in their highly theoretical work on the nature of computing machines. As in engineering, individual members of the departments who were interested in these subjects acquainted themselves with the computer and did their own programming.

Only in the administrative area did a group of computer specialists evolve, because the administrative staff had no intention of becoming computer programmers themselves. A data processing machine was acquired for administration, and a staff of five programmers and a supervisor was hired. These programmers had as their first responsibility the implementation of administrative programs, but in their spare time they also attempted to serve the lin-guistic and information retrieval activities.

As time passed, interest in and demand for the computer's help grew in all areas. The engineering computer center grew as the demand for quantity and quality of computing power increased; it became a complex of equipment and remote communication devices similar to that described in Case 4D. The mathematics department increased its load of computing requirements for numerical analysis only moderately, but the researchers into the theoretical nature of computing machines became interested in programming languages and suddenly developed a demand for computer time to be devoted to "con-versational" experiments with the machine, in which the researchers would attempt to evolve new methods of communication with it, spending extended periods of time at computer consoles developing programs adaptively. The administration's number of applications and demand for computer time grew like the data processing of a typical industrial organization of comparable size. The linguistics and research requirements for computer time grew even more because the kind of file searches and exhaustive pattern studies needed were very demanding of computer time.

The two computer centers of the university grew in every aspect. Much bigger and more expensive equipment was installed, supporting staffs (key punchers, operators, magnetic tape librarians, maintenance personnel) grew, and a higher level of investment and management decisions became associ-ated with the computer centers. The new computers, being far more flexible, were also far more complex than the old ones they replaced. It was no longer possible for the members of the academic staff to spend a few afternoons studying programming and then proceed without further assistance to program their own problems. The machines and the software for them provided so many alternatives, and required consideration of so many procedural rules, that continuously available guidance had to be provided. As a result, many of the less interested faculty members who needed computer assistance decided to have computer programmers do their work for them.

Perhaps most important of all, more and more of the faculty became in-terested in the kind of time-shared "conversational" use of the computer, using remote input-output terminals, that was pioneered by the mathematics department. This technique came to be preferred for the programming and immediate solution of small computational problems of every kind, as well as for the development of the new kinds of programming techniques that members of a number of the departments were now studying. The software for controlling time-shared operations proved to be far more complex than any of the staff had encountered before, and the university was forced to estab-lish a specialty (initially in the mathematics department) where positions as high as associate professor were established for specialists in computer time-sharing techniques.

By the time this stage of evolution had been reached, it had become apparent to all parties that a major change in the method of providing computer resources was needed. After a great deal of study and consideration, a new department of computer science was set up and many of the computer-oriented groups were assigned to it. The new department took over control of all the computers on the campus, and the responsibility of serving all users adequately. All the computer programmers, operators, and supporting personnel were assigned to the new department, and so were a number of the academic groups working full time with the machines. The groups interested in computer theory, languages, and time sharing all transferred to the new department, as did the engineering groups associated primarily with the development of new computer programs. None of the library science people moved to the new department, however, because it was decided that as yet only a portion of their interests would be associated with the new department. Most people thought that eventually the two departments would be combined, though.

The new department is headed by a full professor; it has several other professorships assigned to it plus a hierarchy of lower positions. In addition to the academic positions in the department, there are also a number of relatively highly paid administrative ones, because of the competitive necessity of paying well for competent system analysts and operations supervisors. This poses problems, because for a given level of experience, the administrator tends to be paid more than his academic counterpart; on the other hand, the prestige associated with the academic title remains distinctly higher. It is often difficult for the department head to determine whether a given position should be academic or administrative, and he wishes he did not have to live with the traditional distinctions. He says he is unsure whether he himself is academic or administrative, because the bulk of his time is occupied with personnel and equipment selection considerations, and with budgetary concerns because of the high cost of his department's operations and the fact that the supporting funds come from as many sources as there are using organizations within and without the University. He does insist on continuing to do a small amount of teaching, and he attends a number of academic symposia and conventions. He concedes, however, that it has been a long time since he engaged in significant personal research, which is what he originally thought he would be devoting his career to. ▶

In past years the people associated with computers in universities and research laboratories came from quite different backgrounds and had quite different attitudes from computer people in business organizations. As cases such as this one suggest, however, as time goes on the distinctions narrow. The two classes of organizations become interested in increasingly similar techniques and types of equipment and software, and the concerns of the personnel associated with the machines and their uses necessarily become more similar. Perhaps our observations about computer people and their role in the management of user organizations will eventually apply to universities as well as to businesses.

THE NEW DOGMA AND ITS MISUSE

We have seen that the people associated with computers—the priesthood of the machine—are becoming increasingly important to the organization because of their increasing numbers and impact and because many young people with a high degree of management potential choose to enter this field. However, we have also seen that there is no magic associated with computers that makes a young man into a good manager overnight; it seems to take as long for a computer man to qualify for top management as it does a man following any other road of advancement. Therefore, the impact of computer people as managers has not yet been profound; there will be ample time for organizations to evolve and adjust to computer-oriented top managers. It is not the people—the priesthood—but their attitudes—their dogma—which is having the most rapid and profound influence.

Before a computer can be used, a system design study must be performed to establish the kinds and quantities of data to be handled, the methods of processing routine transactions and exceptions, and the costs and savings involved. As we have seen in earlier chapters, the results of such studies (or system analyses) provide both better understanding of the function studied and a design for a computer-based approach to performing the operation. Usually, the new approach involves less reliance on intuitive and experiential managerial judgment and more on quantitative techniques—an arithmetic determination of the demonstrably correct or optimum action on the basis of numerical formulas derived from knowledge of the process involved. In recent years it has been shown that such quantitative methods, such *system analysis approaches* to managing resources, produce good results in many areas. Tens of thousands of businesses have studied their inventory control policies using the techniques of system analysis, and the total value of inventories maintained by businesses in the United States has dropped dramatically.

According to the National Industrial Conference Board* the sales of United States manufacturing corporations in 1950 (before computers were used by

---

* *Economic Almanac, 1967–1968,* National Industrial Conference Board, Macmillan, New York, 1968.

businesses) totalled $116 billion. In 1966 they were $544 billion, increased by a factor of 4.7. Manufacturers' inventories in 1950 were $31 billion, and in 1966 they were $78 billion, up by a factor of 2.5. If inventories had increased by the same 4.7 factor as sales, they would have been $146 billion in 1966, or $66 billion greater.

Is it to be expected that inventories should bear a direct relationship to sales? Perhaps not, but there is obviously a correlation. And, is the full inventory saving to be attributed to quantitative techniques and computers? Probably not, but there was certainly a substantial effect. Even if only a fraction of the $66 billion inventory "saving" is so attributable, it is more than enough to repay industry's total investment in computers.

Distribution systems, mergers, and civil works (among other things) have proven amenable to closer control when studied using the approaches of system analysis. Perhaps most profoundly, the decisions and operations of the Defense Department have been changed by system analysis. Military defense is now such a complex matter employing so many alternatives, so many sensor and weapon systems of such a high degree of complexity, that no human could possibly comprehend the total picture. The costs of acquisition, maintenance, and operation of these systems are extremely high and interact with and substitute for one another in subtle ways. Without the quantitative techniques of system analysis to evaluate systems and interrelate them by means of mathematical models and simulations, it would be impossible to deal rationally with the kinds of policy decisions, system designs, and procurements that the Defense Department must perform. Beyond a doubt, the procedures and (above all) the attitude embodied in the term "system analysis" have much potency.

System analysis, as an approach to an organization's problems, is not confined to applications of computers. The result of an analysis of an organization's information, production, or distribution system may be restructuring of the organization, a decision whether a merger would be profitable, or a determination of the desirability of building a new warehouse or acquiring a new machine tool. A computer may be used in processing some of the data generated or to support an information system resulting from a system analysis, but the application of system analysis is much broader than the use of computers. Indeed, to many younger managers who have seen the beneficial effects of system analysis, it seems the best general method of controlling and influencing the modern organization. They feel that traditional experiential and intuitive methods of making plans and evaluating alternatives cannot be applied with today's degree of complexity, especially when change seems so rapid and extreme as to invalidate past experience. They see that system analysis is objective and unbiased and permits no favoring of the biases of individuals (even of those initiating studies, as we will see below; some studies have led to results most unwelcome to those initiating them). Some become enthusiastic because they feel that system analysis offers the best way to manage; others become enthusiastic because of their enthusiasm for the computer.

Many managers, not fully understanding what system analysis is all about, nevertheless believe that they must use computers more extensively than they do. Major reasons for this interest are, first, a conviction that with better data and better processing methods better management control becomes possible. Second and perhaps more pressing, many managements feel near desperation in the face of mounting paper work loads, inflationary salary increases, and increasing shortages of competent and responsible personnel. This attitude is reflected in a 1966 policy statement by former Secretary of Defense McNamara which said, "We must develop and install standard data systems within the Department of Defense at a level far exceeding our current practices. These standard data systems must be developed for research and development and operational systems as well as business management-type needs."*

Evidence of this spread of enthusiasm for system analysis can be found everywhere. Business and industrial periodicals devote an increasing proportion of their space to articles about the successful application of quantitative techniques by leading companies, and to tutorial material on data processing and system analysis methods. The papers, seminars, and conversations at conventions and meetings of all types of businesses contain a high proportion of such material. Management courses and summer "refresher" symposia at colleges are heavily devoted to introducing managers to these techniques. Nowhere is this enthusiasm for system analysis more widespread than among younger managers and management trainees, who see their road to advancement paved with system analysis studies that will prove them to be more effective managers than the older, "uninitiated" managers for whose jobs they are competing. The author, in visiting several business schools, found in all of them that the students assumed as a matter of course that they would be using computers on a day-to-day basis to help them in their future managerial planning and decision-making. The business schools have encouraged this interest by extensively revising their curricula to equip students to apply system analysis techniques. For example, in the 1967 catalog of the Harvard Business School† 108 courses are described, ten for the first year and ninety-eight for the second year. Of the ten first-year courses, three devote a sizeable proportion of their content to analytic techniques associated with com-

---

* Secretary of Defense Memorandum, July 29, 1966.
† *Official Register of Harvard University, Graduate School of Business Administration, 1967–1968*, Harvard University Publishing Office, Cambridge, 1967.

puters and system analysis. One of the three courses involves use of the computer for simulating the performance of a hypothetical business, the objective being to give the students simulated practice in management and incidentally make them aware of the computer's potential. Among the ninety-eight elective second-year and doctorate courses offered, no less than forty contain a significant analytic content, either introducing, using, or evaluating the effects of the kinds of technological innovations in business management that can be grouped under the heading "system analysis." Indeed, fourteen of these forty are devoted entirely to the introduction of techniques in mathematics and computer technology. A recent appraisal of the modern business school graduate* said: "Today he comes equipped with . . . cool confidence in the power of mathematics . . . in quantitative methods of analysis and decision making that were not even widely understood, much less widely taught, fifteen years ago."

With the attitudes and skills of the business schools' students shaped this way, there is little doubt that as these men rise to positions of influence, the application of system analysis to management will increase far beyond even its present level.

There are dangers inherent in misuse or overuse of the system analysis technique. The most common of these is establishing erroneous starting assumptions or objectives, "analyzing the wrong system." The enthusiastic supporter of the system analysis technique is anxious to apply it to whatever problems face him. In order to do so, he must be able to assign numeric values to, and make projections for, all the elements of the system being analyzed. In many areas this is possible; all elements of a manufacturing process have costs, production rates, power needs, and the like; all elements of a communications system can be specified in terms of costs, transmission rates, maintenance requirements, and similar measurable factors. Unfortunately, many of the systems to which computer processing is applied have intangible as well as tangible elements. For example, a computer system in a manufacturing company may be designed both to reduce the cost of inventory (a quantifiable, tangible quantity) and to provide greater responsiveness. The increase in responsiveness can be quantized without difficulty, but its value usually cannot. It is assumed that business will increase because customers are pleased by the increase in responsiveness, but the system analysts do not know how much increase in responsiveness will result in how much increase in business. Before the system analyst can get on with the job he must make some assumption for every system element, and in his haste to

---

* Sheldon Zalaznick, "The MBA, the Man, the Myth, and the Method," *Fortune*, May 1968.

proceed he may make an assumption about the value of some intangible quantity (e.g., that business will increase 10% if response time is halved) which is pure guess, and which (if wrong) will invalidate all his subsequent work.

An area where this effort to "quantize the intangible" has been publicly disputed is in the system analyses of defenses against nuclear attack. As efforts were made to design systems to defend the United States against thermonuclear attacks (or deter such attacks), the system analysts applied quantitative values to the destruction that might be caused by such attacks. This was difficult, because the cost of replacing each individual structure within a large city (which can be estimated) is entirely different from the cost of rebuilding the entire city at one time, and there is little experience to support estimates of the latter. Second (and more notorious in the public press) the efforts of system analysts to assign relative values to numbers of human lives caused considerable public outcry. The "relative numbers of megadeaths" discussed in some of the system analysis literature caused a general revulsion. The system analysts generally felt that the fewer "megadeaths" the better; that if one approach would result in thirty megadeaths rather than forty, it was preferable. The humanists were generally of the opinion that any number of megadeaths is so inconceivably atrocious that it is irrational to attempt to make relative distinctions. No value judgment need be made here; it is enough to point out that there can be no logical or rational answers in this area, and all would agree that the cold mathematics of system analysis have a profound inadequacy when masses of human lives are involved. The method is also (though less dramatically) inadequate when applied to many other intangibles.

The second reason why organizations find that they are guilty of "analyzing the wrong system" is more fundamental—the inability to predict future conditions. Many systems being studied cannot be operational for three years, five years, or more, and in such time spans, conditions can change greatly and in unexpected ways. For example, many decisions about investments in new production facilities must be made five to ten years before the production facility is operating. The cost of the capital to be invested in the new facility is always one of the assumptions which enter the system analysis model, and in recent years the cost of capital (the interest rate) has changed so radically and rapidly that many assumptions used in projections have been completely invalidated, and with them the results of the analyses.

Most businesses making investment decisions on the basis of system analysis can do so with confidence that most of the fundamental factors now affecting them will (at least in some measure) still be valid at the time the proposed decision is implemented. Those in the more highly technological areas (e.g., electronic component manufacturing) have a harder time. In five years they may be making products they have not yet conceived today, and any projections of product trends made by today's system analysis may be meaningless. This technological uncertainty affects no organization more dramatically than the Department of Defense, as it plans future weapon systems and forces. Its technological problem is compounded by a political one, because political events can in a few years bring about radical rearrangements of alliances and attitudes. It is not surprising that many Department of Defense system analyses devoted to the planning of doctrines and equipment having long lead times turn out to be invalid in the final outcome.

CASE 8E

◀   At the end of World War II the United States Army had completed fighting its second major war within thirty years on the European continent, and faced the possibility of another one. At that time the threat of a Russian invasion of Western Europe was regarded as serious, and the Army planners, now beginning to use system analysis techniques extensively, addressed themselves with the highest priority to countering this threat.

As technological advances in Army weapons were introduced, the support and maintenance requirements for the weapons grew correspondingly. A modern armored or air-mobile division is expected to move far faster than its predecessors, yet it must be supported with many times the number of supply items, both consumables and parts for the repair of electronic systems, automatic weapons, missiles, and the like. Even the vehicles for delivery of the supplies (helicopters, specialized aircraft) require logistics support of their own, far more complex than that needed for the trains and trucks of an earlier era. Of necessity, then, the Army planners concentrated intensively on designing improved and more responsive systems to control the flow of supplies, using automated communications and computers in the interests of speed and efficiency.

The kind of model the Army planners used to represent the supply problem is shown in Fig. 8-1. It assumes that supplies and equipment will be delivered across a large body of water from the United States or intermediate points, arriving primarily at protected seaports well behind the fighting front, and secondarily at airports closer to the front. The model assumes that there will be a coherent front line, from 50 to 500 miles from the ports at which the bulk supplies enter the system, behind which friendly forces have the terrain under reasonably complete control and on the other side of which the enemy has corresponding control. Between the front and the seaports, the Army organization resembles a "tree" with combat divisions arrayed along the front, divisions reporting in groups to corps headquarters, groups of corps report-

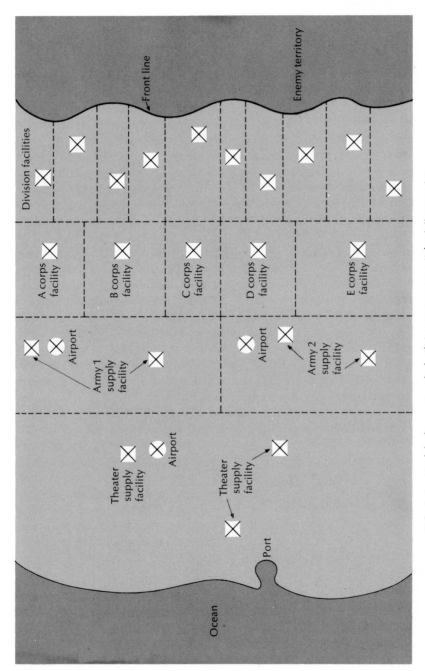

FIG. 8–1 Model of army supply facilities to support a "classic" campaign.

ing to armies, and the entire force under a theater commander. The logistics planners proceeded to divide the responsibilities for supply storage, transportation, maintenance, medical facilities, and personnel support among these several levels of command in an optimum manner. Some facilities were assigned to the division level, others to corps, army, or theater depending on considerations of cost-effectiveness—on what systems analysis had proved to be the optimum balance between minimizing the number of facilities and maximizing the provision of effective support. Computers were to be used to process requests at the various levels, and advanced communication systems were to be used. Computers were also used in the planning to process extensive mathematical models of the system. The Army felt that its logistic planning process had become more effective than it had ever been, and that the plans were well prepared to support the modern Army in a modern campaign.

Events proved otherwise, however. Two wars ensued, in Korea and in Vietnam, and neither conformed to the model of Fig. 8–1. In the Korean War the two ends of the model were as forecast (the seaport to which supplies were delivered and the coherent fighting front that moved back and forth as tactical victories and defeats dictated). However, the war was fought not on a continent but on a peninsula, and as the fighting front moved forward and back, seaports close to the fighting front were won and lost. Thus, it was not necessary (as the model had assumed) to stretch increasingly lengthy lines of communication from the ports to distant fighting fronts; new ones could be established from new ports captured as the armies advanced. Furthermore, the geographic scope of the war was so narrow and the movements of the fronts so rapid that there was no time to establish the ordered echelons of command and supporting facilities envisioned in the model. Most of the detailed plans turned out to be inapplicable, then, and a great deal of hasty improvisation was required.

The Vietnamese war was still different, primarily because there was no clear fighting front. Again the seaports existed, but the enemy was as likely to be found operating nearby as farther away. Combat troops (and their maintenance and support needs) were likely to move to any point in the country, and no position for a supply center was much more secure than any other. Under these conditions, the orderly planning model was almost completely inapplicable and entirely new concepts of logistic organization and support had to be worked out under fire.

It is apparent that the Army logistics planners had prepared themselves to fight the wrong war; that the threat apparent to them at the time never materialized. With the wisdom of hindsight, we can perceive that with the advent of the thermonuclear age the traditional "war of position" had to be modified and that limited wars fought for largely political objectives under entirely different ground rules would evolve. However, in the late 1940's few strategic thinkers were fully aware of this change and none could precisely forecast its nature. As a result, system analysis studies performed then often turned out to be largely meaningless. ▶

The assumptions used in a business system analysis can be equally invalid and it may be equally impossible to know it at the time the analysis is made. The applications of system analysis, then, are limited to situations where there is at least reasonable certainty that the underlying assumptions are correct and where all the variables can be quantized. Even so, the results of system analysis studies must be used with some caution. It is hardly fair to ask the system analyst himself to provide this caution, because unless he is very experienced he is relatively young and preoccupied with his technique, and cannot be expected to have personally experienced these problems. The manager evaluating the results of the system analysis, however, may be expected to have greater breadth of experience and wisdom, and if he equips himself with a thorough understanding of the assumptions that went into the system analysis, he is in a position to sensibly weigh the probable value of the results. In any case, he should be aware that a universal application of system analysis and a blind faith in its results can lead to grievous error.

This care in the application of system analysis is hard to apply, because usually there is no one available with sufficient experience. The system analyst himself, despite good intentions, is likely to have faith in his assumptions. (In fact, more often than not, the assumptions that fail are so fundamental that they were never explicitly stated—such as that the next war will be fought in fundamentally the same way as the last two, or that the company's products tomorrow will be similar to today's). Managers evaluating the results of system analyses are usually ignorant of what system analysis is about, of its weaknesses and strengths; they tend to shy away from this responsibility and even if they assume it, they are inept at finding the weak points in the model's assumptions. Many managers therefore rely on their system analysts to protect them from the consequences of error without being fully aware of the risk involved. As time passes, this situation will surely improve. Existing managers will become more familiar with system analysis, and (as we have seen) new managers are growing up with it.

Fortunately, the senior system analyst is aware of his responsibility and is usually a man or woman of high integrity. He tries to use the best information available, and even his relatively brief experience has probably taught him some humility—shown him that he should carefully specify his assumptions, and objectively identify the areas where his assumptions may be arbitrary or weak. Many system analysts do a good job of protecting management from the consequences of the false assumption, but not all are such paragons. Many are more interested in a quick success or a rapid advance in reputation, and many are so imbued with confidence in their technique that they repeatedly produce overstated and intrinsically misleading results without learning from experience.

Indeed, the "priest of the machine" may be more than simply overenthusiastic or misled—he may be actively dishonest. In the all-too-frequent case where management is reluctant to get involved in the technicalities of data processing, the system analysts and programmers are permitted to have complete control over computer-based systems, and opportunities for such dishonesty arise. Normally, all employees of the firm are subject to checks and balances, to audits and reviews that prevent them having too much authority over financial matters or too much control over valuable company property. In the case of the computer professional, few such checks and balances may exist simply because others in the organization do not have the knowledge to apply them. The result, as Professor Fano of the Massachusetts Institute of Technology implies in the quote at the beginning of this chapter, is that many golden opportunities for dishonesty are offered to the computer professional. An article reviewing this subject* cited some examples:

• The manager of data processing in a New York brokerage firm stole $250,-000 by programming the computer to transfer money from a company account to his and his wife's accounts, and to show that the money had gone to purchase stock for the account. Then, he sold the stock supposedly purchased and kept the proceeds. Because he had complete authority over the data processing operation and because no external audits were applied to his programs, his theft was undetected for several years.

• The chief programmer of a small bank programmed the computer to disregard his own personal checks any time his account had insufficient funds to cover them. The result was an embezzlement of $1357 over a period of about a year. The scheme was discovered only because a computer breakdown forced hand processing of some checks and one of the embezzler's bad checks "bounced."

The author is familiar with another case in which a disaffected employee of a Federal Government agency, feeling that he had been unjustly treated by management, altered a program to subtly distort information contained in the computer's master files. Because the computer continued to process information apparently correctly, it was a matter of several days before operating

---

* Alan Adelson, "Crooked Operators Use Computers to Embezzle Money from Companies," *The Wall Street Journal*, April 5, 1968.

difficulties began to show up and by the time the difficulty was discovered and analyzed a week later, the operation was a shambles. Removing the intentional flaws from the program took several man-weeks, but correcting the files which had been distorted took much longer.

There are other examples, but not a great many. Fortunately, most organizations are not so unwise as these, and have applied at least some elementary financial and managerial controls to their programmers. Also, most computer people are not prone to petty thievery or vandalism; the fact that they regard themselves as professionals and are interested in the respect and admiration of their peers tends to prevent this. With hundreds of thousands of computer people employed by 50,000 or more organizations using computers, however, it is insufficient to rely on professional integrity or general supervision to preclude the possibility of intentional misuse of the computer, and as many professional auditors are quick to observe, improved methods of preventing misuse of the computer are badly needed. Functional managers are learning to devote greater attention to this problem.

A by-product of applying the "new dogma" is likely to be a more rational, less emotional view of the organization and its purposes; when the technique of system analysis is applied, the output is an inevitable arithmetic consequence of the input. Since the results of a system analysis cannot always be predicted, and since those responsible for the study usually have some emotional stake in the results, these can in some cases be surprising.

CASE 8F

◀ A company manufacturing automotive parts stored them in a variety of warehouses around the country. Because the company's pattern of sales was quite fluctuating, management was unable to determine accurately how much of each product line to keep in each warehouse. The primary stock of each part was in the warehouse at or near the plant producing it, but because short delivery times were very important, management was forced to keep at least a moderate supply of every item in every warehouse. They suspected that their total inventory cost was higher than necessary, but they were unable to reduce inventory while retaining responsiveness.

The company established a corporate data processing group whose job, in addition to programming the corporate accounting and financial applications, was to investigate the method of inventory control. This group believed a proper system analysis study would show that inventory levels could be reduced sharply. They thought that by using high speed information systems and air transport they could reduce the number of points at which each item was stocked, but still respond to customer demand at least as fast as at present. They also believed that such a system would require that they assume centralized control and operation of the company's distribution system, because the data processing network on which it would all depend would have to be run at the corporate level.

The corporate data processing group therefore started a formal system analysis of the inventory and distribution system, collecting statistics about the amount, kind, and location of customer demand, matching this with the company's performance in meeting demand, and collecting information about inventories, production capabilities, and distribution costs. When they had adequate information they performed mathematical studies of alternative systems of transportation and storage, expecting to find that the most economical would employ concentrated warehousing at central locations and the use of air transport to fill orders.

It did not work out that way. Most of the parts had relatively low value and high bulk, so air transport was expensive. Also, the cost of information handling and communications would be high with the proposed system. The system analysis proved that a method close to the present one would be best. A varied inventory should be kept at each of the warehouse locations to minimize delivery cost, and each warehouse should decide its own stock levels because of the variations in demand. The use of relatively inexpensive surface transportation would more than offset the cost of duplicate inventories. With this system, incidentally, each warehouse would handle its own information processing and communications so there would be no need for a centrally operated corporate-wide data processing and communication system. The system analysis showed the corporate data processing group that it was in the best interests of the company not to adopt the system plan that would have increased their importance. ▶

In a few cases such as this the results of system analysis studies have been unfavorable to the parties performing them. More commonly, the problem is that the ideal system calls for unwelcome or impossible changes in the organization. Union agreements, for example, while benefiting the company's employees often lead to practices or costs that the ideal plan would do away with. Fair trade or antitrust considerations, community or personnel relations may all render ideal systems unattainable. The system analysis approach is, then, limited in another way: the actions it indicates may be impractical. Managers must be alert to this possibility.

OPERATING AND SUPPORTING PERSONNEL

Every computer system requires a specially trained operating staff. With more than 50,000 computers operating in the United States and an average of at least three operators each, the total number must exceed 150,000. There are even greater numbers of supporting personnel involved in preparing data for computers. Most of these people operate key punch machines and transcribe the contents of documents into punched cards or magnetic tape for computer input. Associated with them are the others who check the accuracy of the work, and the supervisors, teachers, and scheduling personnel required to support the data preparation function. No reliable figures exist for the numbers of data preparation personnel employed in the United States, but since the number of data preparation devices (key punches, verifiers, and the like) exceeds 500,000 and each is operated almost continuously, the number of data preparation personnel must be at least as great. There are also other categories of supporting personnel employed by computer using organizations such as magnetic tape librarians, communications system operators, messengers, and others. It is probably a conservative estimate that as of 1968 there were on the order of 700,000 people employed in the United States operating and supporting data processing systems.

This number is so great that if these people (like the system analysts and programmers) represent a new force or new influence in the organizations that employ them, the influence would be very powerful and pervasive. In point of fact, there seems to be no such overall influence. As Hoos has shown,* most of these supporting positions involve basically repetitive mechanical work, similar to the repetitive manufacturing operations traditionally associated with blue collar employees. Data preparation and operating functions are necessarily routinized to such a degree that employees of average intelligence and limited training can perform them; no freedom to innovate or create is permitted or desired. As we will see in Chapter 10, this leads to certain problems of motivation and identification. Fortunately, many of the people employed in support of computer operations derive some prestige and feeling of self-importance from being associated with the modern, impressive, space age machines. This is just as well, since most of the jobs are intrinsically uninteresting ones. It seems clear that as a generalization such positions are more similar to traditional factory positions than they are to those of the system analysts and programmers responsible for designing and creating the new information systems, and that the supporting and operating people represent no new or different influence. The very fact that more than 700,000 such people could have been hired and trained within a fifteen-year period lends support to this observation. If there were something fundamentally different about them, it would seem impossible to have produced so many, and it must be true that only relatively simple training in new skills is required for these jobs.

---

* Ida R. Hoos, *Automation in the Office*, Public Affairs Press, Washington, D.C., 1961.

SUMMARY

It seems that so far the effects of the "priesthood of the machine" have not been felt very much outside their own areas—the information systems development and computer operations functions which come under their direct control. So far, relatively few of these people as individuals have entered general management or are responsible for policy-making decisions which affect the overall courses of their organizations. This will certainly change, not only because many of the intrinsically most promising management candidates are starting in the data processing function, but also because many candidates for general management (e.g., the students at the business schools) who never intend to work full time in data processing are nevertheless seeing to it that they are equipped with working knowledge of the data processing tool; perhaps they are "lay priests of the machine."

Apparently, we do not need to wait for the computer people as individuals to enter the ranks of management, because their dogma has preceded them. The desirability of quantitative planning, of system analysis, and in general of rational rather than intuitive planning and decision-making has become so widely accepted that many "old line" managers are endeavoring to learn about these methods and use them. This is without question a desirable trend, both because there are many business systems and decisions which can be better dealt with by these methods than by intuitive methods, and also because the increasing complexity of the technologically based organization allows no alternative. The trend also brings with it a danger that too much reliance will be placed on the new methods; that their use is the result of a fad rather than a considered choice of the best planning tool for the job. Presumably this is a self-correcting situation. As time passes, managers enthusiastic about system analysis will discover its limits through trial and error, and increasing numbers of those fully trained and experienced in the art will enter the ranks of management themselves and are unlikely to overuse it. When this time arrives, when it is a routine part of every manager's job to apply "systems thinking" with full knowledge of its capabilities and limits, there will surely be significant differences in the way managers operate and in the way decisions are made. These will be explored in Part IV.

CHAPTER 9

THOSE WHO BENEFIT

According to the assessment in Part I, the beneficiaries of computers should be those who:

> Have large amounts of data to process in repetitive fashion,

> Can surmount the language barrier or pay for programmers and system analysts to do it for them,

> Need to have their data processed rapidly,

> Can change their methods fairly rapidly and in a controlled manner,

> Can afford the computer.

Naturally these conditions can be met only by organizations; few individuals can afford a computer or use its capacity. It should follow that the only individuals in a position to benefit from the computer are employees of organizations large enough to afford them, or individuals who are served by organizations and regarded as important enough to be given access to its expensive services. When the only computers available were large and expensive, this automatically meant that only individuals associated with large organizations could benefit from them. Small computers are less expensive now, but there are still many organizations too small to be able to afford computers. They lack the money needed to acquire the computer, and (more important) the money to perform the system analysis and programming needed to apply the computer to their work. Smaller research organizations, smaller business firms, and most educational systems (school districts and smaller colleges) usually cannot afford computers. Local governments, most hospitals, and all but the largest law enforcement agencies are in the same position. This is unfortunate because while the volumes of data they must process are smaller than those of large organizations they represent just as much of a burden proportionately, and smaller organizations have just as much desire to speed up data processing and to apply sophisticated methods as large ones.

Fortunately, recent trends have combined to make it possible for managers of these small organizations to obtain the services of computers. Groups of smaller organizations having similar data processing needs (such as hospitals or school districts) often find it possible to pool their financial resources and support a computer and its programming staff.

CASE 9A

◀ In California, the Department of Education* has undertaken centralized procurement and programming of computer systems of various sizes which can be used for administrative purposes by school districts of all sizes. Programs for producing such administrative documents as student report cards and records, attendance rosters, normalized test scores, payrolls, financial data, personnel data, curriculum materials, and classroom schedules have all been developed centrally for large or small computers, as needed for the processing required. The programs are generalized to apply to both small and large school districts.

The size and location of the computer used by a school district is dependent on its ability to pay. Small school districts of less than 10,000 enrollment have their processing done at regional data processing centers, of which there are twelve. Medium size school districts of from 10,000 to 30,000 enrollment tend to be able to justify small computers to run those programs of which they are capable, using the regional centers for the remaining work. Large school districts are able to support larger computer systems, and execute more of the programs on their own machines. In all cases, the school district can use whatever equipment it can afford for the applications the equipment can support, and use the larger regional data processing centers for those applications their own equipment will not handle. All school districts obtain the advantages of shared programming, and the State obtains the advantages of uniform accounting and record keeping. ▶

Technology has assisted in making the computer available to small organizations. Remote input-output terminals simultaneously served by a central computer using "time-shared" techniques have made it possible to provide rapid, responsive data processing for many users who need pay only for the amount of service they use. As of early 1969, more than one hundred profit-making time-shared "service bureaus"† offered computational services (primarily for scientists and engineers), with fees as low as $300 per month, including moderate usage. These fees are within the reach not only of small

---

* Alvin Grossman, "The California Educational Information System," *Datamation*, March 1967.
† *The Computer Industry 1968–1973*, Arthur D. Little, Inc., Cambridge, 1968.

research laboratories and colleges, but also of small private engineering consulting firms and businesses.

Another form of "pooling of common interest" is provided by firms that maintain a file of current information in a computer, and lease remote terminals to customers who can obtain immediate access to it. Stock quotation services, which provide the latest prices on a wide range of common stocks and other securities, are available at prices that all but the smallest brokerage firms can pay. Because of these services, practically all brokerage firms, varying in size by a factor of 100 or more, have equal access to current market information. More than 20,000 stock quote terminals have been installed in brokerage firms, so within the limits of the service provided, the power of the computer has been made available to virtually every individual in the securities industry. Similar developments have occurred in some of the sciences. Medical researchers, for example, need information retrieval services which can recover existing information about the effects of drugs and chemical compounds on humans and laboratory animals. A government organization (the National Institutes of Health) and a number of private ones (notably Chemical Abstracts Service) provide computer-assisted information retrieval services for these researchers at modest fees, and it may be said that virtually every medical researcher, no matter what the size of the organization with which he is affiliated, has a nearly equal capability to use the power of the computer to recover and examine data dealing with the effects of drugs and chemical compounds.

These efforts are spreading the benefits of computers already realized by individuals in large organizations to individuals affiliated with many small ones. Therefore, when we review the classes of individuals who benefit from the computer, we can generalize almost without regard to the size of the organization involved.

In the remainder of this chapter we shall examine the benefits computers have brought to the various classes of individuals affected by them.

MANAGERS

As we saw in Chapter 5, the top managers of organizations using computers have been affected relatively little so far, because their concerns usually involve intangible and subjective factors with which computers cannot deal. A large proportion of top management's time is associated with the selection and motivation of subordinate managers, and the computer can be of little help in performing this function. The business decisions made at the top management level involve such matters as mergers, commitments of capital to long-term development projects, and evaluations of probable moves by competitors. These also involve intangible factors, and such long lead times that the computer's data can rarely be of assistance. However, we have seen that the computer's usefulness is "creeping up" the management ladder, that its ability to simulate the effects of alternative decisions improves as its files and the programs for performing simulations improve. As time passes, then, the abilities of computers through the programs and the files with which they are equipped will be increasingly useful in the decision-making functions of top management, though it seems too much to hope that all of top management's functions will eventually employ the computer.

There are exceptions to this generalization, particularly in organizations where the primary responsibilities are associated with the management of an extensive system of resources and its proper employment to meet varied demands. In such organizations the computer is already of very direct assistance to top management.

CASE 9B

◀ Each of the major river systems in the United States (such as the Mississippi, Ohio, Columbia, and Arkansas) have been equipped with dams, dikes, retaining walls, artificial channels, and the like that control the flow of water in the rivers of the system. The U.S. Army Corps of Engineers is responsible for maintaining these facilities as well as for planning new ones.

Under normal circumstances, the flow of water in the various parts of a river system must respond to conflicting demands. Considerations of flood control suggest that the reservoirs at the upstream end of the system should be kept as empty as possible, to provide capacity for absorbing the runoff from sudden rain storms. Considerations of irrigation, on the other hand, indicate that sizeable quantities of water should be kept in the upstream reservoirs so that in the event of drought there would be as much as possible to keep the river levels up. Considerations of navigation and electric power generation suggest that rates of flow and the depth of channels should be kept reasonably constant. Considerations of recreation suggest that the surface area and shoreline of reservoirs be kept constant to fit facilities and beaches at fixed sites.

In normal times, managers of the complexes of dams in each river system compromise between these demands, and operate the dam gates so as to discharge amounts of water which satisfy most of the requirements adequately while considering both the irrigation and flood control needs. If a heavy rain storm should occur anywhere in the river system, however, the operating rules should change accordingly. Some reservoirs should start emptying as rapidly as possible so as to be ready to absorb the increased runoff. Which reservoirs should be emptied, and by how much, depends on several factors such as the size and location of the rainstorm, the operator's knowledge of how rainfall in that vicinity affects the various tributaries, and considerations of the down-stream effect of the increased flow. The decisions should be made as rapidly as possible after receipt of information that the rainfall is occurring or expected, so that the system of reservoirs can be prepared as completely as possible before the surge of water arrives.

The computer has been applied to this management problem with great success. During the design and implementation stages of the computer program for control of a river system (which takes many years to complete), much time and effort is spent obtaining and correlating historical records of rainfall and stream flows throughout the river system's watershed. This work results in a model suitable for storage in a computer's files of how the river system responds to the various amounts and distributions of rainfall on record. This model is then used in designing the dams and other works to be built in the river system, the objective being to attain the desired degree of control under all likely conditions at minimum total cost.

After the river basin has been equipped with most or all of the planned facilities, the computer model is put to use to assist the management function. Fluctuations in demand for water (e.g., variations in irrigation requirements and power generation capacity) are fed into the computer which, using its model, computes the optimum way to release the necessary quantity of water from the reservoirs in accordance with the pre-established requirements for navigation, flood control, and future irrigation. (Because the interaction of all the flows in the river system is very complex, the computer's speed is required to produce the optimum answers quickly. Without it, decisions would have to be based solely on experience plus a few calculations.) Then, when an unexpected storm occurs, as soon as data about the location and amount of rain begins to be collected and fed to the computer, it provides predictions of the flows to be expected in all the streams. It also suggests the actions to be taken downstream and predicts their effects, providing an optimum reaction to the emergency almost immediately. ▶

In this and similar instances, then, the computer's ability to handle the interactions involved in large systems and complex simulations has already made it useful in the broadest of resource management responsibilities.

"FLICKERING" MANAGEMENT AUTHORITY

In the past, only those at the highest level of the organizational pyramid were provided with a sufficient breadth of information to deal with matters involving all parts of the organization. The junior manager working within sales, manufacturing, or accounting knew nothing about the current operations of the others. The data existed only within the departments, and was brought together with data from other departments only for reports to the highest level of management. If a junior manager had an idea for some change in his organization's operations, he had no way of evaluating its effect; he had no information with which to demonstrate that it had validity. All he could do was submit his idea to senior management who (being otherwise occupied, and because of the junior's relative lack of seniority and prestige in the organization) might follow a natural tendency to overlook the idea or take it lightly. This tendency was strengthened because most juniors' ideas, derived from imperfect knowledge, were unrealistic. The junior manager suffered from being "low on the totem pole," low in the hierarchy of seniority, and also low in the hierarchy of information availability. Only the most senior were provided with company-wide information, which automatically made them the only ones capable of thinking in company-wide breadth.

As we have seen, an increasing number of organizations have found it advisable to store operating data about their departments in computer files, with the data standardized so that the files may be combined in support of computer procedures to optimize operations. With access to the computer provided by time-shared terminals (though this is not necessary; any manager with enough authority to request a computer run can obtain service) the junior manager has access to all the company's operating data and any simulation and prediction programs that may have been prepared. He, like anyone having access to the computer, is able to use its facilities to test the consequences of a possible new venture. If the president tests the consequences of an idea of his, the computer will produce the best answer its data and programs are capable of producing; if the most junior manager in the organization (assuming he has access to the computer) tests an idea, the computer will produce an answer of equal quality. In such a situation the junior manager no longer need submit only an unsupported recommendation to management, but can test it as thoroughly as more senior managers can, using the same resources. (Indeed, it is frequently true that the junior manager is more familiar with the computer and its use, and may be able to use it even more effectively.) The junior manager's recommendation can now be accompanied by the results of the computer-developed forecast evaluating the desirability of proceeding with it, and the fact that the originator of the idea happens to be low in the hierarchy becomes irrelevant.

Many ambitious junior managers, having such a tool at their disposal, rise to the opportunity and make greater efforts to conceive and test novel and original ideas for new policies and ventures. Top managers, perceiving the increase in the creativity of their subordinates and now provided (for the first time) with thorough evaluations of new ideas, usually encourage this experimentation. The effect is that the authority for originating and testing ideas for change "flickers" within the management structure of the organization. He who has the idea is the one who temporarily has the authority to proceed with its analysis, to the point where analysis proves the idea desirable or not.

This "flickering authority" is a novel thing, made possible by the general availability of information and the means of manipulating it. In the past, where the availability of information paralleled the hierarchy of the management structure, authority for originating change was necessarily concentrated at the top. Now, with equal information facilities available at all levels of management, authority for originating change is likely to be found where the idea is found, whether this be at the lowest or highest level. "Flickering authority" is new, and its effects are not clear; however, it may lead to significant alterations in familiar methods of management. The junior manager has a powerful new incentive to be creative and to think beyond the bounds of his (probably) still relatively narrow job, because he knows he has the tools to evaluate his idea, and he knows that if the evaluation is successful, the idea will receive full attention and he will receive credit for its possible success. Top management is strengthened because it is no longer the sole source of well-considered innovations; enthusiastic junior managers are increasingly using the predictive models in the computer to test and contribute an increasing number of ideas.

CASE 9C

◀ A major oil company, interested in expanding retail gasoline sales, had for some years been pursuing a policy of distributing its credit cards as widely as possible. Experience had long since shown that possession of the company's credit card would increase the average driver's consumption of the company's products.

As time passed more and more avenues for distribution of credit cards were explored (e.g., to employees, to stockholders, to holders of other types of credit cards, to those who returned coupons in advertisements). Manageagement finally came to consider a simple "broadcast" mailing of credit cards to individuals who had not requested them, on the assumption that even though many cards might be thrown away, the more cards delivered the better.

Discussion about the pros and cons of this "broadcast" mailing of credit cards centered around the cost of distribution, the fraction of those receiving credit cards who would use them, and the average amount of usage. Computer programs were used to test various aspects of the economic viability of the scheme, but it was not yet clear which course of action would be followed.

A junior planner became troubled about another aspect of the matter—the possibility that "broadcast" mailing of credit cards might put them in the hands of so many poor credit risks that the company would lose a great deal of money through defaults, failures to pay for credit purchases. He mentioned this but attracted little notice; it was generally assumed that the amounts of individual losses would be too small to matter.

The company had computer data available about credit risk as a function of family income, employment, and location of residence. The worried junior manager, on his own initiative, instigated a computer run that would correlate this credit risk data against a typical mailing list that would be used in broadcasting the credit cards; the names and addresses to which the credit cards would be sent were correlated with the credit risk data by residence location. At the end of the computer run, a total would show the probable total default losses associated with the planned distribution of cards.

The junior manager was supported by the computer. It appeared that the probable default losses associated with the planned mailing list would be much too high to be acceptable. The junior manager prepared a report including the computer's virtually unquestionable demonstration that the losses would be too high, and presented this to the managers responsible for the program. They almost immediately accepted the results, because even the proponents of the program could not argue for long against the computer's statistical correlation of credit risk with the mailing list intended to be used. They chided themselves for failing to appreciate the desirability of correlating the credit risk data with the mailing list, and proceeded to abandon the scheme.

The junior manager received praise and a salary increase as a result of his initiative, and felt that he had learned a significant lesson. When he simply reported to the manager in charge of the project that he was concerned about the question of credit risk, his concern was essentially ignored as simply a matter of inexperience. By using the computer's data and statistical findings to prove his point, however, he rendered his inexperience irrelevant and accomplished far more in both his company's and his own interests. He made a private vow to ally himself with the computer more intimately in the future, because apparently his interests could be enhanced by its proper use.

The managers in charge of the project were relieved that they had been spared the consequences of their error, and made their own private vows to use the computer more in their future planning. At the same time, they came to realize that with the aid of the computer, the junior managers were in a better position than before to assist them and stated that in the future they would encourage junior managers to do this sort of analysis more and would listen to them more. ▶

Apparently, "flickering authority" should benefit all parties. The junior managers will benefit because their ideas are likely to receive more careful consideration and early success, while senior managers should benefit because they will have more ideas to choose from, more creativity applied to their company's interests. One might expect that senior managers would feel threatened by greater delegation of authority to junior managers, but there is no evidence that such a phenomenon will generally exist. For one thing, credit to the junior manager is given only after solid achievement; the fact of having an idea and of using the computer is of no value unless the idea proves worthwhile. The junior manager who becomes a "threat" is the one who has a succession of good ideas that prove valuable, and most senior managers are objective enough to appreciate that any such man deserves a place in their ranks whenever he can be found. More important, the fact that authority "flickers" within the ranks of management does not mean that responsibility flickers. The senior managers retain the responsibility for the company's operations, and therefore for the success of any innovation being considered. So long as this is so, they will presumably also retain the lion's share of the credit for its eventual success. It does not appear difficult to share the credit for a successful venture between a junior originator of an idea (a staff contribution) and the more senior managers who oversee the idea's implementation and exploitation (a line contribution).

This "flickering authority" is just emerging; there are relatively few clear-cut cases such as the above. It seems clear that the principle will become increasingly pervasive and important, however, as the availability and value of the computer programs and files describing organizations and their relationships with one another and the public increase. The probable corporate effects will be explored further in Part IV.

ADMINISTRATORS

In many organizations, administrative managers have benefited more than any others from the appearance of the computer. Administrative managers are concerned with details of the hiring and administration of personnel at the operating level, with providing supplies and facilities to support the organization's operations, with controlling overhead and supporting budgets, and with many incidental accounting and record-keeping functions. Long plagued by the squeeze between rising operating costs and the need to control overhead budgets, they have often received a powerful helping hand from the computer. Case 9A, for example, referred to computer services provided to assist the administration of school districts in California. The administrators in the district offices and the schools are able, with the help of the computer, to schedule their classes more efficiently, exercise greater control over their payrolls and operating budgets, and to maintain more useful student records while at the same time reducing or holding constant numbers of clerical personnel. Administrators of hospitals have benefited as much, or even more.

CASE 9D

◀ The administrator of a small hospital (120 beds) recently found herself working sixty-hour weeks attempting to keep up with her job. She had to schedule nurses, janitors, food service employees, and other service personnel. She had to manage inventories of surgical, housekeeping, and medical supplies and she was responsible for the hospital's accounting. This accounting centered around the preparation of bills for each patient, with an increasing variety of billing methods. Some were in-patients and some were out-patients; the billing systems were different for each. Some of the patients were charity cases; others received various benefits from insurance plans, Medicare and Medicaid. She had to oversee the preparation of the necessary forms and submissions for each plan, taking into account each patient's individual arrangements. Furthermore, she thought it important to be able to present each in-patient with a final bill immediately upon discharge, because experience had shown that the likelihood of collecting the full amount was much higher if the bill could be presented immediately rather than mailed later. Unfortunately, the doctors were not consistent in providing advance notice of the time of discharge of their patients; they reserved the right to discharge a patient any time an examination convinced them the patient was fit. As a result, the objective of having bills ready at time of discharge was never fully met.

The administrator attempted to perform all these functions with a clerical staff of four people. In earlier years, before the medical expense reimbursement plans had become so numerous and the complexity of inventories and services had increased because of more specialized medical techniques, four clerks were enough. Recently, the increasing complexity of the work had overloaded the four clerks and forced their working hours to rise to an unwelcome level. The administrator was very anxious not to increase the number of clerical employees because, even with increases in rates, costs had risen so much that the hospital was having an increasingly difficult time making ends meet.

The State Blue Cross agency, a large organization with much data to process, had long since installed computers for its own purposes. It had become concerned about the ability of the administrators in the smaller hospitals to handle their data processing loads, because the Blue Cross agency needed timely and accurate data from them in order to perform its functions satisfactorily. The Blue Cross agency became aware of the success of counterpart agencies in other states in providing data processing services for small hospitals, charging a fee that would offset the cost of the service and, at the same time, solving the problems of data gathering. They therefore developed such a service themselves and offered it to the small hospitals in the state.

The administrator was offered a service that would require her to prepare punched cards corresponding to all the accounting transactions taking place in the hospital (items chargeable to patients' accounts, issues from inventory, assignments of nurses, time cards recording duty hours, etc.). A remote input-output terminal connected to the Blue Cross computer was to be installed in the hospital; it would include a typewriter and a punched card reader. As each batch of cards was prepared it was to be entered in the terminal and transmitted to the computer, which would then perform several functions. It would automatically prepare the hospital's payrolls and mail the checks from the Blue Cross offices. It would schedule the assignments of nurses to duty stations given the number of stations, the availability of nurses, and the expected demand. It would automatically prepare patient bills and prepare notices of overdue accounts. It would automatically prepare reimbursement request forms for submission to the medical expense reimbursement plans applicable to particular patients. It would keep track of inventory issues and prepare reorder notices, and it would prepare periodic accounting reports. Moreover, whenever a patient was discharged, the system would permit the administrator to initiate a request through the keyboard of the remote terminal for an up-to-date bill. The Blue Cross computer would immediately prepare and transmit an up-date bill to the typewriter, so that by the time the patient was ready for discharge, the bill would be available for presentation.

Because more than fifteen hospitals were signed up for this service during the implementation stage, the cost to the hospital in question was little more than the cost of one additional clerk, and the savings from increased collections and improvements in inventory management were expected to offset it. The hospital administrator, then, accepted the service joyfully. Her work week and those of the four clerks dropped back to normal levels, the ability to provide up-to-date patient bills upon discharge was achieved for the first time in the history of the hospital, much of the onerous data handling required for accounting purposes left the hospital entirely, and in every respect the administrator's situation greatly improved. ▶

The administrator's job is not threatened by the computer, because the planning, personnel administration and overall responsibility remain; there is no reduction in importance or prestige. The computer is an unalloyed blessing to the administrator, then, taking over quantities of increasingly onerous data handling work and leaving him freer to attend to broader aspects of his administrative responsibility.

EMPLOYEES

The employees of computer-using organizations have been affected by it in proportion to the amount of their work taken over or assisted by the computer. The following groups of employees have been strongly affected and have clearly benefited.

The greatest beneficiaries are, of course, the computer people themselves: the "priests of the machine" who were discussed in the preceding chapter. They owe their livelihoods to the computer, and many of them believe that by basing their careers on the methodology suggested and supported by it, they can advance far into the ranks of management. However true that may be, we have already seen that the imbalance between supply and demand for trained computer people has caused salaries to rise sharply, so the data processing system designer and programmer is clearly far better off because of the computer than he would be if only less powerful data processing tools of more limited scope were available.

Many computers are used to provide information to the sales person or customer representative. The objective is either to provide him with complete information rapidly so that he can serve the customer more adequately, or to increase his chances of making a sale. In either case the employee himself benefits because his job has been simplified, because the customer with whom he deals is more satisfied, or because his sales record is better. It is obvious, for example, that the computer-based reservation systems used by virtually all airlines have been of great assistance to the agents at the ticket counters. Before the reservations systems became available, the agents in a given city would sell airplane seats from "blocks" of reservations assigned to them, frequently telephoning or telegraphing the airline's central service if their demand exceeded the supply assigned to them or if the flight requested was not one for which they were regularly assigned blocks of seats. The customer would have to wait for one or perhaps a series of messages to be exchanged; he would often not be able to obtain confirmation of reservations for several days. The agent would have to spend considerable time on the individual situation, probably generate many more pieces of paper, and maintain long lists of unanswered reservation requests to which he should attend. Despite these efforts, flights would often be oversold or reservations unrecorded, and the hapless agent would then have to deal with the irate customer. In practical fact, it is inconceivable that today's volume of air travel could be handled on a reservation basis without the aid of the computer-assisted reservation service. The conditions existing at ticket counters today and the work load of the ticket agents are bad enough. In the absence of the reservations system, conditions would be nothing short of chaotic.

Many other examples exist where the computer provides this kind of assistance to sales personnel. A case as widespread as that of airline reservations can be found in the stock brokerage business, where almost every customer representative has access to a stock quote terminal connected to a computer that can provide current price information on any security. Without such a service, the customer representative (like the airline ticket agent) would have to place individual calls, provide poorer service, and spend far more time attempting to answer the customer's questions about stock prices.

It is in the interests of both the organization and the sales person for him to contact as many potential customers as he can. On the other hand, the chances of making a sale are often enhanced where a degree of personalized service is provided. The salesman must decide between offering such special service to a particular prospect and thereby enhance the sale, and moving on to another prospect. In some cases, the computer can provide a degree of personalized service without requiring a corresponding investment of the sales person's time, so he can do both.

CASE 9E

◀ A life insurance salesman must ordinarily convince his prospect that he is underinsured; that he should acquire an additional policy. In order to do so, he must obtain data about the prospect's present financial arrangements: his income, his assets, his present life insurance policies, the present and future value of his retirement plan, and the like. With this data the salesman must project the income available to the prospect (or his survivors) at various times in the future and under various circumstances, and compare this with the income they would need to maintain a satisfactory standard of living. Since this kind of projection often involves compounding interest or retirement plan contributions over a period of many years and must consider the combination of a variety of incomes and expenses, the salesman must spend considerable time developing it.

Many of the life insurance companies use computers to help their salesmen develop these projections. The salesman completes a form with financial data about his prospect, then sends the form to data processing personnel who prepare punched cards containing the information and feed it to a computer that makes the projection or series of projections the salesman has requested. Within a day (or less if necessary) the results are available to the salesman. During this time he has been free to call on other prospects, so he can call on many more prospects than he could when he had to perform the projective analysis calculations himself. ▶

Of course, only a minority of sales people and customer representatives receive such services. In many cases their jobs are such that computer services would not help them. In others, the computer programs that would provide the assistance they could use have not yet been developed. Nevertheless, the number of sales people already helped runs into tens of thousands.

When computers are used to schedule production operations and therefore issue instructions to production personnel, it usually is assumed that the employee receiving the instructions suffers a reduction in initiative or motivation.

CASE 9F

◀ Case 1H described an automated bakery using computers to operate the mixers that prepare batter for large quantities of cakes. An employee watches the mixing sequence to make sure nothing goes wrong, and at various points in the process he adds small quantities of special ingredients that it is not economical to provide through the automatic system of pipes and conveyors. When he is to add an ingredient, the mixer stops and signal lights display the instruction for him. After he completes the operation, he restarts the automatic process.

Certainly one might assume that nothing could be more demeaning than this. The employee is not only subservient to the machine's orders, but plays only a minor role in the process; the computer adds most of the ingredients from automatic systems and directs all the mixing. The employee "plays second fiddle"; he is required only for the addition of minor ingredients not worthwhile handling through the automatic process.

In fact, the employees operating the mixers generally prefer the automated process over the earlier one where they operated the mixers manually. In the past, it was up to them to initiate and stop each step in the mixing process at the right time, to accurately measure the quantities of material being added to the mixer, and to rigidly follow prescribed "recipes" all through the working day. Addition of the wrong amount of an ingredient or failure to follow the mixing sequence exactly usually resulted in the spoilage of as much as 500 gallons of batter having a substantial value. A severe dressing down, if not dismissal, would result. The employee was therefore "on edge" all day, repeating a mechanical process endlessly but always with alertness and care lest a costly mistake be made. Now, with the computer on the job, his responsibility is greatly reduced because it is much less likely that he can cause an expensive error. He still has as much work to keep him busy (there are fewer employees per mixer), but now it is up to the computer to make sure that the recipe is followed accurately each time. The employees generally find this a more satisfactory condition. ▶

It is more likely that the supervisors of production operations will be hurt by the computer, because their decision-making functions are directly superseded. Experienced foremen who have throughout their careers exercised judgment in scheduling operations and managing personnel based on accumulated experience, will inevitably object to the loss of responsibility and suffer in morale. Some organizations have intentionally planned systems that obtain the advantages of computer control of production while retaining an area of responsibility and judgment for the foremen, happily combining the benefits of both to the advantage of all parties.

CASE 9G

◀ An automobile manufacturer has a crew headed by a foreman assigned to each work station on the assembly line. Each station can perform only the set of operations possible to the machines at the station and the skills of the crew, but considerable flexibility is possible in assigning individual workers having multiple skills or different levels of skill. Before the computer became available, it was customary to provide the foreman with the day's work schedule and allow him to assign his personnel in accordance with their availability and skills. He considered such individual factors as vacations, the increasing skill levels of new employees in training, and details such as a particular employee's head cold or dislike for another.

When a computer was installed to schedule the operations of the work stations, it was provided with codes describing the skills and experience levels of the employees assigned to each work station. Theoretically, it could have scheduled the assignment of individual employees as well as the foreman. Practically, it could not consider changing and intangible factors affecting work assignments. The planners of the computer-based system, appreciating this, refrained from incorporating a computer program to schedule employees. Instead, the computer would present the daily requirements to the foreman as before (supplemented by changed requirements caused by events during the day). The foreman would then make his personnel assignments to meet the requirements and report back to the computer any overload or slack at his work station. The computer would then combine the foremen's reports and adaptively reschedule the work, so that lightly loaded work stations could help out those that happened to be undermanned. Furthermore, the computer would verify that the foreman had done what appeared to be a satisfactory job of associating the necessary skill and experience levels with the tasks to be performed.

The results suited all parties. Management was able to obtain more adaptive and detailed scheduling, resulting in higher efficiency. They were also protected against the effects of foremen's errors in scheduling, because the computer checked each assignment for gross errors. The foreman approved of the process, because with the computer's help any emergencies at his station (the sudden illness of one of his people, a broken machine, or a sudden surge in requirements) could be handled by rapidly rescheduling as many other work stations as necessary; this had never been possible before. The foremen also appreciated the computer's verification that they made no gross errors in their assignments.   ▶

In some cases, professional employees performing repetitive work have been helped considerably by the computer. In many schools, for example, the work load of teachers has been reduced. Case 9A explained how a network of centrally programmed computers in California has assisted in the management of the public school system. Much of the work performed (student test scoring, grading, and record keeping) is work which previously had to be performed by the teacher. This voluminous clerical work interfered with the teacher's ability to attend to and assist the students, so the reduction in clerical and administrative work load on the teacher is of obvious benefit to all parties. The teacher will benefit further when computer-assisted instruction comes into widespread use for teaching simple skills and facts; such work occupies a great deal of teacher time without fully utilizing the teacher's abilities. It has been well demonstrated* that computer-assisted instruction does at least as well and perhaps better than a human teacher in "drill and practice," because individuals can work at their own pace with the endlessly patient machine. A combination of the computer in drill and practice with the teacher in the more sophisticated areas of concept communication and understanding will apparently form a powerful team in which the abilities of both parties are best utilized. Computer-assisted instruction is still in its infancy and is very little used on a regular basis, but clearly as its use increases both the teacher and the student will benefit.

Computers do the work of literally armies of data processing clerks who would otherwise be needed to operate accounting machines and adding machines, maintain files, sort documents, prepare bills, and generally perform repetitive and largely mindless data handling functions. These jobs were always relatively unpopular because they offered very little in the way of interest or creative potential to the worker. The clerks who remain are now dealing primarily with exceptions and special processing cases that the computer cannot be programmed to handle. Most of these positions offer intrinsically more varied and interesting situations for the clerk. The job of the data processing clerk has, on the average, been upgraded to a level where most of the jobs are more interesting.

It might be said, then, that clerks have benefited from the assistance of the computer. In the process of assisting them the computer has abolished many of their jobs, though, so it is open to question whether one should

---

* Enoch Hays, "CAI: A Commencement," *Business Automation,* November 1967.

consider this a benefit or not. Furthermore, as was noted in the last chapter, the use of the computer brings with it a large number of new repetitive jobs in data preparation. The girl who used to operate an accounting machine is now likely to be found operating a key punch machine. Whether she has benefited from the change is questionable.

SCIENTISTS AND ENGINEERS

Next to the data processing professional, the individual benefiting most from computers is probably the scientist engaged in research. Some branches of science have advanced into areas of complexity that could not have been reached without the computer's help. This was pointed out in Chapter 1 and is exemplified by cases such as Case 1C. In other cases the computer's contribution has enabled scientists to perform research in areas which could otherwise have been approached only with extreme difficulty, if at all.

CASE 9H

◀ A biologist wished to investigate the relationship between movements of the eye and electrical signals in the brain. He hoped as a result of his work to be able to relate mental functions to physical effects to a degree never possible before.

The biologist surgically implanted electrodes in the heads of a group of cats so that he could measure electrical potentials in their brains as they performed certain actions. He also fabricated contact lenses that would fit over the cats' eyeballs, and attached to the contact lenses small mirrors on stems so that they projected out from the eye. An experimental apparatus was arranged so that a light beam reflected from the mirror attached to the contact lens and fell on a group of photoelectric cells, as shown in Fig. 9–1. When the eyeball moved, the mirror would move with it and the reflected beam of light would move across the photoelectric cells producing electric signals that would indicate the speed and amount of the eye's movement.

The experiment's objective was to stimulate eye movements of the experimental cats by flashing objects into their fields of vision, and then record both the movements and the simultaneous electrical potentials occurring in their brains. There are many electrical potentials in the brain associated with various bodily functions, thoughts, and perceptions, and the biologist knew it would be very difficult to separate those associated with the eye movements from others recorded by the electrodes. Therefore, the experimenter anticipated that he would have to run a great many trials with both the same and different cats so that by statistical correlation he could discover which brain potentials were associated with particular eye movements.

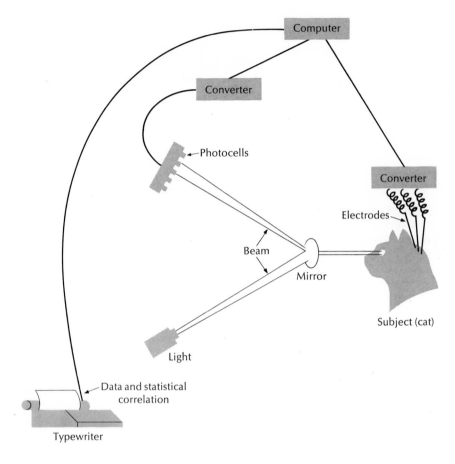

FIG. 9–1 Apparatus for correlating eye movements with brain potentials.

This was easier said than done because the animals' patience was limited and only a small number of readings could be taken at each session. While the cats were not in actual pain, it was nevertheless necessary to restrain their movements during the experimental sessions and the contact lens on the eyeball was an irritant. After a few minutes the cat's mounting impatience would distort its responses and the biologist would have to release the cat and allow it to rest before undertaking another session. The biologist knew he would have to conduct many trials, because many different eye movements would have to be measured repeatedly in numerous cats so that statistically valid correlations could be obtained.

Ordinarily the data from an experimental session would be collected and analyzed afterward. Only then would the biologist discover whether a successful correlation was obtained between a given eye movement and a set of brain potentials. Sometimes the correlation would be clear quickly and many of the repetitions would be wasted, and sometimes no correlation would appear and the session would have to be repeated. Much of the time in the experimental sessions would be wasted, then, because of the biologist's inability to know how the correlations were developing. To remedy this, the biologist connected a computer to the devices reading brain potentials and to the photoelectric cells recording eye movements. As the experiment progressed, converters would change the signals into digital form and the computer would execute a statistical program to determine whether statistically valid correlations were being obtained from repeated trials of the same eye movement. The results were printed by a typewriter at the site of the experiment, so when a correlation was obtained the biologist would immediately be informed and he could change to a different movement or terminate the session. The biologist was therefore able to make more progress in a given session, and the number of experimental sessions was greatly reduced. Without the computer to tell the biologist when he could leave a particular eye movement and move to another, far more sessions would have been required —to the point where the research would have been impractical. ▶

Engineers have also benefited, because the computer enables them to perform design calculations more rapidly. The engineering time per job is reduced, and the number of alternative design solutions that can be tried is increased. The computer's benefits have sometimes gone beyond this simple role as a fast calculator; in some areas it has made possible the application of entirely new design methods.

Often no theoretically "perfect" solution to an engineering design problem can be determined, because the exact mathematical relationship between the elements of the process in question is unknown, or because the equations describing the relationships are too complex to solve. In such cases the engineer cannot predict with certainty how a change in the design would affect the results. There is always some knowledge of the action of each element of the system being designed, though; the individual relationships between one variable and another can be observed from experience. The problem is to predict what effect each element will have on the whole. In these cases it becomes possible to build a model of the system being designed in the computer, making parts of its program represent each element of the system and using its speed to compute the effect of a change in one element on all the other elements and on the performance of the whole.

Case 9B illustrates this design process. The engineers designing the complex of dams, dikes, and levees to control a river system cannot represent all the interactions of the streams as mathematical equations; there would be too many, and the effect of each on every other would not be known. They can, however, make a mathematical representation of each separate stream and each intersection with another stream. When rainfall is assumed to occur in one part of the watershed, its effect can be examined as it "moves downstream" by steps. First the increased flows in the tributaries can be seen, and the time and amount of runoff to the secondary rivers observed. As these join the main stream, the height and timing of the flood crest emerges. The effect of a dam at a particular point in a secondary river can be tested under various rainfall assumptions, and dams can be "moved" until the engineers are satisfied that the minimum number of dams give adequate control under all expected rainfall conditions.

Their job is not yet done, because they are not always free to locate dams in the ideal sites. Perhaps a town or a national monument might be inundated by the reservoir, or perhaps the location might be uneconomic for generating power. These and other offsetting considerations lead to compromises with the ideal model, and require additional design work to be done.

With the computer's model such runs can be performed economically and rapidly, and the design is improved in two ways: First, because many more trials have been made, the ideal is more likely to be approached. Second, the effect of each element of the system on every other has been considered, so the precise requirements for each dam are known. This could not be done before, so the requirements for the individual dam were less perfectly known and for safety's sake they were overdesigned.

This leads not only to better engineering but to different engineers. In the past, engineers concentrated on carefully setting up and executing mathematical formulas to determine the characteristics of the thing being designed. The computer does this for the engineer, but it also invites him instead to develop models such as the above. The engineer becomes less of a mathematician and more of a model builder, and the skills required are considerably different—in fact, the entire approach to the job changes. Traditional distinctions such as that between engineers and architects become blurred, and we can see that the engineers of the future will surely differ in nature from those of today. This subject will be explored further in Part IV.

THE PUBLIC

Few individuals own computers in their own right, and few have access to computers except as employees of organizations owning them. Therefore, the private individual must receive the benefits of computers only indirectly.

The public as a whole presumably benefits from the increase in scientific knowledge made possible by the computer, and stockholders benefit from the increased efficiency in their companies' operations made possible by use of the computer. Such benefits (while unquestionably real) are diffuse and unmeasurable, but there are also clear-cut cases in which sizable segments of the public have benefited directly from the use of computers by organizations. It is evident, for example, that the public has benefited directly from airlines' use of computer-based reservation systems. The air traveler today can easily make and change reservations and construct complex trips made up of many interconnecting flights, some belonging to other airlines operating in other parts of the world, and is free to change his mind at any time and location. This facility is probably in part responsible for the great popularity of air travel, because without the computer no individual ticket agent could have immediately available information about alternative flights or about flights between points not under his immediate jurisdiction. Days would be required for reservation confirmation, so the public would have to submit its requests for reservations well in advance of the intended trip and be permitted to make no changes thereafter. Obviously, travelers and their use of airlines would be constrained by this inconvenience.

The investor in securities has also benefited from the availability of computers to the firms serving him. In addition to the routine data processing tasks of handling transactions and customer accounts, computers universally perform the collection and dissemination of current stock price information. The investor obviously likes to be easily able to obtain current quotes on his stock; this has probably been associated with the great increase in public interest in securities trading which has occurred during the last decade.

CASE 9 l

◀ Publicly available price quotations have been available for many years for stocks traded on the exchanges, first through the ticker tape and then through the computer-based quotation services. However, the many stocks traded "over the counter" (between dealers by telephone, not at centralized exchanges) have only recently had the benefit of quotation services. In February 1965, the first quotation service for over the counter stocks was instituted and price quotations began to appear on a daily basis in newspapers and (to a degree) in stock quote services handling the stocks listed on exchanges. Since then, these over the counter stock quote services have grown so that now reasonably current quotations are readily available to the investing public for most of the common over the counter stocks. The availability of quotations is thought to have increased public interest in the over the counter stock market and led to increased trading activity; trading volume estimates support this opinion. A private report in 1965 showed that as of August 1964 (about six months before the over the counter quotations began to become available) the volume of shares traded over the counter was about 2.5 million per day. At the same time the New York Stock Exchange was trading about 4.4 million shares per day, so the over the counter stock volume was about 56% of the New York Exchange volume.

As of June 6, 1968* it was estimated that the over the counter trading volume had grown to about 21 million shares per day versus approximately 14 million on the New York Stock Exchange: 150% of the Exchange volume. Thus during 3½ years since over the counter stock quote information became available, the trading volume grew from 56% of that of the New York Exchange to 150% of it.

This undoubtedly has occurred for many reasons other than the availability of quotations. For example, many new companies having a high degree of speculative interest have been formed during the period and are being traded over the counter. However, many speculative companies are also listed on the Exchange. It seems logical to impute a good deal of the relative increase in volume to increased public interest caused by the increased availability of quote information. ▶

Some services which could not exist without the computer have been received enthusiastically by the public. The credit card is an outstanding example; it is so popular and widely used that it has become a major force in the nation's financial system. Without the computer to process the myriad individual transactions associated with credit cards, to post each to the correct card holder's bill and to correctly compute and pay all of the various commissions and charges involved, the widespread use of credit cards would be impossible.

Statistics on the overall growth of credit card usage are not readily available, but the growth has clearly been striking. In one class of credit cards, those issued by banks, it was only after a period of experimentation during the 1950's marked by caution and the development of data handling systems that banks began aggressively offering credit cards in the early 1960's. These bank credit card plans grew rapidly and proliferated: as of early 1968 more than 1000 banks were associated with a credit card plan, and the larger plans exceeded six million card holders each and typically were growing between 30% and 50% per year. This growth rate is underscored by a report by the Comptroller of the Currency† that as of October 4, 1967, the amount of consumer credit extended under bank credit card plans stood at $838 million, up 28% since April 25 of the same year—less than six months.

---

* *The Wall Street Journal,* June 6, 1968.
† *The New York Times,* November 8, 1967.

The public clearly likes credit cards. Credit card plans could not exist except at high cost without computers to process the masses of small transactions involved, so the computer has directly benefited the public by making these plans possible.

STUDENTS

Students in an increasing variety of subjects benefit from the availability of computers. The main reason is that although students must learn to do arithmetic by hand, once they do so the performance of it in support of other work is time-consuming labor. In advanced areas of mathematics, the sciences, and statistical studies in economics and sociology, the working out of arithmetic problems becomes an increasing burden. Teachers are limited in the complexity and size of problems they can assign to students because of the time needed to perform the elementary computations involved in finding the answers, and the interest of students is greatly dissipated by the need to spend time on laborious and error-prone calculations. If computers are available to help the students with their arithmetic, the assignments they can handle become more extensive, complex, and realistic, and the student's interest in the creative and challenging elements of the problem is stimulated because he has less laborious computation to do. In a civil engineering course at MIT, for example, students who were assigned problems in developing two-story structures now, with a computer available, practice the design of twenty-story buildings.* Students generally respond to the availability of computers with enthusiasm—"They have no fear of them," states Professor Anthony Oettinger of Harvard. "The problem is to keep them from getting addicted."*

As we have seen previously, computer-assisted instruction in the teaching of rote subjects and drill and practice skills seems to have a potential equal to or (because the progress of the individual student controls the speed of the teaching program) superior to that of a human teacher. It appears likely that in industrial and armed forces training, and in grade schools where simple skills are the primary subjects taught, computer-assisted instruction may become very general.

Computer-assisted instruction can be applied to drill and practice teaching of facts, and to the teaching of complex operating techniques when equipment simulating the operating environment is driven by the computer.

CASE 9J

◀ Astronauts training to "fly" the Apollo project's lunar module can practice with a device called the "Full Mission Engineering Simulator" operated for

---

* *Time,* May 19, 1967.

NASA by the Grumman Aircraft Engineering Company.* This simulator is a full-scale model of the lunar module, contained within a chamber that has relief maps of the lunar surface projected on its inner surface as well as star maps simulating the appearance of the heavens as they would appear to astronauts piloting real lunar modules. A model of the command ship from which the lunar module will leave and to which it will return is also suspended in the chamber. The astronauts "fly" the lunar module, and as they operate its controls, computers receive the control impulses and compute the resulting motion of a real lunar module in flight. The computers then compute the relative change in appearance of the environment that would be caused by the motion. Finally, the computers send signals to move the projectors and models in the simulator. The command ship becomes closer or further away, turns or moves from side to side as the astronauts manipulate the controls of the lunar module; the sky and lunar surface move correspondingly. Each action and reaction is simulated in the exact manner that it will occur in a real flight of a lunar module. In the simulator the astronauts can "learn to fly" the lunar module, and can perceive the precise effects of their "flying" as they will appear during the real mission. By means of the computer-driven simulator, then, it becomes possible to train pilots thoroughly in handling the lunar module, even though it is impossible to provide risk-free training flights in advance of the real thing. ▶

Similar computer-controlled flight simulators have been used for years to train pilots of commercial and military aircraft: the resulting reductions in training costs and accidents are inestimable. There have also been some experiments with the use of simulators for automobile driver training, and it is hoped that someday through the use of simulators drivers can be taught how to react in danger situations without the unacceptable risks and costs that would accompany the real thing. Hopefully, as time goes on, the teaching of operating skills of many kinds will be simulated using mockups of the equipment or vehicles involved, with computers used to make the mockup act like the real thing. Much money could be saved and (more importantly) higher levels of skills may be obtained, particularly in dealing with emergency situations.

The computer can sometimes be used by the teacher to establish understanding of a concept in the mind of a student. The process of developing a computer program to solve a problem forces the student to think in an analytical and logical way about the nature of general solutions to the problem, which is often what the teacher wants him to do. Because computer pro-

---

* *Computing Report,* International Business Machines Corporation, September 1967.

gramming requires perfect logic and imposes strict discipline (the computer will expose all imperfections), this can be a very effective tool in developing analytical skills. On the other hand, it can sometimes backfire.

CASE 9K

◀ In a high school where the students had access to a computer, a mathematics teacher assigned computer programming tasks (which the students enjoyed) to illustrate some of the concepts of mathematical analysis. One student was assigned to write a program that would find the square root of two accurate to four decimal places. The teacher knew that the students had not been given any general method for finding square roots, and he hoped that in developing a computer program the student would work out a general method for finding square roots by himself.

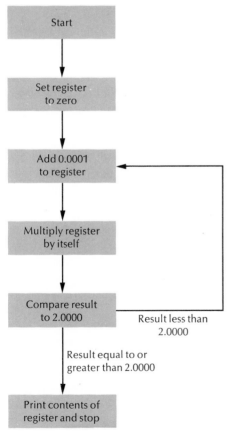

FIG. 9–2 Student's computer program for finding the square root of two.

The student turned in the correct answer, but his computer program for finding the answer seemed to have no relationship to any known method for finding square roots. The teacher looked at the program, and found that it worked as shown in Fig. 9–2. The program set a storage register to zero, then added 0.0001 to the register, multiplied the resulting number by itself, and checked to see whether the result was 2.0000 or greater. If not, the addition and multiplication were repeated. Finally (after 14,143 repetitions) the register reached the value 1.4143, the square root of 2.0002. The computer printed this number, and the student presented it to the teacher along with the program in satisfaction of his assignment. The teacher ruefully accepted the result, but realized he had failed to appreciate that the student could use the speed of the computer to circumvent the intent of the assignment; to find the answer by "brute force" rather than by the kind of analytical thinking that was intended. ▶

Despite such examples as these, it is unquestionably true that most students are interested in learning how to program the computer, and that the discipline involved is closely related to the analytical discipline of mathematics and the sciences. The teacher whose students have access to a computer has a powerful new tool both for increasing the complexity and scope of their assignments, and for helping students develop their analytical skills in a manner they regard more as play than work.

SUMMARY

It is clear that millions of individuals have benefited directly from computers. Top managers of organizations are beginning to be helped significantly as computer-based simulations that help them with their planning functions are improved. Junior managers and management trainees are benefiting far more because of the "flickering authority" that develops; they are enabled to contribute more effectively to their organizations' planning while in junior positions, and presumably to have their merits appreciated earlier. Many administrators and employees of organizations have been helped because their jobs have been simplified or because they can be more effective with the computer's aid. Sales people and customer representatives sometimes receive such assistance, and professionals such as teachers increasingly use computers to perform their more routine work. Scientists and engineers benefit particularly, because the computer has made it possible for them to do routine work faster, to penetrate areas which were impractical or impossible without its support, and to use simulations to develop better engineering designs than was possible using the old "cookbook" methods. Students benefit because the labor of hand calculations in working out problems is reduced, so the creative content of their work can be increased and the problems they practice with can be more like those of real life—in fact, simulators for teaching operating skills are nearly indistinguishable from real life. Finally, the public is benefited both indirectly and in a number of direct ways because computers make possible a number of very welcome public services. Without question, use of the computer has brought great benefits, not only at the level of the organization (as we have seen before) but also at the level of the individual. A manager finding that a proposed computer application is one of the types discussed in this chapter may, then, be confident that it will be of genuine potential benefit to the individuals concerned.

CHAPTER 10

THOSE WHO SUFFER

*"Our society not only fails to ask for or expect any depth of commitment
from the individual; in a curious way it even discourages such commitment.
Perhaps nothing is more effective in suppressing any spirit of endeavor on
the part of the individual than the overpowering size and complexity of
the joint enterprise in which we are all supposed to be participants."*
JOHN GARDNER

The computer, more than any other single object, is the symbol of this size
and complexity in the public mind. It symbolizes impersonality, conformity to preestablished patterns, "reduction to a number," and impossibility
of changing the status quo because of the colossal inertia associated with "the
system" that characterize the popular image of the modern organization. One
may justly plead that it is unfair to cast the computer in the role of "heavy,"
and assert that the computer is merely a passive tool carrying out the wishes
of its owners. The computer is no more than a symptom, not the disease itself.
On the other hand, the contribution of the computer to making the giant,
monolithic organization of today possible is profound. Without it, many of
the objectionable characteristics of the modern organization would not have
developed, because the organizations we know could not exist. In the absence of the computer, many of the great industrial and governmental enter-
prises of today would either be impossible or would have to exist in entirely
different forms, forms which (for all we know) might reflect a greater hu-
manism and concern for the individual. Up to a point it is fair to blame the
computer because its capabilities have made possible the existence of the
organizations to whose weaknesses Mr. Gardner refers; it is rightly taken as
the symbol of both their efficiency and speed and of their impersonality and
complexity.

It is fair to recollect at this point that the computer and the techniques it
supports are viewed by many as a source of new opportunity: the computer

professionals whose entire careers are made possible by it, the younger managers whose careers can be benefited by the "flickering authority" the machine and its techniques make possible, the employees whose jobs are simplified and whose income is enhanced by the support of the computer; all these become more committed rather than less. But there seems little question that such people are a minority. Anyone reading the daily newspapers is aware that the majority are concerned and anxious, if not dismayed, by the "computerized society" of which Mr. Gardner speaks. To the degree that each of us shares this feeling, he has suffered because of the computer. Furthermore, the manager of a computer-using organization must be aware that its employees and customers are part of this majority.

Beyond this general disenchantment caused by broad trends of which the computer is a symptom and to which it is a contributor, there are specific classes of individuals who can be seen to have suffered in concrete ways because of the use of the computer.

MANAGERS

The senior managers of organizations should be expected to benefit heavily from computers. (Otherwise, why install them?) As noted in the last chapter, sometimes they do. In a surprising number of cases, though, top managers have been disappointed by the lack of direct assistance provided to them by the computers in their organizations. Some even feel that their jobs are more difficult with the computer than they were before.

CASE 10A

◀ The chairman of the board of an electric utility describes himself as being concerned primarily with two factors: the profitability of the company as it exists today, and the planning of the company of tomorrow. When computers were installed for customer billing and to perform engineering design calculations, the chairman was enthusiastic; he hoped for assistance from them.

The chairman's first disappointment came when he found himself getting profitability information more slowly (instead of more quickly) than before. The computer programs for handling customer bills and accounting transactions were so designed that all the detailed processing runs for a month had to be completed before the summary reports of interest to the chairman could be prepared. It took several days after the end of the month to complete the detailed runs; only then could the processing of the summary accounting reports start. Under the previous manual system, clerks could start accumulating information and develop rough totals for the monthly accounting reports while the last documents were still being processed, so at the end of a month only a final few documents remained to be added to the accounting reports. Since this required only a day or two of work, the accounting statements appeared very soon after the completion of the detailed processing. Since the computer could not even start the summary accounting processing until all the detailed work was done, it took several more days than the manual system had, and the monthly reports were slower getting to the chairman and the other executives.

The chairman's second disappointment came when he found that he was less able to ask for special reports and analyses than he had been before. It had been his custom upon reviewing the monthly accounting reports to ask for further breakdowns and explanations of unusual or unexpected figures, so that he could determine whether action was required or not. His questions varied, but whatever they were the answers became available in a day or two. A few clerks would review the detailed data associated with the area and prepare a report for him. After the computer appeared, he found that a request for special analysis would require a new computer program to be prepared that could review the magnetic tape files and select and tabulate the information he wanted; the process would typically require three weeks instead of a few days.

The chairman's third disappointment came in the area of planning. Each major decision about the installation of a new generating facility, transmission line, or major substation involved millions of dollars and a number of years for planning and construction. To be economical, each should return profits for at least twenty years. Projections of demand for electric power were of crucial importance, then, and a long time horizon was required because it took (on the average) about five years between perception of a change in demand and the installation of major facilities to meet it. The chairman hoped that with the computer processing data about trends in population, industry, and consumption of energy, he would be able to obtain better information than ever before on which to base the company's decisions about installing additional facilities.

He found that the computer's power demand forecasts were to be prepared for only one year ahead. He objected that so short a forecast would be useless for his purpose, but he was answered with the explanation that the only detailed data available for computer processing dealt with present and short-term future demand; that figures from which long-term trends might be developed were available only as broad, overall estimates not suitable for computer processing. The chairman observed that these estimates were already available to him, so he might as well forget about using the computer in his long-range planning. The computer people agreed; it was mutually concluded that the computer would not be used for long-term planning until more detailed data about demand became available.

The chairman's hopes for assistance from the computer were completely disappointed. In the profitability and financial control area he felt that he was worse served by the computer than he had been by the earlier manual system because regular accounting reports were slower in appearing and because his requests for special reports were less well met. In the planning area he discovered that the length of time with which he had to be concerned, five to twenty years in the future, was so great that no detailed data with which the computer could work would be available. He conceded that while the computer was essential for use in customer billing and detailed engineering work, and while the company could not do without it, it was useless to him. ▶

Some day the chairman may receive better service; the computer may become more useful to him in both areas. Developments in computer and programming technology promise to help him in obtaining and analyzing accounting data; someday he may be provided with an inquiry terminal from which he can obtain current profitability figures at any time, and which will permit him to ask questions about the figures which will produce successively greater detail until he is satisfied that he understands the situation he is investigating. It can be questioned (as we have seen in Chapter 2) whether detailed data by itself will ever answer the questions he asks about causes and potential cures, but at any rate his desires for current and selectively detailed information may well be met soon. The detailed data needed for better long-range planning may also become available. Because computer-oriented techniques for developing statistical forecasts and detailed plans are so effective, the desirability of obtaining statistical data for long-range planning has become much greater. Many organizations need it—not only utilities, but also major industrial and commercial firms and local, state, and Federal government agencies. Each collects part of the planning data useful to it and (usually) shares it with the others. In five or ten years, when extensive time series of varied and accurate data have become available, the computational capabilities of the computer may be able to assist the chairman in his long-term planning.

Conditions are improving, then, but they improve only slowly and in the meantime many of the enthusiastic managers who had expected direct, immediate assistance from the computer remain disappointed.

Another problem which has afflicted many managers of divisions within large organizations is loss of control over their internal information processing functions. Most divisional organizations decentralize authority and responsibility, and intend the general manager of the division or president of the subsidiary to have full authority over all operations within his organization. Data processing within the division is one such area, important to the manager because it provides control information not only to himself but to all other levels of management; it also supports scheduling functions, purchasing and inventory control decisions, and many other operating areas closely associated with the profitability of the division. Most division managers logically feel that control over the data processing in their divisions is as important to their performance as control of any other function.

As we saw in Chapter 6, however, divisional managers are losing this control. For a variety of reasons it is becoming advantageous and economically necessary for corporate staffs of large organizations to standardize and develop data processing systems, and for corporate management to require that the divisions adopt the systems and conform to them. Often some programming and computing resources remain under the control of the division manager, but usually they are in sufficiently short supply that after the corporate needs receive first priority very little is left. Managers of divisions are presented with new problems of an interpersonal or political nature when they become dependent for the first time on information systems developed by and responsible to managers outside their divisions.

CASE 10B

◀   A large international corporation headquartered in New York operates subsidiaries in several European countries. The subsidiaries have manufacturing plants, warehouses, and networks of sales outlets of their own, but they are all accountable to headquarters in New York for their performance. Over the years each of the European subsidiaries evolved its own information system— the network of reporting, communications, and data processing that seemed appropriate to its size, the country in which it operated, and the desires of the particular individuals in charge.

Headquarters in New York was concerned with the efficiency of data handling throughout the organization, because there were continual problems with late, incomplete, and inconsistent data submitted by the subsidiaries. Often requests for improved or standardized data were met with pleas that a particular subsidiary's internal data processing was in difficulty, or that the information required in its particular country differed from that needed in other countries; headquarters would be asked to settle for incompatible data. Headquarters finally decided that these excuses were not sufficiently valid, and that it would be desirable to centrally develop a data gathering and reporting system which would serve its own needs and those of all the subsidiaries. The corporation believed that the large and experienced data processing staff in

New York could design a system better than that of any of the subsidiaries, and that all would benefit from the improved information, shorter reaction times, and standardized content of reports that would result.

The managers of the subsidiaries unanimously objected. Each of them felt that in one way or another the information content of the proposed system was unsuitable for his particular company and country, and that he would lose rather than gain in the value of operating information presented to him. Several of the managers of subsidiaries that had previously used only small computers or manual data processing complained that new equipment costs would be imposed upon them, because they would have to acquire more expensive machines to perform the data collecting and processing specified in the corporate system. Finally, the subsidiaries agreed that collection and transmission of information in the quantity and form required by the corporate system would impose increased clerical burdens on their people. Salesmen would have to learn new coding systems and get used to different and more voluminous reports, more keypunch personnel would be required to prepare punched cards, new clerks would have to be hired, and present employees used to existing procedures and reports would have to learn new ones.

Not stated but suspected by corporate management, the managers of the subsidiaries also objected because the details of their operations would be more "visible" to headquarters. Any staff planner or ambitious junior manager at headquarters could anonymously examine details of the operations of any of the subsidiaries, because much more detailed information in standard and easily processed form would be available there. The managers of the subsidiaries would potentially be exposed to more detailed and frequent reviews of their operations, often without knowing that the review was taking place or having an opportunity to explain the facts or defend themselves.

Corporate management was taken aback by the vehemence and unanimity of these objections, and modified the system accordingly. It was "scaled down," and the subsidiaries were permitted more freedom to collect data as they wished for their own operations and later to convert it into the form required by headquarters. Also, many assurances were given that performance reviews would not be performed without the knowledge of the subordinate managers, and that every effort would be made to have the corporate information system respond adequately to their needs as well as to the corporation's. Having made these changes and representations, however, corporate management persevered with the project and insisted that the corporate information system go ahead. The subordinate managers, for their part, were slightly mollified by the changes that had been made but remained opposed to the corporate system. With varying degrees of resignation, though, they finally accepted it as an economic necessity. ▶

This is far from a universal reaction (though all of the subsidiary managers in this case shared it). In many organizations, managers of divisions have difficulty with their data processing, and appreciate that the kind of modern information systems they would like can be obtained only through pooling of the corporate resources. In other cases, managers feel that information systems are not so critical; that if they have a reasonable voice in specifying the functions of the system, they are quite happy to have someone else develop it for them and deal with its problems. But, unquestionably, most managers of divisions in organizations where data processing is being centralized suffer some degree of loss of authority in the process.

Sometimes the effect of the computer goes deeper; because of it, the business using it changes in unwelcome ways. Such cases are exceptional, because the information system of an organization usually plays a subordinate role; its nature is determined by factors involving the manufacturing and sale of some product or service. The information system cannot change these, and must conform to them. In some industries the procedures are less constrained and the availability of information causes them to change, though, so the computer has a greater effect. We have already seen that in the securities industry the availability of computer-based information has (apparently) expanded and changed the market. It is not too surprising to learn that the way in which the business is done, and the roles of the managers and decision makers have been significantly changed in the process.

CASE 10C

◀ Traditionally, dealers in the over the counter stock market would buy and sell as "principals," taking ownership of the securities they buy from or sell to their customers and attempting to make profits for their own accounts by selling at prices higher than they paid. For example, a dealer discovering from the activities of his customers that interest is growing in a certain stock might buy a block of it from another dealer, hoping that his customers would continue to bid its price up and that he could make a profit by reselling the stock to them. In the process he would charge his customers "what the traffic would bear"; they would defend themselves by contacting a number of dealers offering the stock, comparing prices, and taking the best.

Once over the counter stock quotations became readily available, this pattern changed. The quotations reflect the prevailing price, so all dealers and customers are equally knowledgeable. Few dealers will take the risk of deviating very much from the prevailing price (buying higher or selling lower) unless they have an unusual quantity of stock to sell, or a large order to buy. Instead, they buy or sell as the customer's "agent," executing his order at the prevailing price and charging him a commission for the service. As agent, the dealer attempts to make no profit on the transaction but charges his customer a commission comparable to the commission charged for executing an order at a stock exchange. The dealer's income is determined by the commissions earned rather than by profits made on his inventory of stocks. The pattern of "agency" business is quite different from that of "principal" business, because profits depend on volume of commissions rather than skill or luck in buying and selling. Agency firms emphasize larger numbers of customers, and employ larger numbers of less skilled people; there is less room for the small entrepreneur. The people involved emphasize different skills, and while the public interest is better protected in that the individual customer obtains the benefit of the prevailing market price, he no longer has the option of "catching" a dealer with a price out of line with another dealer, and making an extra profit in the process.

No statistics are available to show the degree of change from principal to agency operations among over the counter stock dealers, but it is generally agreed in the industry that the change has been very extensive since the appearance of public price quotes since 1965. Firms preferring agency business have grown and prospered, while those preferring principal business have been forced to change over or have been "squeezed out"—some have benefited, and some have suffered severely. This, then, is a case in which the computer's handling of information not only benefited the public (or most of it), but has changed the nature of an industry serving the public, harming many of the firms in the process. General implications of this kind of change will be explored further in Part IV. ▶

We can conclude that in some industries where the availability of information is associated with the way business is done, the positions of even the top managers are radically changed because the computer can affect the methods of doing business, the customers, and the market. The dislocation and change involved are bound to hurt many who do not take readily to the new way of doing things. There is a corresponding advantage to the new managers who are at home in the new version of the industry, but in the immediate term there is confusion, dislocation, and unhappiness.

As demonstrated in Chapter 4, there is ample proof that computers can benefit the day-to-day operations of many organizations. We saw in case after case that the computer's ability to relate all the organization's data together in assigning resources to meet demands, or in scheduling operations, makes possible much higher operating efficiency. It should follow from this that the managers of operations benefit. Because the machine has taken over much of the routine decision-making formerly associated with operations and is doing the job better, the managerial and supervisory personnel associated with operations should be pleased.

In fact, this does not necessarily happen. Many of those responsible for managing the operations of organizations spent many years learning to make accurate and rapid decisions that would efficiently allocate and schedule the organization's resources, and have difficulty adjusting to the fact that the computer has rendered these skills valueless.

CASE 10D

◀ A Navy supply center has the responsibility of providing spare parts and supplies on demand to ships working in or visiting the geographic area in which it is located. A high value is put on turnaround time, the time needed to retrieve the required items from storage and transfer them to the ship, take care of the paperwork, and permit the ship to be off again, thus clearing a berth for another ship that may be waiting. Obviously, turnaround time will be of critical importance in wartime, so it is felt important to continually practice keeping it low in peacetime.

At the same time, pressure is maintained to reduce the value of inventories maintained at the supply center. Since appropriations are limited and both the cost and range of items which have to be carried are continually increasing as weapon systems increase in complexity, every effort is made to reduce the quantities of supplies at the center to a bare minimum. This objective, of course, is in conflict with the objective of keeping turnaround time to a minimum. With low inventory levels, "stock-out" conditions are more frequent, and each "stock-out" probably requires the ship to wait while the desired item is procured from another source.

The scheduling of order filling operations and establishment of inventory levels was the responsibility of a group of senior petty officers and civil service workers, all of whom had been at the center for long periods. They had become skilled in reconciling the conflicting objectives of minimal turnaround time and minimum inventory levels, because they had learned to anticipate demand on the basis of experience and intuition. When they learned, for example, that fleet operations were scheduled in the northern part of their area, they could make educated guesses about the timing and quantity of requests for items of cold weather equipment and adjust inventory levels in anticipation of demand. Similarly, they would study transfers of ships into and out of forces operating in the area, and adjust their inventories accordingly. They felt that experience had made them very skilled at setting inventory levels and scheduling the replenishment operations for ships calling at the center, and that they were doing a good job.

A computer was installed to schedule operations, keep track of inventory levels, and originate orders for replenishment of inventories. The center's management had become convinced that its mathematical rules for scheduling would produce the highest possible efficiencies, and that its rapid handling of individual transactions would reduce turnaround time. Also, management felt that clear cause and effect relationships determined demand, so on the basis of accumulated statistics and information about ship movements and transfers, the computer was also programmed to establish desirable inventory levels. After a period of program debugging and improvement, it became evident that the computer, with its statistical rather than intuitive approach, was enabling the center to maintain its record of turnaround time (and in some cases improve it) while handling increasingly complex inventories without any increase in inventory investment.

The petty officers and civil servants that had been associated with the operation were retained—in fact, their number was increased. The increasing work load involved in handling complex electronic and missile supplies and spare parts more than offset the work taken over by the computer. Furthermore, many of their original responsibilities in areas such as physical management of materials, personnel administration, and assisting ships to determine their needs had not been affected. There was, then, no unemployment caused by the computer.

There was unquestionably a drop in morale, however, evident not only to the personnel directly affected but also to all of the center's managers including the commanding officer. The petty officers and civil servants involved in controlling operations had taken particular pride in their ability to make intuitive scheduling and inventory level decisions, and regarded these as the most important and rewarding part of the work. The remaining areas of personnel administration, customer assistance, and materials management had never been regarded as of primary significance or interest. Most of the men had spent years improving their ability to make the scheduling decisions and felt theirs was a complex art in which it took many years to become proficient. When they saw that a machine was able to do this work faster than they could, and as well or better, they suffered a severe loss of self-esteem, and their feelings were evident in their actions. They put in time rather than (as before) enthusiastically devoting themselves to doing the job as well as possible. They took up other interests, requested transfers to other jobs, retired early, and generally showed a tendency to want to leave their positions as soon as possible or to augment them with other interests. Perhaps most significant, they changed their attitude in advising promising juniors. The operations supervisors once actively sought others to follow in their footsteps. Now, when asked they would advise the juniors to look elsewhere for opportunities. ▶

Are such men members of management or merely supervisory employees? This is only a matter of definition, because in many smaller organizations, the highest position in operations still involves making day-to-day decisions in matters of detail. Regardless of the definition, such people have a difficult time adjusting to the computer's success. The computer is (if well programmed) a clear improvement, so they have no grounds on which to criticize its introduction; there is no way to soften the psychological blow of observing it performing better than they ever could the functions they spent a lifetime learning. It often develops that the incumbent manager of operations can never adjust comfortably to the new world in which the computer is making his detailed decisions. In a striking percentage of cases, the appearance of a computer to perform resource allocation and scheduling functions in operations is followed within a year or two by a change in the management of operations.

As we saw above, some managers have been disappointed because the computer turns out to be of no help to them. Others have found that a problem they thought was within its capability was, in fact, not; that intuitive as well as deterministic factors enter into the solution to the problem. These managers are disappointed by the computer's inability to exceed the limits of the mathematical and numerical procedures with which it has been equipped.

Such cases arise when the data about a situation are slow in coming, and managers feel they must make a decision and take action quickly. Sometimes they will infer the probable nature of the situation from the initial data, and will have long since committed themselves before enough data accumulate to enable the computer's rigorous mathematical logic to agree.

CASE 10E

◀ When a submarine is attempting to stalk and attack another submarine, it ordinarily wishes to remain hidden from its enemy as long as possible. It will try to run quietly, and obtain information about the enemy only by listening to the noises he makes. The direction from which the noises come is easily determined, but the attacking submarine must know more than just the direction to the target. The target's range must be known (so that the attacker may be sure he is within torpedo range and the torpedo's controls may be set appropriately) and the target's course and speed must be known (so that the torpedo can be aimed to intercept the target rather than pass behind it). It is possible to determine all these from the bearings obtained from listening to the target's noise, if a series of observations are taken over many minutes and plotted on a chart as shown in Fig. 10–1. One's own position is known, and the series of changing relative bearings to the target can be plotted. After a while, it becomes clear that only a single, constant-speed, constant-course

Set of Target Bearings Relative to Submarine

Time	2110	2113	2116	2119	2121
Bearing (degrees)	275	279	288	300	320

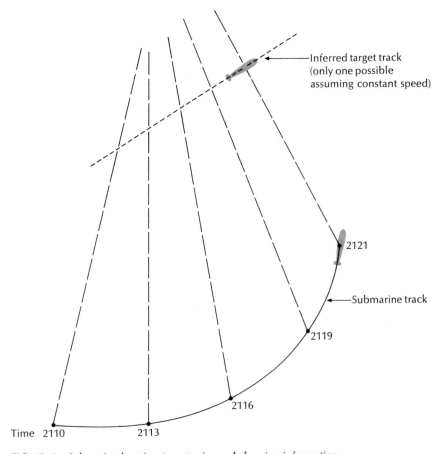

FIG. 10–1 Submarine locating target using only bearing information.

target track is consistent with all the bearings. (If the target changes course or speed, another series of bearings is needed.)

Because the precision of the solution can be improved if the computations are done arithmetically instead of graphically, and because time is of critical importance (the target may become the attacker any minute), the Navy experimented with computers that when fed the target bearing information, would produce the solution as soon as possible.

Submarine commanders generally found the computer to be of little use, despite its apparently perfect applicability to the problem. Surprisingly enough, the computer was too slow. Its mathematical program required a certain number of bearings showing a certain rate of change before it could produce a satisfactory solution. The submarine commanders, receiving and plotting the same data, could make educated guesses. They could guess from the sound of the target's propellers what kind of ship it was and approximately at what speed it was moving, then change course to obtain a bearing that would test the hypothesis. They could guess whether it changed speed or course based on changes in the target's sound, and again alter their own course. These judgments were imprecise, and so could not be programmed into the computer. With their help, however, the submarine commanders could become reasonably certain about the target's position, course, and speed, and set and fire their torpedoes many minutes before the computer could provide a completely certain mathematical solution. Desperately anxious to fire his torpedos as soon as possible (before being fired at), every commander would fire on the basis of educated guesswork rather than wait for the additional bearings needed to produce a perfect solution. The computer, being unable to guess or establish hypotheses that could be tested by maneuvering, was inevitably slower (and therefore useless). Despite the purely mathematical nature of this problem, then, the computer was unsuited to it. ▶

In many an apparently precise, logical problem there is more intuition and human judgment than meets the eye, especially if there is pressure to take action before perfect or complete data become available. In such cases, the computer can be much slower than the manager.

We saw that the computer makes possible management by exception, the identification by preprogrammed rules of exceptional and unusual conditions, which are the only ones normally reported to management. This is often implemented as *responsibility accounting,* in which profit centers are established in the organization and each manager is given full responsibility for his profit center. Only deviations from the pre-established profit plan will call corporate attention down upon him; otherwise he is free to run his activity as he sees fit. This is a desirable principle in many respects and has attracted many organizations. However, it contains some potential pitfalls that can actively harm the managers involved.

Case 5J spoke of an electric utility company which had adopted responsibility accounting and whose top management were very happy with it. However, the case also described the plight of a maintenance supervisor, who in trying to play by the rules and not be penalized for exceeding his budget, did what he knew was an inferior job. Rather than deviate from his budget by spending additional funds to provide the company with a sound facility when an unexpected construction condition arose, he arranged to meet the original budget by doing a marginal job though he knew it would be necessary to repeat the work within a few years. This man was resentful of a system that forced him to take short-sighted action, but felt that he had no choice because the system of rewards was centered around meeting or bettering the established profit targets, and doing poorly (and having the attention of management called to one's activity) invariably meant censure.

He was probably wrong, of course. Surely his management would have preferred him to approach them with a justification for exceeding his budget, and they would probably have authorized the exception and thought highly of him for appreciating its necessity. Unfortunately, in many organizations subordinate managers are not sufficiently close to top management to understand their motives or anticipate how they will react to a situation. Subordinates often feel that they must protect themselves by hewing to the line and obeying the established rules. When these rules are based on numerical measures of performance (as they invariably are in computer-based responsibility accounting systems), subordinate managers tend to exaggerate the importance of the numbers more than management intended. They attempt to find ways of beating the system, and often succeed by artificial tricks such as transferring overhead charges to other profit centers, postponing capital expenditures, or arranging to be credited with an unfair share of a revenue item which must be divided arbitrarily among several participating profit centers. Such attention to sterile political and accounting tricks can do the organization nothing but harm. At best, it diverts the manager's attention from the real work of the organization. At worst, it creates dissension among the subordinate managers and an entirely false impression of the state of affairs in the minds of the top managers. Management by exception is a two-edged sword, then, because arbitrary or erroneous definition of the measurement rules can cause active harm to the organization by inducing managers to concentrate on them rather than on the interests of the organization.

EMPLOYEES

Clerical employees are frequently displaced by computers that take over their jobs. It follows that clerical employees should be among those who suffer most because of the computer, but this has not generally proven to be true. Two forces have alleviated or prevented this suffering.

First, almost every organization has relatively high clerical turnover as the young women who make up most of the clerical force get married, change jobs for reasons of personal preference, become pregnant, or for other reasons leave their present jobs. Clerical force replacement rates of 20% per year are regarded as low, and in some organizations they run as high as 50% per year. When a computer system is introduced that will take over the jobs of existing clerks, it usually takes two or more years to reach full operation. During that time normal attrition among the previously employed clerks is almost invariably enough to accomplish the reduction in force the computer will accomplish. Second, throughout the "age of the computer" most organizations have experienced such an increase in the complexity and quantity of clerical work that few have been able to reduce their total clerical force even with the help of the computer. The chairman of a giant New York bank says,* "Not a single person has lost his job because of automation" in his bank; indeed, he observes that the bank employs more clerks now than it did before it had computers. He feels that the computer has no more than enabled banks to maintain their clerical growth at a reasonable rate and says, "Without automation to handle the twenty billion checks that will come flooding into U.S. banks by 1970, bankers would have to hire every American woman between the ages of 21 and 45." Many other similar statements could be cited: the most obvious possibility for clerical suffering, displacement from jobs because of the computer, does not appear to be significant.

On the other hand, some more subtle effects of the computer have caused clerical workers associated with it to feel that they have been harmed. Machines do not work at the tempo of humans. A computer can be run continuously for nearly twenty-four hours per day, seven days per week, but cannot speed up. A human can hurry, but cannot work many more hours than he would under normal conditions—especially if he is hurrying. It can be very frustrating for a clerk anxious to hurry in order to meet a heavy work load to be forced to continue working at the usual pace because the computer cannot speed up, but to be asked to stay six or eight hours overtime in order to get all the work done (while knowing that perhaps two hours overtime would have been enough if the work were done manually and an increase in speed was possible). The machine's tempo becomes most irritating when it is providing real-time support to clerks or customer representatives, because real-time systems slow down as work increases. Airline ticket agents, for example, must await the computer's reply to inquiries they make about reservations for passengers. At rush hours, when long lines of passengers are standing at each ticket agent's position, the number of inquiries to the computer increases. Because its processing speed remains constant, waiting lines of unanswered inquiries develop and the ticket agent is required to wait longer at the very time when fast answers would be of the greatest value. At off

---

* George Champion, Chairman, The Chase Manhattan Bank, N.A., *Automation, Capital and Economic Growth*, published by Chase Manhattan Bank.

hours (when business is slack) the computer can provide instant service, but then it matters less. It has been noted* that under such conditions the frustrated human tends to uselessly re-enter his query time and again, even though he knows re-entry is useless. He nevertheless finds it an outlet for his frustrations, because the computer's response to peak loads is exactly the opposite of what the employee would like to see.

The clerical worker also seems to suffer from anxiety when she knows her work will be fed to a computer rather than to another clerk for further manual processing. She somehow feels that the machine's icy intolerance of error or deviation from established procedure provides a subtle form of pressure on her; she worries more about precision and accuracy than when she deals with humans who either adapt to her deviations from procedure or politely (rather than formally, through her supervisor) call errors to her attention. There is no easy way of knowing whether this anxiety reaction is general or simply occasional, but the author's experience indicates that a significant percentage of clerks feel that their jobs are less pleasant now that computers are associated with them.

While the computer rarely causes firings or layoffs of clerical workers, the same cannot be said of clerical supervisors. The supervisor is probably settled in her or his job, and has neither the wish nor the opportunity to move readily to another. The particular function the supervisor is responsible for may not exist in any other organization or may be obsolete everywhere, but it may be all that the supervisor has learned in the course of his career. Turnover in supervisory positions is far lower than turnover in the clerical positions supervised, and cannot be expected to accomplish reductions in force levels.

When a computer takes over a major clerical function of a large organization, entire clerical units may be done away with and the positions of the supervisors of those units, so the problem of supervisor displacement is fairly common. Sometimes parts of the supervisor's job remain but usually (as we saw in Case 10D) not enough to prevent the supervisor from feeling severely injured. Often nothing of the original job remains, and the organization is faced with the problem of dealing fairly with a loyal, long-time employee whose skills are absolutely useless either to itself or to any other organization.

Organizations take various approaches to this problem. Retraining for other jobs is immediately thought of, of course, and sometimes works. But veteran clerical supervisors are often slow to learn entirely new areas of work and find it difficult to adjust to the reduction of responsibility that inevitably goes with transferring to a new area. Sometimes early retirement can be ar-

---

* Harold Sackman, *Computers, System Science, and Evolving Society,* Wiley, New York, 1967.

ranged for older supervisors, though complications can arise from the nature of existing retirement plans, union agreements, and the like. The supervisor can simply be fired, usually with a large "conscience bonus" intended to make all parties feel better about it. Most managements will avoid this at almost all costs, however, and keep veteran supervisors even in essentially useless "make-work" jobs; the reputation for replacing loyal veterans by machines capriciously and on short notice is one they simply cannot bear to establish— either in the employees' minds or in their own.

Where supervision of production facilities is performed by the computer, a similar displacement of veteran supervisors occurs but it is less severe, because (as we have seen) a need continues for experienced human surveillance over the "automated" operations. In production-oriented activities supervisors are often members of unions too, and seniority helps them. Junior employees are "bumped" according to existing seniority agreements, and the supervisor keeps his job while a younger (and hopefully more mobile) employee loses his. However, these factors only blunt the blow; the fact remains that the obsolete supervisor is one of the classes of people most adversely affected by the computer, and as the application of computers to operations spreads this problem is likely to worsen.

Certain classes of skilled operating employees are also subject to replacement by the computer. Usually these are not the employees who handle the direct tools of production: as Case 1H and Case 9G illustrated, the totally computer-controlled production operation is still a rarity and nearly the same number of skilled operators is still required both to perform parts of the production function and to monitor the automated ones (performing lubrication, changing tools, and correcting malfunctions). However, when operating employees deal with information rather than directly with the tools of production the computer is more of a threat to their jobs.

CASE 10F

◀ When a ship is designed, a process called "lofting" must be performed. Put in its simplest terms, lofting is the process of converting the naval architect's design into the detailed drawings needed to tell the shipyard exactly how to cut and assemble all the structural parts. During the lofting operations thousands of blueprints are developed for the individual plates and structural members of the ship. Hundreds of thousands of elementary calculations have to be performed to determine the thicknesses and shapes of metal to be used, and thousands of details must be considered such as the locations and sizes of holes in interior plates and bulkheads for the lines carrying electrical wiring, steam, cold and hot water, and air. The lofting operation involves relatively simple calculations and routine decision-making, yet the complexity of a large ship is so great that tens of thousands of man hours of labor are involved.

The U.S. Navy Ship Systems Command has for several years been supporting the development of procedures for performing the lofting process automatically by computer. The thought is that a computer could be provided with a description of the naval architect's plan for the ship. Suitably equipped with programs for computing stresses and for making the geometric calculations and decisions needed to produce drawings, the computer could then perform the lofting. The computer can operate plotting boards to produce the engineering drawings to be given the shipyard, but it might even go a step further. If the shipyard is equipped (as many are by now) with numerically controlled metal cutting tools that work from punched paper tapes, perhaps the operation of preparing scale drawings for the plates can be completely done away with, and the shipyard can be provided only with small drawings for human review plus the paper tapes to directly operate the shipyard's metal cutting machinery. Additional savings would result, because one of the most expensive parts of the lofting process is drafting. Thousands of hours are spent simply producing drawings after the design is complete.

If this project is successful, the Navy will be able to obtain ship designs much more quickly and at far less cost than ever before. However, hundreds (pernaps thousands) of specialized low-level engineers and draftsmen will be permanently displaced because the computer will, at one stroke, have eliminated all the jobs in their field. ▸

This displacement of draftsmen may occur in other industries too, because numerically controlled machine tools are coming into widespread use. As they do so the development of increasingly sophisticated computer programs for producing the control tapes continues. If the time comes when the designer of a mechanical product can transmit his design directly to the machine tool with the computer's help and leave records of the design stored only in the computer, then the engineering drawing will become largely obsolete. The tens of thousands of drafting positions now existing throughout industry will then be greatly reduced in number, and no comparable positions are evolving anywhere else.

The displacement of draftsmen has not occurred yet; it is still conjectural. A similar class of skilled operating employees who deal primarily with information are the operators of typesetting machines, and their displacement has already occurred. For a number of years computer programs have been available that can perform the typesetting function at much higher speed and lower cost than humans. The computer systems for this purpose are steadily improving, lately through the development of computer output devices that can produce finished pages of book quality text for direct transfer from cathode-ray tube displays to lithographic reproduction plates. The introduction of these computer-based typesetting systems has been slowed by typesetters' unions which have acted to protect their members' jobs. They have in many cases successfully negotiated agreements with publishers to retain typesetters on the payroll, or to make payments to the union for the members' benefit, that reduce the impact of the sudden dislocation. Over time, however, the trend is inexorable; there are already fewer typesetting jobs available than there were before the computer was introduced, despite a great increase in the total number of printed documents produced.

To summarize, groups of employees such as veteran supervisors and practitioners of operating skills that are performed better by the computer have been badly hurt by it. However, these groups probably do not include a great number of people; by and large, the major displacements in clerical and production operations have involved a change rather than a reduction in the total number of jobs available. Perhaps more pervasive, though less demonstrable, is the harm caused by the computer to the employees who work with it and are supposed to benefit from it: the clerks who work within computer-based systems or who obtain information from them.

SCIENTISTS AND ENGINEERS

In Chapter 9 it was observed that scientists have been among the prime beneficiaries of the computer. The benefit is not without exceptions, though; there are cases where using a computer has misled or hindered the scientist in his work. Its use to simulate experiments that are not actually performed can lead to systematic error. If false assumptions are built into the computer program performing the simulation or if faulty mathematical relationships are incorporated, the results (though consistent with the simulation model) may be completely inaccurate. Too much reliance on simulation without experiments that would show the scientist he has made false assumptions can lead to false results and wasted work.

CASE 10G

◀ For many years astrophysicists have been studying the processes by which new stars are formed in condensing interstellar dust clouds. Since it is obviously impossible to set up laboratory experiments that duplicate the formation of stars, the concentration has been on theoretical mathematical investigations of the process. One approach has been to establish mathematical relationships that describe the actions of cosmic dust clouds under the influences of gravity and other forces, and to simulate their actions over millions of years at high speed with a computer. An orderly series of events takes place in the mathematical model: condensation of the gas, progressive heating, and eventual initiation of the thermonuclear reaction of the young star. A broad correlation was established between these theoretical models and observation of the conditions existing in young stars, and it began to appear to many astrophysicists that the computer models had led to a complete understanding of the process of star formation.

During the 1950's the attention of astrophysicists began to be focused on a class of stars called "T Tauri stars" (named after the identifying symbol of the first of the class discovered). More than one thousand T Tauri stars have now been detected in the galaxy, so they must be considered a relatively common type of young star. These stars, apparently still in the process of approaching a stable condition, turned out not to fit the model. They have extremely active and luminous atmospheres, they eject massive quantities of surface material, and they vary widely in brightness; none of these effects are predicted by the mathematical models of star formation. The processes involved are still a "complete mystery."* Apparently some oversimplifications have been built into the present models of star evolution, or some of the processes that occur during star formation are completely unknown (and, naturally, not included in the models). If the T Tauri stars had not been discovered, if the discrepancies between their actions and those predicted by the stellar evolution models had not been noted, astrophysicists might have been misled for many years into thinking that the process of stellar evolution was fully understood, that the computer models could be expected to reliably predict the series of events that occurs during the formation of any star. ▶

The computer may mislead the scientist or engineer by fostering overreliance upon it. We have seen that techniques based on the use of the computer, loosely grouped under the term "system analysis," have been very useful in complex engineering development and production projects including military weapons systems (such as the Polaris missile system) and aircraft and space vehicle development. Many scientists and engineers whose careers have been associated with these programs have come to rely on system analysis techniques, and on the computer to support the techniques. When these scientists attempt to attack problems in different fields, they naturally tend to believe that the techniques they have found useful before will be applicable again.

The attention of the day is focused on sociological and economic problems of urban blight, ghettos, transportation systems, and welfare programs. Many of the organizations that have been effective in technological areas are

---

* George H. Herbig, "The Youngest Stars," *Scientific American*, August 1967.

attacking these problems, and numerous government and industrial leaders have spoken of the advantages to be expected from applying system analysis techniques to these sociological and economic problems. It may be that there will be such advantages. In at least some areas (such as transportation, where statistical models can be completely accurate) these techniques may be very useful. However, one may legitimately question the degree to which computer-based, quantitative system analysis can be applied to problems of human society, which ultimately are fundamentally spiritual. It seems likely that some of those familiar with the usefulness of the system analysis approach but less familiar with its limitations may have overrepresented its ability to solve socioeconomic problems.

There is one respect in which all scientists and engineers unquestionably suffer to some degree: in the desperate struggle they must make to keep up with the pace of change. As we saw in Chapter 3, there are many reasons for the headlong rush of innovation and introduction of new techniques, but the computer is at the root of many of them and is a legitimate symbol of the continuous change and evolution of techniques. Scientists whose results and ways of arriving at them were the focus of attention yesterday now find themselves obsolete because new techniques with which they are unfamiliar have led to new results. Engineers suffer even more, because often their careers are based on the use of design methods they learned in school, and which are known to produce satisfactory and safe products because of generations of experience. Now that revolutionary computer-based design techniques have appeared which make possible more efficient and economical designs, the older engineers are in a quandary. If they adopt the new techniques (assuming they have enough mental flexibility and retain enough learning ability to do so), they will have joined the "new wave" and will be able to produce better designs. However, they will no longer have complete confidence that their designs have adequate safety factors and are able to respond satisfactorily to unexpected conditions.

Herman Kahn of the Hudson Institute* has spoken of the computer as a force causing "knowledge turnover." He selected as an example the computer industry itself where (he says) engineering knowledge must be reevaluated and upgraded at least every two years. He observes that peak salary is reached when engineers are thirty-one or thirty-two years old, and that unless they move into administration, salaries subsequently decrease. This anomalous situation surely results in unhappiness for the "aging" engineers of thirty-five and over who find themselves already obsolete.

---

* *Electronic News,* January 1968.

Whether the pace of innovation in engineering and science is too fast or too slow does not concern us here. It is sufficient to note the suffering, dislocation, and extra effort required of scientists and engineers simply to maintain themselves current in the area they once thought they understood, and the computer's role in causing it.

THE PUBLIC

The most obvious form of public suffering attributable to the computer occurs when a computer-based information system on which the public is dependent breaks down. It may break down because of mechanical failure, though usually the system's designers will have provided backup equipment so mechanical failure rarely causes much difficulty. A more common source of failure is inadequate programming, the failure to take into account all the exceptions or special conditions that will arise. When the system and the organization employing it are unprepared to deal with all situations, the public can suffer and the individual who is the exception may find himself attempting to correspond with a system that persistently misclassifies his problem. Most of us have our personal experiences with such situations; Case 2F, a possibly exaggerated description of an impoverished old lady being mistreated by a computer, can represent them all. Such difficulties arise from human failings, of course; failure of the system's human designers to anticipate the special cases and provide for them either in the computer's programs or by clerical procedures.

A source of public distress more directly associated with the nature of the computer is the frequent failure of the computer-based information systems when overloaded. As was noted before, computers cannot speed up when peak loads are experienced; they can simply be run longer. In an economically managed installation computers will normally run 100 hours per week or more, so the reserve capacity to deal with unexpected loads may be very small. Human-based systems can be augmented by adding more people or by simply asking the existing people to work faster and longer until the peak is eliminated. Sometimes additional computers can be added to augment computer-based systems too, but often the job cannot be divided between two machines because it is designed for step-by-step processing by one (i.e., a given program requires as input the output of another program). In such cases the organization employing the computer can find itself helplessly falling behind in its data processing without seeing any easy solution short of reprogramming the work load for a large machine or for multiple machines.

CASE 10H

◀ During the 1967 to 1968 period the securities industry experienced a tremendous growth in trading volume which overloaded most firms' data processing facilities. The author's own experience is apparently typical. After ten years of association with a large securities firm during which time his accounts were handled perfectly, he experienced increasing difficulty during late 1967 and early 1968. Confirmations of securities purchases and sales came more and more slowly, but the firm nevertheless continued to insist on payment for purchases within four days of the trade date. Finally confirmations stopped coming altogether; special efforts were needed to obtain "duplicate" confirmations for originals that had never existed. Receipts for documents and payments for securities sold slowed down to such a degree that follow-up requests were invariably required to obtain them, often with two or three weeks extra delay. Statements showing the status of accounts, usually received regularly on a monthly basis, became erratic and stopped altogether for three months. At this point the author's confidence was sufficiently shaken that he requested certificates for the securities held for him by the firm, and then waited eight weeks before they appeared.

The cause of this is clear. The large securities firm with which the author dealt had committed itself to the use of a relatively large computer for its routine data handling, and had allowed what it considered a reasonable safety margin of extra capacity to handle peak loads. The activity during 1967 and 1968 far outgrew the safety margin provided, so the machine fell behind in its processing. It could catch up only when light trading days or holidays occurred, and by postponing less essential work such as statement preparation indefinitely. There was no way for the firm to augment the machine's capacity except by preparing new system designs and programs for a larger machine or multiple machines, because the processing was so arranged that each successive program had to await the completion of the preceding one. Thus, the author (and apparently other customers of the securities firm) suffered until an entirely new computer-based system could be designed and installed to cope with the extreme increase in activity. ▶

According to many authorities the public will suffer when personal data (e.g., income tax, credit, and police records) become centralized in computer files and too readily available. An invasion of privacy issue has been raised on the basis that individuals are entitled to confidential treatment of personal data about themselves and assurance that this data will not be released to individuals or organizations not specifically entitled to it by law. It is feared, for example, that if an individual's arrest record becomes available to a credit bureau, or if his credit rating becomes available to a potential employer, irrelevant or misinterpreted information may be misused to the individual's detriment. In many cases unfavorable entries in such records can be explained by the individual or eradicated after the legal need for them has passed. But if the records are permanently stored in computer files, the individual may not receive a chance to explain them, or an opportunity to either review the records or initiate permissible changes to them.

Much of this personal data is already stored in computers. Various organizations such as credit bureaus, the Internal Revenue Service, the Social Security and Veterans Administrations, large metropolitan police departments, the Federal Bureau of Investigation, and many other agencies have computer-based files containing quantities of personal data. These files are scattered at present, usually well protected from inquiry from individuals outside the organization, and in any case accessible only with difficulty and expense because of the inflexibility of current computer systems (an ill wind that blows public good!). The files are stored in incompatible codes and media, and no general efforts have yet been made to bring these files together, considering the immense cost of converting them into standardized form. A federal data bank has been proposed* but so far it is only a concept and has been much criticized by the Congress. It can probably be stated that little new loss of privacy, little new public suffering has occurred because of centralized, computer-based personal files. The worry is for the future, though, as the files grow and the machines become easier to use; the possibility of future public suffering is a very real one which must be considered carefully. The future possibilities are treated in Part IV. For the moment, it is sufficient to conclude that increased availability of personal data caused by the computer has not yet resulted in general public suffering, though individual instances may well have occurred.

SUMMARY

It is interesting to observe that most of the categories of individuals who can be shown to have suffered because of the computer—managers, employees, scientists and engineers, the public—are the very same categories of individuals who were shown in the previous chapter to have benefited from it. The hypothesis begins to emerge that the computer is an unalloyed blessing to very few individuals and, conversely, an unalloyed evil to very few. To most, it seems to represent a package of new opportunities and new constraints, offering powerful new freedoms and methods combined with a loss of old flexibilities and a group of new problems. This hypothesis will be explored in Part IV,

---

* Alan F. Westin, *Privacy and Freedom*, Atheneum, New York, 1967.

in which the evolving pattern of opportunities and constraints will be projected into the immediate future, and the resulting effect on the next generation of individuals and organizations using computers will be assessed. Regardless of what the future may bring, it is already clear that the organization using computers will encounter a mixed pattern of gains and losses. Its management must be prepared to exercise wisdom and care if the net gain is to to be maximized.

Part IV | THE NEXT GENERATION

CHAPTER 11

CONCESSIONS DEMANDED BY THE COMPUTER

"Each man must learn how to give up his own particular way of doing things, adapt his methods to the many new standards and grow accustomed to receiving and obeying directions covering details, large and small, which in the past have been left to his individual judgment."*
F. W. TAYLOR

In Parts II and III of this book the effects computers have had on the organizations and individuals using them were reviewed. Computers have been in use for more than fifteen years but many of these effects have only recently begun to become apparent, and will probably develop much further in the future. This enables us to predict with confidence at least some parts of the unfolding pattern of the computer's effects, and of the changes it will cause. This prediction should provide useful guidance to the manager of the organization using computers, and to the individual working with or dependent on it.

The process of change takes time. The constraints on the rate of change derive from human and organizational inertia—a combination of rational and unrational reasons why decisions to discard old methods and adopt new ones may be delayed after the new method is perfected. Probably the effects of the computer that we can predict with confidence will take many years to develop to their full; another fifteen years may well be required. In fifteen years an entire new generation of professional people, managers, and employees will have emerged, and an entire new generation of organizations (or changes to existing organizations) will have appeared.

This and the following two chapters are devoted to exploring the logical extrapolations to their complete form of the effects of the computer that we have identified in the preceding chapters. No attempt is made to speak of the further future or to discuss the possible effects of hypothetical new develop-

---

* F. W. Taylor, *Shop Management*, Harper, New York, 1919.

ments in technology; even these will probably take an entire generation of individuals and organizations to become fully realized after they appear.

We have explored the limitations of the computer and the negative effects and harmful changes it has caused in the organizations and individuals associated with it, so we can understand the concessions that those who choose to live with the computer must make. This chapter will discuss these concessions, these modifications of behavior which the next generation will have to make in order to live with the increasingly pervasive computer, and to manage organizations in which it is increasingly important.

INDIVIDUALS IN PRIVATE LIFE

As uses of the computer expand and as private citizens encounter it increasingly in their affairs, they will apparently have to make certain concessions to it. A well-established concession which continues to irritate many of us is the requirement that we "become a number." Because of the difficulties machines (and, for that matter, people) have in dealing with individual names and addresses in full alphabetic form, machine-based information systems have for years required that individual customers, accounts, employees, etc., be identified by numbers. All of us wish to retain and emphasize our identities as individuals, so this symbol of depersonalization is naturally unwelcome. It would be nice if developments in computer technology or in computer programs offered hope that this situation would change, that in the future the information systems with which we must deal could "recognize" us as personalities rather than by impersonal symbols. Apparently this will never happen, though, because problems of separating similar or identical names and addresses (distinguishing children from their parents and the like) cannot be solved by man or machine unless other information is given. If "John Smith" and "John Smith, Jr." live at the same address and if John Smith, Jr. forgets to append the "Jr." to his name when he, say, applies for an insurance policy, neither a human nor a machine at the insurance company could avoid sending his mail to his father. Whenever individuals deal with machine-based systems, then, they must be willing to adopt impersonal but completely unambiguous identifying codes to avoid error and become resigned to "becoming a number." Since we may presume that individuals will deal with machine-based systems more frequently in the future, it is to be expected that individuals will encounter this necessity and be forced to make this concession more often.

Actually, though, the individual may find this concession less burdensome in the coming years. In the past, information systems have grown up independently of one another and in each identifying numbers were assigned to individuals as the system's designers saw fit. As the individual deals with more and more systems there are more and more numbers which he must be ready to provide, either through memorizing them or being able to retrieve some document on which the number is recorded. For most of us the number of different codes or identifying symbols by which we are known has become ridiculously large, and after using them for a period of years we are apt to have memorized a formidable list of such numbers.

CASE 11A

◀ The author deals with (probably) an average number of computer-based information systems, more than some individuals, less than others. He has not memorized most of his identifying codes; most are needed infrequently enough so that it is more convenient to find a document containing the number. In some cases, the number is never needed except in association with a document containing it (e.g., a utility bill stub). However, some of the numbers referring to him are used so frequently that he has memorized them. Those immediately coming to mind are:

> 2996
> 01742
> 185–274
> 820–20888
> 579–38–1670
> 558502–1615
> 617–369–5101
> 550–96–96–6
> 617–864–5770–530

The above numbers all refer to the author in one connection or another, and identify him to one information system or another. Most individuals have probably memorized approximately as many numbers that refer to themselves. ▶

Different systems are, of course, concerned with different facts: the geographical location to which a piece of mail should be sent, the telephone terminals that should be interconnected, the identity of an individual paying a tax, claiming a benefit, or charging a purchase. Nevertheless, more numbers are assigned to individuals than are necessary, and it would be in the interest of all parties to standardize numbering systems and reduce the number of different ones. Such standardization is already occurring. For example, Social Security numbers assigned to individuals are already used by the Internal Revenue Service and recommended by the American Bankers Association for identification of credit card holders. Many other organizations also make use of the Social Security number; it seems a foregone conclusion that it will become the standard individual identifier. Similarly, since the Post Office Department instituted Zip Codes they are increasingly used by industrial firms to identify localities within which street names are unambiguous.

In the future, then, we will unquestionably (and unfortunately) be required to identify ourselves by number even more frequently than now, but there is every likelihood that a few numbers will suffice for all identifications, and that the great number of unrelated codes now assigned to an individual will be reduced to a more manageable group. This will be a convenience to him and to the organizations whose computer systems deal with him. Whether the individual will become any more "depersonalized" by this process is debatable. Perhaps so, but it is certainly reasonable to think that an individual who can be depersonalized by a process so superficial as using a code must be a shallow individual indeed.

One of the reasons for installing computer-based information systems is to save personnel costs by reducing the numbers of employees involved in simple, routine tasks. Among these tasks are customer contact functions such as selling tickets, collecting tolls, taking orders, and making reservations. If such transactions are simple and routine, both parties can benefit from having the customer transact his business directly with the machine that keeps the records. If he knows just what he wants and his primary objective is immediate service, often the machine can provide this more effectively than a human. (When such operations involve exceptions, requests for consideration of special cases, or simply the straightening out of confusion, human employees of the organization offering the service must and will be provided to deal with the customer.)

As computer programs become more flexible and capable, we can therefore expect to see human customers being asked to deal more frequently with the machines. This is to the customers' benefit because they receive more responsive service at (hopefully) lower cost than before, but the individual must make concessions because he must learn to communicate with the machine on its own terms. As we have seen in previous chapters, computers are unable to use language in the loose, symbolic, evocative sense that humans automatically do. Computers are also unable to perceive relationships not previously incorporated in their programs, or to work at the preferred tempo of human activity. Apparently none of these limitations of computers is about to ease in any fundamental way, at least during the next generation. It appears that it is the human who will have to modify his behavior, who will have to learn to adapt his language to that of a programmed machine and to adapt his preferred tempo to that of the machine. This is not a function of rank or station; it applies equally to an organization's President and to its least important clerk or customer.

Does this mean that private individuals will have to become computer programmers? Certainly not in the sense that computer programming is a highly skilled profession involving a great deal of theoretical knowledge about how computers work. But we have seen that programs for particular applications of computers can be so designed that commands can be given to them in terms close to the English language. Case 2D, for example, discussed an information retrieval program which required the operator to know nothing except how to operate a few buttons. The terms the operator could use to structure questions at various levels of abstraction were displayed by the machine in increasingly specific order, and the operator had only to select the appropriate terms to identify the data he wanted the machine to retrieve from its file. Such computer programs that guide the human in phrasing his questions in terms the machine can "understand" have a very interesting future potential, and can probably be applied widely. For example, if a human is dealing directly with a computer to obtain a ticket to a baseball game, all he may need to know in advance is that he should push the button marked "tickets to baseball games." At that point, the machine will display schedule information and ask him to specify the date he prefers, then display the choice of seats and prices available for his decision. The machine will require nothing of him but selections between alternatives it offers, plus a few specific facts such as date and credit card number. In dealing with such a system, the human needs to have learned something about how to communicate with machines, but does not have to be skilled in programming.

There is ample evidence that humans can and will make the concession of learning machine language when it is in their interest. In using the telephone system, for example, all of us have learned how to program a complex data processing machine using a variety of commands.

CASE 11B

◀ At his place of employment, the author has telephone service typical of that available in most offices. In the course of using the telephone to place a variety of long-distance, personal, and business calls, he has learned to issue the following variety of commands to the telephone system:

1   Signal to secretary (intercom button).

2   Signal to another extension within the building (dial the extension).

3   Signal the company operator for placing calls to be billed to clients (dial "O").

4   Connect the telephone to outside line (dial "9").

5   Signal any telephone within local calling area (dial number after obtaining outside line).

6   Signal any telephone with the regional area code but outside the local calling area (after obtaining outside line, dial "1" and then the telephone number).

7   Signal any telephone within the direct distance dialing system (obtain outside line, dial "1," dial area code, dial telephone number).

8   Signal the information operator in any city (obtain outside line, dial "1," dial area code, dial "411").

9   Place credit card call (obtain outside line, dial "O," dial area code and telephone number, be prepared to orally repeat previously memorized credit card number on demand).

Probably most businessmen are familiar with all of these procedures and sometimes others, and almost every private individual in the country is familiar with at least some of them.   ▶

Many computer programming languages include no more different kinds of commands than these, and many computer users have learned nothing more complex than these requirements of the telephone system. Most future computer-based information systems with which the private individual will have to deal will probably be equally simple, so it can be expected that the public will be able to understand them.

Will humans be willing to take the trouble? Humans have been willing, by and large, to learn how to issue commands to the telephone system. There was resistance to learning how to use the direct distance dialing system, but by the simple expedient of reducing the rate if the subscriber uses direct distance dialing, the telephone company has obtained almost universal compliance. We can expect that the next generation of private individuals will also learn the languages of whatever information systems they find advantageous to use, particularly individuals who have grown up with computers as familiar tools of education and the home. This is even more true of managers whose jobs can be done better with the computer's help. Time and effort—concessions —will, however, be involved in learning these languages.

In most cases, the machine language which the individual must be prepared to "speak" is that of the keyboard; he will depress keys on a telephone or a special keyboard to instruct the computer. Technology may make possible variations such as the use of a finger-touch on a TV tube screen to select one of a list of choices displayed on the screen, or direct communication by voice between the human and the computer. Of course, we will not see computers conversing in free language with humans (at least not in the next generation). In Chapter 2 we saw that even when computers appear to accept commands in human language, they are really accepting only symbols with meanings far more restricted than their meanings to humans. Within this limitation, though, technology already makes it possible for machines to distinguish certain specific sounds from one another, including specially inflected versions of the ten digits plus a few other syllables which the machine is able to separate from all others regardless of the accent or pitch of the particular voice. We may find private individuals being asked to learn such a spoken machine language, a set of ten to twenty specific sounds which the machine will recognize. These sounds will be related to words, but will have only the specific meanings associated with the information system.

In the process of learning machine languages, individuals must learn at least a little about computers; the next generation will have to take more trouble to understand the strengths and weaknesses of computers than their predecessors did. In this respect, they will be making a concession. They will have to learn yet another complex technical subject in addition to all those the private individual of today is expected to know. This may not be as serious a concession as it sounds, however, because little special study may be needed. The process of "growing up" with computers as part of the environment may automatically provide the needed education. Already the average educated person understands more about computers than he did ten years ago, usually not because he has made any special effort to become familiar with them but simply because he has run across them frequently in his reading about current events or business matters, and he has encountered them in his dealings with organizations providing services to him. The manager, particularly, has been encountering computers increasingly frequently.

If computers become widespread tools of education, the familiarization of the average man with them will be greatly accelerated, and it seems inevitable that programmed teaching (probably using computers to a considerable degree) will be in widespread use within a few years. Our exploration of this subject in Chapter 2 indicated that the primary uncertainty is over the degree and timing of computer assisted instruction, not over its possibility.

But if children at impressionable ages are forced to work with computers during their education, is it not possible that their individuality may be stifled, that they may become so used to obeying the rules of a programmed machine that they become little more than programmed machines themselves? The answer to this question seems clear: it is summed up effectively by a question and answer taken from an interview with a professor who has been using computers in a college course.*

---

* John G. Kemeny, "Education," *The General Electric Forum*, General Electric Company, Winter 1967–1968.

Question: "There has been much said and written about the machine taking over and people becoming just numbers. Would you care to comment on this?"

Answer: "In freshman class last year I read a quotation indicating just this fear. Completely unexpectedly, the entire class broke into uproarious laughter. Suddenly I realized that here were students who had all sat at a computer teletype. They knew not only what was right, but what was wrong with computers. There was no question in their minds as to who was boss and who was slave."

If those who work with computers are going to become depersonalized and mechanical, surely some of the tens of thousands of computer programmers who have spent as much as fifteen years working with the machines should show these effects. Most of us are acquainted with some computer programmers, and surely we would agree that few of them have become depersonalized and mechanical. In fact, as a group they tend (in the author's judgment) to be the opposite: a generally highly cultured, interesting group of people with as much interest in artistic, social, political, and family matters as any other group with a corresponding educational and economic background. More evidence could be cited, but it is probably not necessary to belabor the point further. He who would maintain that those who work with computers become like computers themselves has to be one who has never associated with such people.

It is undeniably true, however, that the discipline imposed by the computer affects the people who are exposed to it. Computer people learn "systems thinking," as we saw in Chapter 7. They develop an ability to think in terms of processes and systems and learn to solve problems in analytic and methodical ways. One finds computer people using flow charts to express travel directions, or everyday procedures such as starting a car in cold weather. So, while we concluded that the computer does not have the superficial effect of making people act like it, it nevertheless subtly influences their mental attitudes by enforcing an analytical and logical discipline upon their thinking. Previously, only scientific or engineering training included such discipline. As this discipline of systems thinking spreads beyond computer technicians to managers and professionals of all kinds, a larger percentage of private individuals will be included. As all children become exposed in some degree to this influence during their educations, it will become more or less universal. Is it a bad influence? Perhaps not; perhaps an improvement in the mental discipline of the average individual may be entirely to the good. On the other hand, this system of discipline certainly requires a degree of change and at least a moderate concession in changing most individuals' habits of thought.

Loss of personal privacy is another concession the individual may be asked to make, because there are many reasons why files of information about individuals should be consolidated and made more readily accessible.

> When a policeman arrests an individual suspected of a crime, it would be desirable for any record of previous arrests anywhere in the country (or for that matter, anywhere in the world) to be made available to the policeman immediately.

> As we saw in Chapter 1, the duplicate filing of requests for income tax refunds became such a widespread form of fraud that the Internal Revenue Service was forced to install a centralized computer system containing all taxpayer records, so that every claim by a given taxpayer would be processed centrally no matter where he had resided previously.

> The fraudulent use of credit cards is a serious problem; wherever a card is presented, the organization asked to honor it should be provided with information about all previous uses of the card and the credit standing of its holder.

> Most of us would agree that drivers' licenses should not be renewed without consideration of the individual's medical history and recent arrest record, regardless of where the arrests or medical records may have been recorded.

Some files of information of a personal nature should be combined and made more readily accessible, then, and as the economics and processing power of modern computer systems makes this possible, it is being done.

As the centralization of personal records increases, however, serious concern arises about the individual's loss of privacy. The concern is not that new or more detailed information about the individual will be recorded; it is already recorded. The concern is that by bringing the information together in a central file easily accessible by people and organizations unknown to the individual involved, a biased and unfairly complete exposure of the individual's past will be too widely available. The protection now afforded to the individual by the practical difficulty of obtaining information will be lost.

CASE 11C (hypothetical)

◀ In the year 1979, Mr. William H. Smith applies for a universal credit card. The Credit Card Bureau, as a matter of routine, obtains a copy of his personal dossier from the Federal Central Records Service. A review of the dossier indicates that Mr. Smith has never used credit extensively, so his present credit rating is based only on mail-order book club and utility billing experiences. He has always honored these commitments, but they provide too little evidence to establish a solid credit rating. The Credit Card Bureau therefore looks further into his dossier, and observes that Mr. Smith has been:

> Convicted of car theft and of failure to honor a court imposed financial obligation,

> Three times convicted of disorderly conduct,

> A member of the Communist Party,

> Court-martialed while in the Army for desertion in the face of the enemy,

> Divorced twice.

Concluding that this is evidence of a thoroughly bad character and that his credit history is too weak to support a favorable credit rating, the Bureau refuses Mr. Smith's application for a credit card. This is a great inconvenience to Mr. Smith, because much of the economy of 1979 is geared to the use of the universal credit card and he will find his business and personal affairs a good deal more difficult to manage.

If Mr. Smith had been asked, he could have explained these blots on his record in the following manner.

When he was in high school he was once involved with a group of his friends in a drinking bout that culminated in a "joy ride" in a car which had the keys left in the ignition. Shortly before the boys planned to abandon the car and go home, a police cruiser stopped them arrested them all, and they were subsequently convicted of car theft. Since it was the first offense in each case all the sentences were suspended and Mr. Smith, chastened by the experience, avoided both overindulgence in alcohol and any similar pranks thereafter.

When he was in college, Mr. Smith became involved in a movement of protest against the college authority. As an act of defiance he joined the Communist Party and resigned from it after graduation from college, having taken no part in Communist movements or activities. He was also involved in noisy and violent demonstrations which led to three arrests for doing minor damage to the University buildings. In each case he was convicted of disorderly conduct, but the nature of each offense was minor and only minor fines were assessed.

After graduation from college he was drafted and sent to Viet Nam. A patrol of which he was a member was ambushed, and Viet Cong mortar shells hit the trucks the patrol was escorting. One of Mr. Smith's friends was trapped in one of the trucks, and Mr. Smith heard his cries as the truck burned. Mr. Smith jumped up from his position in the defensive line and ran back to help his friend. The commanding officer called on him to return, but he ignored the command, and at the truck found that his friend was dead. The officer reported Mr. Smith's disobedience as desertion in the face of the enemy; he was court martialed. The circumstances of his action were explained by the defense, and he was let off with a letter of reprimand.

Mr. Smith involved himself in two unsuccessful marriages after leaving the Army. He was required to pay alimony to both wives and found this a difficult financial penalty. He later found that his first wife was living with another man, and felt it unfair that he should have to continue paying her alimony. He therefore stopped, and she sued him. The court ruled that he was still liable for the alimony payments since she was not legally remarried, and ordered him to resume payments (which he did).

Mr. Smith had been employed respectably for ten years since leaving the service, and the only blot on his record during this time was occasioned by a stand on principle (the refusal to pay alimony) with which the court did not agree. All of the earlier convictions were associated with extenuating circumstances of one kind or another which probably could have been explained to the satisfaction of the Credit Card Bureau. If Mr. Smith had been given the chance to explain or even to enter the full story in his dossier, the judgment might have been different.

The more salient question is: What business was all this of the Credit Card Bureau's? The only judgment relating to Mr. Smith's financial soundness was his refusal to pay alimony, and he made good the payments after the court decision against him. Every other aspect of his credit history was without blemish; if the Credit Card Bureau had seen only financial information, it might well have issued Mr. Smith his card and in relying on the nonfinancial information it exceeded its authority and competence. ▶

Such a case is by no means inconceivable, and as of now Mr. Smith would have little or no form of redress available to him. If access to complete files of personal information becomes as unrestricted as this case implies, great harm may well result to many individuals.

This danger has been broadly recognized, however, and national figures (including some Congressmen) are advocating preventive and restrictive legislation as well as technical barriers implanted in the information systems to prevent their unauthorized or unfair use. In his excellent book* Professor Alan Westin advocates that computer programs accept only inquiries accompanied by "passwords" carefully kept secret, reject invalid questions, and maintain records of activity including identification of questioner and question. He also advocates the establishment of certain overall legal and regulatory principles. They center around the idea that each invasion of privacy must be individually justified by the courts, and that every such invasion must be

---

* Alan F. Westin, *Privacy and Freedom*, Atheneum, New York, 1967.

monitored after the fact for compliance with the original intent. Specifically, he suggests:

1 Individual justification of each invasion of privacy,

2 Proof that no alternative legal means could be used,

3 Proof that the technique to be used is effective in principle,

4 Demonstration that it is impracticable to gain the consent of the party whose records are to be reviewed,

5 Specific restriction on the scope, duration, and operation of each review, followed by monitoring of compliance,

6 Government sponsored development of protective devices and measures of redress that can be used by individuals and organizations,

7 Establishment of explicit sets of standards and codes of conduct for employers, professionals, and others having individuals' records at their disposal.

He believes that if statutes are enacted at the Federal and State levels incorporating these principles, and that if suitable judicial and review bodies are set up including procedures for individual redress, that satisfactory privacy protection can be obtained.

The only ways to completely prevent the loss of individual privacy are to stop recording the information or to bury it intentionally in inaccessible files. Neither is sensible, because files of information about lawbreakers are legally necessary and desirable, and the social and economic benefits of consolidating some of them are overwhelming. Of course, access to the files should be restricted by law; a particular investigator should be given access to only a small part of the files. In most cases the individual in question should also be informed that reference is to be made to his dossier, and in many cases (such as voluntary credit checks, and applications for driver's licenses) his consent should be mandatory before the reference is made and the portion of his dossier to be released should be under his control. Finally, the individual should be guaranteed the right to review the records about himself and to freely insert qualifying or explanatory information. He should also have the right to petition the courts for erasure of information he believes is no longer relevant or valid. These principles, combined with the legal protections advocated by Professor Westin, should go far toward minimizing further loss of privacy.

There are no restrictions that cannot be circumvented, though, either by clever private individuals hoping to gain advantage over others or by governments determined to "root out subversion," "get something on the crooks," or otherwise willing to wink at legal constraints on their powers, with the tacit cooperation of the public and the courts. The possible protections of public privacy are in no sense absolute; the possibility—indeed probability—of misuse of the information is very high. We must conclude pessimistically that the very existence of the information will suggest its misuse, and that the only way to absolutely obviate this is to not record the information in the first place, which is unreasonable. We must also conclude that the managements of organizations possessing such information have a continuing responsibility to monitor its use.

If the public wants the services of computer-based information systems, it must pay for them in one way or another. Computers and their programs are expensive, and though these costs are declining, they will remain significant indefinitely. This is true even when many remote users share the costs of a computer, because some of the costs involved in remote use of computers are not likely to decline very much, such as the costs of telephone lines between the individual's home or place of work and the computer he wishes to use. Perhaps most significant, the user must be equipped with a device for two-way communication with the information system, as the subscriber to telephone service must be equipped with telephone instruments. This device (or *terminal*) must have certain capabilities if it is to provide the desired services. If the user wishes to buy tickets for travel or for entertainment events, the device must be able to display available space to him and then print some form of ticket which will constitute the buyer's evidence that he has bought the space. In fact, if any form of purchase or commitment is made by the individual through his terminal, he will presumably require a printed document of some kind as evidence of the transaction. Some possible services involve the retrieval of sizable amounts of information (such as investment advisory services, and reservation systems providing descriptive information about hotels). If such services are to be used by the individual, his terminal must be able to provide high-speed display of information in sizable volumes, perhaps using a television-type display tube. Naturally, the individual must also be equipped with means of entering his questions or demands into the information system. Keyboards for both alphabetic and numeric entry, and probably slots for inserting the credit cards that the public will usually use to make payment, must also be part of the terminal.

If the individual is to be provided with varying information services, then, he will need a terminal in his home or office equipped with alphabetic and numeric keyboards, a special reader for credit cards, a television-type display, and a printer. Such terminals cost thousands of dollars today and even though their costs will probably drop significantly, they will remain far above the cost of television sets, stereo phonographs, or any of the familiar consumer electronic items. Combining the high cost of the terminal with the cost of the telephone line and a fair share of the cost of the computer system providing the service, it is evident that the private individual of the next generation must either be prepared to pay a high price or to do without the services as an individual.

Compromises are possible, of course. One highly plausible scheme would provide terminals to communities instead of individuals. One can envision a travel agent's office (or perhaps a branch bank or drugstore) equipped with terminals for public use that could communicate with a variety of services of interest to the local businessmen and individuals. Many people could then share the terminals, paying only toll charges according to their amount of use. Such an arrangement would have the incidental advantage that the staff of the bank, travel agency, or store would be available to assist customers in the use of the terminals, to collect cash when necessary for the purchase of a ticket or other item, and even to publicize the availability and merits of new services.

Even if community use of terminals turns out to be the answer to the cost of providing information systems for the public, there is still a toll charge to the individual which may be significant. Clearly the advantages of the systems are not pure gain to the private individual since he must make the concession of paying for them, while also making the more subjective kinds of concessions discussed above.

INDIVIDUALS IN ORGANIZATIONS

Individuals will also be required to make concessions in their roles as employees and managers of organizations using computers. They must be willing to work with the computer, to provide it with instructions in the form and manner in which it requires them. As we saw above, the computer cannot be expected to adapt to human languages, preferred pace of work, or pattern of social graces and intercommunication. The individual will be required to make the adaptation, to make allowances for the rigidity and lack of personality of the machine, and to live with and compensate for its weaknesses. Again the possibility arises that the individual will become "depersonalized." Experience indicates, however, that the more the human working with the computer becomes depersonalized and mechanical like it, the less successful the combination of man and machine will be. Apparently the truly effective information system is one in which the computer does the calculating and filing, and leaves to the humans the exercise of judgment and intuition.

CASE 11D

◀ A manufacturing company specializes in making parts for engines, transmissions, and other mechanical assemblies used in aircraft. They are prepared to make thousands of different parts to order, usually in relatively small lots and with a high cost per item. The production schedule changes every day in response to emergency orders for parts; the schedule of each work station on the production floor is flexible and still developed on an intuitive basis.

Since the runs are small and many different parts may be in production at a given time, automatic assembly lines have proved impractical and the company relies on manual movements of material. A group of employees is responsible for moving raw materials and partly finished work around the production floor, from the stock room to the work stations and between work stations as series of machining operations are performed. It is important that these employees provide prompt service to every work station requiring materials or partly finished parts from other work stations, but at the same time efficiency dictates that they make as few trips as possible, making as many pickups and deliveries as possible on each trip. For years the employees who move the materials have competed with one another to provide good service while at the same time making as few trips as possible during the day.

A computer was installed by the company to control inventories and to produce payrolls for the production employees based on the complex piecework schedule worked out with their union. It was hoped that the computer would also eventually assist the complex production scheduling operation. After a number of years of experimenting with production scheduling programs, each more effective than the previous one, the programmers felt that they were in a position to deal with the highly volatile nature of the production schedule, to completely schedule each work station and the movement of materials on the production floor. However, trial runs of the scheduling program encountered complications. Small impediments in the flow of work (a broken tool, a worker taking a break, an aisle temporarily blocked by a machine being moved) would impede the planned flow and make small adaptions necessary in the ideal sequence of pickup and delivery. Most of these small, temporary impediments were not reported to the computer because most of them were cleared up within a few minutes, but it was found that if the movement of materials rigidly followed the machine's schedule, a significant amount of delay and inefficiency would result from the failure to take account of them.

The system designers finally settled on a compromise. The computer would schedule the anticipated work load for each work station, and from this develop a "need list" of raw materials and semifinished parts for that work station, and the expected time each would be required. These need lists would be delivered by a computer output device on the production floor to the employees responsible for moving materials, and each employee would develop his own sequence of movements to satisfy the demands of the need list while adapting to any impediments to his movements that existed at the moment or occurred during the day.

The result was satisfactory to all parties concerned. The efficiency and responsiveness of the production process improved, and the employees responsible for moving materials felt that their jobs were more interesting. They were given clear-cut assignments (the demands they were expected to satisfy during the day were made clear and explicit), but they were allowed to use their initiative to solve the intellectual problems of which pickups and deliveries to incorporate into each trip, taking impediments into account. The man and the machine worked together to use the best abilities of both in optimizing the movement of materials. ▶

As the pace of change has accelerated in the past few decades, individuals have been forced to learn to live with it, to adapt, and to learn new jobs and methods when necessary. We have seen that the computer is a major element in the process of change in organizations and that its influence has forced a great deal of adjustment, sometimes with very unhappy effects. As computers move further into the operational decision-making processes of organizations, this problem will surely become worse. For one thing, we have seen that computer-based systems are more difficult to change than manual ones, that the inertia of existing systems increases as the number of computers and computer programs involved increases. This increased inertia can be illustrated by considering the degree of difficulty a manager has in changing a clerical system, as the degree of automation of the system increases:

1 If a manager wishes to change a clerical system in which the work is done by hand, he prepares a memorandum describing the change and circulates it among the employees. After a day or so in which they become used to the new method, ask questions, and iron out difficulties, it is in operation.

2 If the employees are using keyboard-operated accounting machines to support the clerical system, the process is similar. However, a technician must be called to make changes in the "motor bar" which determines the functions the accounting machines will perform as the operating keys are depressed. This may take him several days: first, he must convert the description of the new method into the machine operations that must be performed; second, he must then change each of the machines. The clerical employees must wait until he is finished before they can start to practice with the changed methods.

3 If the clerical operation is performed by punched card machines, the manager must describe the change he wants to the supervisor of the punched card system. A new sequence of machine operations will then be designed by the supervisor to accommodate the change, and for each of the machine operations needed, a new control panel for the machine used in the operation must be prepared. It is also likely that punched cards with different formats must be obtained for the changed system. This requires designing the new card, communicating the needs to a printer supplying the cards, and waiting for a stock of the new cards to be delivered. Test runs must be performed to make sure that there are no errors in the control panels and that all conditions have been accounted for. After this has been done and the new cards have been received, the new system is ready to go into operation. Then a training period must be allowed for the personnel operating the punched card machines. In total, the time required for implementing a change using punched card machines may be a week or two.

4 If a computer is involved in performing the clerical operation, the manager must communicate his requirements to the chief of data processing, who probably assigns the task to one or more of the programmers employed by the company (assuming one is available for assignment at the time—often, new jobs must go to the bottom of a waiting list). They must review the program presently being used for the operation to become fully familiar with its details. They must then design the necessary changes to the program, and convert these changes into machine language. As in the punched card system, any new forms, cards, or supporting procedures must also be designed and the necessary items procured. The programmer must debug the changed program because errors or oversights are likely. Because of the subtlety of some of the possible errors and the difficulty of perceiving all oversights using test data, it will probably seem wise to run the changed system for a while in parallel with the old one so that the results can be compared and the adequacy of the new system can be verified. After the results of the parallel operation have been judged satisfactory, then the old system can be abandoned and the new one accepted. This procedure, from initiation of the change by the manager to completion of the parallel operation period, is likely to take one or two months even for a simple change. Thus we can see that the manager's ability to cause changes in clerical systems has decreased since computers have taken over clerical functions formerly performed by simpler machines or by hand.

Another constraint on the manager's ability to cause changes in data processing is that he will often have less authority over it. When a division of a large organization has internal line control over its data processing function and wishes to make a change, it is free to do so. However, if its information systems are dependent on a corporate data processing organization, the division must negotiate for the changes it wants and perhaps be refused. Even if the need for the change is accepted, no programming personnel may be available for the job. Also, the division may be asked to make internal changes because the data processing organization wishes them made for reasons (hopefully) of benefit to the overall organization, but not necessarily to the division. As we have seen, for economy and because of the increasing complexity of modern information systems, large organizations are tending to centralize their data processing functions at the corporate level, so this situation will be encountered by more and more managers of divisional operations. For them the pace of change is as fast as ever, or faster, and the environment in which they seek the changes they want (and accommodate to those required by others) is more complex and hard to deal with.

Managers of both small and large organizations are presented with a more fundamental problem by the computer: the demand that they learn the techniques of system analysis and quantitative management which it embodies. Managers may or may not elect to learn these techniques and to apply them to their operations, but increasingly it appears that if they are to remain competitive, managers must at least become sufficiently familiar with the techniques to be able to evaluate their applicability. Willy-nilly the manager must learn something about system analysis, because the least that will be required of him is that he reject its use on rational grounds rather than simply those of ignorance. (Hopefully most managers will find some use for the knowledge, because there seems to be an increasing degree of truth in the system analysts' claims that their techniques are the best for controlling modern, complex organizations.)

The process of applying system analysis will require additional concessions. To most organizations the systems approach is new, and quantitative techniques have not been applied before. No matter how competent or experienced the professional personnel developing the plans may be, their experience with the company's problems is likely to be limited. Conversely, if the individual attempting to apply the techniques is an experienced manager only partly trained in the new methods, he is likely to make both technical and practical errors. Traditional techniques of intuitive or experiential management, while sometimes becoming obsolescent, have the great virtue that there is a body of experience supporting them. The manager using traditional techniques is unlikely to make gross errors, and will probably anticipate the drawbacks of proposed changes. When the techniques of systems analysis are being applied for the first time, though, the whole situation will be new; there will be no body of experience to guide those designing and implementing the new system. Thus, many new mistakes will be made and many organizations will surely have to pass through a learning period before they are as good at managing in the new way as they were at managing in the old.

The requirement that managers become familiar with the new techniques applies particularly to the financial officers, accountants, and auditors who are responsible for the safety of the organization's assets and their protection from misuse. A programmer or systems analyst having uncontrolled freedom to manipulate financial files has (as we have seen) opportunities to evade conventional accounting controls in order to defraud the organization. It is self-evident that the only way of completely preventing this is for the auditors or financial officers to become the programmers' equal in knowledge of the techniques being used to manipulate the files, and to be able to review with the programmer the operations being performed and verify that they are acceptable.

Many similar concessions will have to be made by scientists and engineers —sometimes even to a greater degree. There is no question that every future physical scientist, engineer, and (later) every member of the medical, economic, and social science professions will have to become intimate with the computer as part of preparing for his career. This does not seem to bother the students; they rarely seem to feel that they are making a concession in learning about computers in colleges and universities. In fact, we have seen that the reverse seems to be more common. The colleges and universities usually have more trouble providing enough computer time to satisfy the demands of eager students who wish to experiment with computers than in forcing students to undertake the subject. Nevertheless, the students are indisputably making a concession. The curricula for technical students are already overcrowded with material necessary for proficiency in their fields, and the pressure seems to increase every year. Whether they are willing to take time to learn about the computer is not so important, perhaps, as the fact that they must do so in addition to finding time for all the other subjects.

The scientist or engineer already practicing his profession is in a more difficult position. He has spent his career working with now obsolescent tools, and he may be less able to adapt to new methods than students still in school. He is probably also busy studying the continuing advances in his professional field, and may have little time to devote to the subject of computers. For him, the concession of time and effort may be greater than that for students.

Scientists and engineers are likely to be more seriously hampered by a subtle problem which could, in time, seriously affect their entire professional fields. As we have observed, they are increasingly coming to depend on the computer to process experimental data while experiments proceed, and to help guide the course of experiments. Furthermore, scientists and engineers are learning how to simulate the processes they are studying in computers, enabling them to work in areas that would otherwise be impractical and reducing the investment of time and money needed for experiments. The computer's assistance is tremendously beneficial, unquestionably, but does it contain some implied constraints? Will the scientists and engineers be led insensibly into paths of investigation which can be dealt with using the by-now familiar computer tool, rather than those which are intrinsically the most promising? How does a scientist or engineer diverge completely from the accepted and familiar area of investigation when a tremendous amount of computer programming has been invested in the simulation models and experimental setups of the familiar area, and none in the new? Will there be an inertia of developed computer programs and data files that favors continued exploration of old fields and makes it practically impossible to start new ones, just as there is with clerical systems? These questions cannot be answered yet. The influence of the computer in science and engineering is still new and growing, and in no field has the computer become so basic a tool that it could have reached such a position of influence. The next generation of scientists and engineers will answer these questions, however, and it is to be hoped they do not find that in order to obtain full benefit from the computer they have had to make the concession of being virtually unable to move into new fields.

ORGANIZATIONS

The adaptations which organizations must undergo as they put the computer to increasingly widespread use will involve painful changes, including concessions of present ways of doing things. One of the most evident derives from the breaking down of traditional structures in the organization. In Chapter 6 we examined the computer as a force for centralization of organizations, and concluded that while no abrupt or absolute centralization was likely to occur in most, nevertheless existing chains of operational command are often being shortened and functions are being combined so that the computer's ability to interrelate data from different areas can be utilized. In most organizations existing lines of demarcation between functions have evolved over many years, are understood by all, and are implicit in the employees' and managers' views of themselves and their present and future places in the organization. When major changes occur in these lines of demarcation, much confusion necessarily ensues. Even though the new information system may be working in a matter of months or years, it is likely to be many years before all of the employees have become comfortable with their new image of themselves and the organization. Inevitably, increased confusion and uncertainty is a concession the organization must make to using the computer in ways which cause changes in traditional, functional structures.

Another aspect of this confusion results from the creation of a new information-processing "shadow organization" alongside the existing structure.

Figure 6–2 depicts the kind of data processing organization, semicentralized and involving dual reporting relationships for data processing personnel, which seems to be coming into existence in large, divisionalized organizations. This "shadow organization" clearly involves new difficulties of intercommunications and reporting relationships for the organization and its employees. We observed above that the manager wishing to make changes in his division's data processing may no longer have the authority to do so, and may be forced to negotiate with a central organization. Similarly, the organization's ability as a whole to modify its information systems now involves the concurrence and teamwork of many parties, including the data processing organization in its entirety and (to varying degrees) the managers and operating personnel of the divisions. This is not impossibly difficult; many examples can already be found where such teamwork occurs smoothly. But without question the organization has been forced to permit a new form of organizational confusion to come into existence.

To develop and implement complex data processing systems requires a sizeable investment and the contributions of an extensive professional staff. Presumably it is the larger organizations who will be able to afford these investments; the smaller ones will not. It may be feared that small organizations might be forced out of business because of the efficiencies gained by large competitors through the use of computer-based systems. We have already seen that this is not always so, because small organizations are sometimes better at providing the personal services individual customers want. We have also seen that the techniques developed by large organizations can frequently be put to use by small ones without duplicating their investment. The computer manufacturers make available "packaged" application programs for the small organization, and data processing service companies are increasingly offering the kinds of services to small organizations which demand a sizeable development investment. Groups of small organizations (in effect) share the service bureau's cost of developing the services to which they subscribe. The smaller organizations therefore have a chance to make use of some of the data processing techniques that larger competitors have the resources to develop internally. However, they must make severe concessions to do so. The small organization no longer has the ability to design the information system which best suits its precise needs: it must adapt to the decisions about file structure, format of accounting reports, data that should and should not be incorporated in the files, and method of processing that the computer manufacturer or the service organization has decided will represent the best compromise for all. In adopting such a compromise, the small organization gives up much of its freedom to perform its data processing in its own way, and almost completely gives up its freedom to request changes and modifications

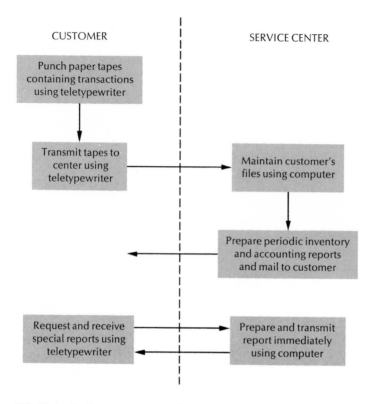

FIG. 11–1   On-line accounting and inventory control system provided by service center.

to data processing procedures. Experience shows that no organization lightly gives up these freedoms.

CASE 11E

◀ In 1964 a data processing service organization was formed with the idea of providing on-line computer services to small organizations performing warehousing and distribution services. The service was to work as shown in Fig. 11-1. A teletypewriter terminal was to be installed in each subscriber's office, and with it he would prepare punched paper tapes containing all of his inventory and financial transactions. These would be transmitted to the service organization's computer, which automatically updates and maintains the customer's files. At weekly and monthly intervals, as needed, inventory and accounting reports would be automatically produced and mailed to the customer. Also, at any time, members of the subscribing firm's management could request reports from the computer through their teletypewriter, reports showing a variety of information about balances of individual inventory items or groups of items, or up-to-date accounting trial balances.

The service organization developed a set of computer programs which it thought would do these things adequately for a wide variety of distribution organizations, and proceeded to attempt to sell the service. Immediately it ran into difficulty, because every firm approached was dissatisfied with some aspect of the standard programs. The prospective customers either wanted to keep additional information in the file records of the inventory items (such as style codes or automatic reorder points), or they wanted reports that differed in format or nature from those the service had planned. They also wanted changes in the responsive reporting facility which permitted the manager to obtain special reports through the teletypewriter. Each potential customer had different ideas about what he wanted to ask, and about the form in which he wanted to see the information.

The service organization, dismayed by the diversity of customer interests and anxious to get its business started, agreed to many of the requests for special modifications to the program packages. Sometimes they asked for and received special fees for performing the program modifications. They then undertook the special programming for ten customers, a job that completely occupied the programming staff the service organization was capable of supporting for a year and a half. The organization had hoped to have forty or fifty customers at the end of the first year and a half, and realized that even though it might in many cases be paid for the special programming needed, it would never be able to grow fast enough if each customer was permitted to ask for program modifications to suit himself.

The service organization made a concentrated study of the program modifications that the initial customer group had asked for, and found ways to incorporate the most commonly desired ones into the standard service offering. This work involved still more programming time; it was more than a year later that the organization began to offer its expanded service to potential new customers. They were more successful this time, and were able to add an additional fifteen customers without requiring more program modifications. Nine out of ten prospective customers still found the program package too restrictive, though, so for the second time the standard service offering was redesigned and expanded to incorporate more variations. Finally, nearly four years after the organization had started, they found they had a service offering which would appeal to a large percentage of potential customers without modification. As they entered their fifth year of operation, they had increased their subscribers to sixty and finally saw a possibility of becoming profitable. ▶

This experience is significant, because we know that the pressures to use automatic data processing would make most of the small organizations approached by the data processing service company anxious to use its services. Most were probably willing to compromise their preferred ways of keeping files and presenting reports to the greatest extent they felt they could, but nevertheless only a minority could do so enough to accept the service. Probably the sixty existing users of the service feel that in accepting even the current refined and sophisticated version of it they are making severe concessions with respect to what they would ideally like.

We see, then, that a generalized "computer utility" is no panacea, that the very differences between organizations that enable them to survive competitively preclude their using identical information processing services. Computer utilities in the form of data processing service companies offering packaged services can sometimes help, but concessions must be made to the standards required and freedom is lost.

One of the worries which the smaller organization faces in using a common data processing service is loss of privacy; the possibility that competitors, government agencies, or any party they would rather protect their data from may gain access to it. This worry affects the larger organization as well because once data is stored in standard form in any computer, the ease of access to it seems to lead to requests (sometimes having the force of law) that the data be made available. Increasingly, for example, state and federal agencies require the contractors carrying out public works projects to submit detailed planning documents and status reports in unprecedented detail. The contractors generally resist this requirement, at least at first, not so much because they are doubtful of meeting their commitments but because they fear that they will lose control and flexibility in managing their own resources. Their fear is, of course, justified. The contracting agency, given the data and ability to use it, will certainly second guess the contractor's planning to a greater degree than before. It has a right to; it is paying for the work and so long as its intervention is competent, the results should be (and often are) satisfactory to the contractor as well as to the agency. Unquestionably though, the contractor (and any other organization in a similar position) has conceded a degree of its privacy of information and its freedom to conduct its business as it sees fit.

The problem of loss of privacy, then, affects organizations as well as individuals, though in the case of organizations it is possible that the major loss of privacy has already occurred. Government requirements for reporting detailed data are already so extensive, and the ability of government agencies to second guess private organizations' operations so limited because of lack of staff or technical competence, that the further reporting made possible by computer-based information systems may involve little additional loss. In fact, the simplification of the reporting process resulting from reporting everything in standard, machine-readable form may be more of a boon to the private organization than a disadvantage.

Sometimes loss of privacy of business information can lead to mutual disadvantage to firms competing with one another; in order to obtain the benefits of computer and communications systems, they must lose competitive advantage. Case 10C described the change in the nature of over the counter stock trading caused by the general availability of price quotations for the securities traded. Formerly, the firms in the business were able to release their quotations only selectively, to change them rapidly without the knowledge of their competitors, and to quote different prices (if they saw fit) to different customers. This freedom has been virtually taken away by the public availability of current "typical" quotes, and as we have seen, the result has been that most firms now conduct business as agents (executing orders at the "typical" price and charging a commission), rather than as principals (attempting to make a profit on the difference in price between the wholesale market and the retail price they can charge the customer). Perhaps this particular change was in the interest of the public (the Securities and Exchange Commission thinks so*) but it certainly involved a major concession on the part of the firms in the over the counter stock trading business, a concession so great that they were forced to change the fundamental nature of their business.

Effective use of the computer within a large organization leads to standardization of data files and the programs used to manipulate them. Beyond this, if organizations wish to cooperate with one another in the exchange and processing of data (e.g., for economic models, or for the interchange of business statistics) standardization will be needed among them. Standardization, of course, involves both concessions and costs. Concessions are required because standard ways of reporting and processing data may be less than ideal for any of the individual organizations adopting the standard, and costs are involved in converting existing files to the new standardized form, changing data collection procedures to comply with it, and preparing programs that will produce the standardized results. Also, additional data processing equipment may be needed by the individual organizations participating in the standardized system.

CASE 11F

◀ Through the World Meteorological Organization nations are supporting a global atmosphere research program. The ultimate outcome of this program,

---

* *Special Study of Securities Markets*, Securities and Exchange Commission, 1963.

hoped to be realized by 1977, is a system in which all the world's weather data are processed by a network of computers with information communicated among them in a standard form and processing done in a common manner. The result, it is hoped, will be weather forecasts for any area two weeks or more ahead.*

The computers required to process and intercommunicate all this data are expected to number 256, each about the size of the largest ones available today, which cost on the order of $5 million apiece. The cost of these, plus the costs of weather satellites and other networks of sensors for gathering the required data, will total billions of dollars to be shared among the participating countries. The results will be of unquestioned benefit, but in order to participate in the program and obtain the results, each subscribing nation will have to invest a substantially greater sum than its present meteorological system has required. ▶

Even within an organization the cost of standardization may be great. Case 6A, for example, reported that a single mail order sales organization had to invest $600,000 to convert its catalog mailing files to a standard form. While exceptionally high, this investment indicates the kind of concessions organizations attempting to standardize internal data files must make.

SUMMARY

The overall picture is sobering. Organizations are being forced to change, leading at best to confusion and at worst to complete revolution in the way they do business, sometimes to the detriment of profitability. They are forced to adapt to standards, both internally and externally, that constrain their ability to process data as they wish and which invite exposure of their affairs to competitors and to public agencies. At the same time their data processing systems become more rigid and less adaptable than any they have previously had. This forces them to plan information systems so accurately that they will remain suitable for the necessary term. A manager in an organization that has been forced to make these changes might be forgiven for viewing the whole idea of using computers with skepticism. Individuals, too, may be subject to skepticism about the computer's benefits after reviewing the tangible and intangible concessions it demands.

Fortunately, these concessions will not have to be made overnight. The rate of organizational change is constrained by fundamental factors which will not change: human factors such as the ability to absorb changes and willing-

---

* *The New York Times*, February 1, 1968.

ness to adopt them, economic factors involving the displacement of existing personnel and resources and the development and conversion costs of new systems, and the inevitable shortcomings of the planning process—imperfections not foreseen in the planning stage, delays for shakedown and debugging, and difficulties of standardizing on new intracompany and intercompany information systems. Surely a full generation must pass, of both individuals and organizations, before the changes can be expected to be complete. Perhaps even more than one generation will be needed. It is a striking fact that the quotation that opens this chapter, predicting just such concessions as we envision here, was written fifty years ago—in 1919—and its prediction is still not fulfilled.

CHAPTER 12

OPPORTUNITIES OFFERED BY THE COMPUTER

*"The electronic computer has a more beneficial potential for the human race than any other invention in history."**
RAY EPPERT, former President, Burroughs Corporation

We have looked at the benefits computers have brought to individuals; we can combine these with new applications and trends and predict with some certainty additional opportunities that will be offered by the computer in the immediate future. As we have already seen, the "immediate future" is likely to take ten or fifteen years to develop because of the constraints on the rate of change and the time necessary for newly developed computer applications to become perfected and widespread. We are again speaking of the next generation of individuals, organizations, and managers concerned with the use of computers.

INDIVIDUALS IN PRIVATE LIFE

In today's society the individual has many needs for information. He is interested in travel reservations and routings, stock quotations, telephone numbers, availability and prices of goods, and general information of many kinds. Much of this information is provided satisfactorily by present sources; it is unlikely that telephone directories, road maps, or encyclopedias will soon be replaced by new media. Some kinds of information are subject to rapid change, however, and any printed documents are likely to be out of date by the time they are referred to. Reservation information for airplanes, hotels, and entertainment events is typical; computers are already in widespread service in the reservations area and can be expected to proliferate in the next few years. The availability of airplane seats is now almost universally accessible to individuals everywhere through the network of computer and com-

---

* Gilbert Burck, *The Computer Age,* Harper & Row, New York, 1965.

munications systems connected to every airline ticket office and many travel agents. Similar interconnected networks for hotel reservations are growing rapidly, and others for entertainment events are apparently going to follow. As the coverage of these services becomes more universal, usage will increase. This will make it economical to provide more input-output terminals of reservation systems nearer to more individuals, further improving the service. There is a "snowball" effect, then, leading to reservation systems both more universal and useful in their coverage and more readily accessible.

Another class of information in which many individuals are interested is price data for stocks, bonds, mutual funds, and other types of investments. As we have seen in cases cited in previous chapters, computer-based security price information systems are already in widespread use within the brokerage industry; the salesman handling an individual's account almost always has a computer input-output terminal near him that enables him to answer questions about prices. The availability of this information is spreading; the individual soon may be able to obtain it directly. In one city, for example, one of the UHF television channels is devoted to displaying the ticker tape from the New York Stock Exchange; information about prices of other securities and changes in the price indices is interspersed with the ticker display. In another city one of the large brokerage firms is experimenting with direct connection of the public telephone system to its stock quote service, using a computer output device that plays back prerecorded words selected by the computer. This system, when working, will permit a customer of the brokerage firm to dial a special number which connects him with the firm's securities quotation system, then dial the identifier of the security in which he is interested and obtain an oral quotation of its current price, all without occupying one of the firm's representatives. These systems, combining the computer's ability to digest information with the public communications network's ability to distribute it, make available to millions of individuals information which only a few years ago was restricted to a relatively few firms subscribing to the ticker tape service.

Each of these systems requires the individual to learn its language (its operating procedures and codes); having made that concession, he will then have at his disposal a convenient means of obtaining accurate information he could previously obtain only with delay and difficulty using the services of other individuals. At present most such systems have to do with reservations or securities information, but they may be applied to many other kinds in the next generation. Even if no new areas are developed beyond those currently being exploited, it is safe to say that the private individual in the next generation will be provided with computer-based systems for the retrieval of information which will make his life simpler and more convenient.

Many of the computer-based information systems now being developed by organizations have as one of their objectives the improvement of service to individual customers. When most organizations' computer programs are first developed, they are "bare bones" programs incorporating nothing more than a rigid, minimal set of operational procedures needed to carry out the organization's basic data processing. As we have seen, this can lead to mishandling of customer relations where special circumstances exist, to increased time delays, and to a general increase in the rigidity of the organization. This is changing as computer programs evolve beyond the "bare bones" stage, and many organizations feel that they are now able to develop information systems that will provide more customer convenience than they could ever offer before.

CASE 12A

◀   A bank in a large city must compete vigorously with others to attract individuals' checking accounts. It reduced its service charges as far as practicable, introduced preprinted personalized checks, convenient local branches, and other competitive aids only to find them matched by other banks. The bank acquired a computer some time ago to process checks and, in attempting to develop additional services, thought of exploiting the computer's ability to handle great quantities of detailed data at little additional cost by offering data processing services to customers. Perceiving that many of them used household budgets, the bank decided that it could introduce an automatic budget accounting system which would work in the following manner:

1   The customer would give the bank a list of account names (e.g., food, rent, or taxes). The bank would then set up in the computer individual magnetic tape records for each of these accounts within the customer's overall checking account record.

2   The customer would code each deposit made in his account in accordance with the account numbering structure he had set up. He could put all of a deposit into one of his budget accounts, or distribute it among several as he chose.

3   The customer would write on each of his checks (in a special box) the account number of the budget account to which this check should be charged. The bank's computer would then charge the check to the indicated budget account. (The cost of keypunching the additional code for the customer's budget account is virtually the only additional cost the bank would encounter.)

4   At the end of each month the customer's statement would list the deposits and withdrawals for each of his budget accounts, as shown in Fig. 12-1. The

John and Mary Doe 12 Main Street Concord, Mass. 01742 550–96–95–2	Beginning balance		591.46
	Ending balance		642.14
	Deposits	3	724.69
	Withdrawals	11	674.01

01 Rent
Beginning balance   .00
Ending balance   .00
Deposits   228.61
Withdrawals   228.61

02 Food & Entertainment
Beginning balance   25.50
Ending balance   18.40
Deposits   198.00
Withdrawals   38.65
                         19.80
                          5.00
                         28.60
                         44.50
                         38.05
                         30.50

03 Insurance
Beginning balance   .00
Ending balance   (25.30)
Deposits   200.00
Withdrawals   150.00
                        75.30

04 Clothing
Beginning balance   255.50
Ending balance   240.50
Deposits   .00
Withdrawals   15.00

05 General
Beginning balance   310.46
Ending balance   408.54
Deposits   98.08
Withdrawals   .00

FIG. 12–1   Bank statement for automatic budgeting checking account.

customer's budget account number and name is printed over each associated list of checks and deposits, and the starting and ending balance in each is shown as well as the total balance in the customer's account.

The bank hopes that this automatic budget accounting system will attract many depositors who find it inconvenient to maintain budget records of their own. (Of course, they are still required to establish appropriate account numbers and accurately and consistently code deposits and withdrawals; the bank cannot do that for them.) The system is not in operation yet, so the bank does not know what competitive advantage will be gained from it. It feels that the experiment will be inexpensive, however; the programming investment has not been high and the increase in operating costs will be of very little significance. ▶

In addition to adding new services customers want, organizations are attempting to use computers to improve existing services by reducing customer waiting time and work loads on employees. These efforts are particularly promising in the social services, where the tremendous growth in case loads and a shortage of professionals has created a crisis in customer handling. In Case 1E we reviewed efforts to use the computer to help the medical profession with diagnoses, patient monitoring, and medical history record management. A primary objective is to reduce the amount of professional medical time that must be spent with each patient without reducing (indeed, sometimes increasing) the quality of medical care. Welfare agencies have a similar problem: an explosively increasing number of cases and increasingly complex regulations for protection against fraud, combined with inadequate professional and clerical staffs. Many are turning to computer and communications systems to help solve this problem and, hopefully, provide better service than ever before.

CASE 12B

◀ The Massachusetts Division of Employment Security is in the process of installing a state-wide network of computer input-output terminals connected to a central computer.* The purpose of this system is twofold—first, to virtually eliminate fraudulent claims; second, to provide on the spot preparation of unemployment benefit checks.

When a claimant enters a local office to collect an unemployment check, he will present an identification card containing his name and social security number and a ledger card to the operator of a typewriter-like terminal. Both cards are placed into the terminal, the identification card in a special slot and the ledger card in the platen of the typewriter-like device, which also holds the blank check forms. The information on the card is transmitted over telephone lines to the computer center in Boston, which verifies the claimant's record and eligibility and calculates his benefits. It immediately sends the information back to the typewriter, which then updates the claimant's ledger card with the date, amount of payment, and the claimant's balance, and simultaneously typewrites the check for him. In addition, the system will perform by-product functions such as statistical studies on unemployment patterns, financial accounting, and possibly in the future a matching of unemployed workers with unfilled jobs anywhere in the state.

The present system of forwarding the claims to Boston, preparing the checks in batches, and issuing them by mail involves long delays because of

---

* *Management Consultant's Bulletin*, RCA Information Systems Division, Camden, N.J., June 1968.

heavy work loads, and permits occasional fraudulent or duplicate claims to be honored. The new system should both solve the existing problems and provide an instantaneous service to the eligible claimant which (it is expected) will be greatly appreciated. ▶

Now that organizations are acquiring the experience with computer systems that enables them to add conveniences to the already perfected basic data processing programs, the individual will frequently benefit. The organizations will, too; simplicity and rapidity in providing service simplifies the organization's job, and competitive advantage can be gained.

In Chapter 11 we discussed the loss of privacy individuals might suffer if centralized files of personal information are stored in easily accessible computer systems. Some centralization of such files seems inevitable because of the social value gained, particularly in connection with welfare and law enforcement. Another potential benefit from such centralization of personal files may be a gain in convenience to the individual. Today, the private individual must spend a great deal of time filling out forms as he applies for loans, charge accounts, licenses, employment, security clearances, schools, medical services, unemployment and welfare benefits, and so on ad *infinitum*. He must repetitively record information (often in multiple copies) which he has frequently recorded before: how many times has each of us written on a form his name and address, social security number, medical history, employment history, education history, awards, honors, arrests, etc.? The process is boring and irritating and therefore error-prone, and the number of forms the individual is required to fill out seems to increase inexorably.

If centralized, comprehensive personal information files exist in computers, this process can be greatly simplified. When an organization needs information about the individual, it could obtain this information directly from the centralized file service instead of requiring the individual to recite it in detail. The organization would presumably prefer to; the information from the centralized file will be legible (no small advantage!) and will be complete, accurate and honest (if the provisions governing its entry into the file are rigorous). When the individual himself provides the information, the possibility exists that he will err, omit relevant information, or make false statements. Organizations must go to considerable expense to verify the individual's statements, expense which could be greatly reduced if a centralized file of accurate information were available. The individual's privacy could still be protected; he would have to authorize the file service to release that portion of his individual dossier which is relevant to the subject.

The individual might be provided with a simple form such as that shown in Fig. 12-2. It would contain spaces for the individual's name and identifying

---

RELEASE OF PERSONAL DATA

Releasing Individual

Name ————————————————

Address ————————————————

————————————————

Social Security Number ——————————

Recipient

Name ————————————————

Address ————————————————

————————————————

Identifying Number ——————————

Data To Be Released (check)

Bank accounts ☐

Insurance coverage ☐

Educational history ☐

Military service record ☐

Police record ☐

Family history ☐

Credit status ☐

Welfare eligibility ☐

Employment history ☐

Medical history ☐

Residence record ☐

Honors and awards ☐

————————————————————

Signature

————————————————————

Notary

FIG. 12–2   Hypothetical authorization for release of personal data from centralized file service.

number (presumably social security number) and for the name and identifying number of the organization or individual to whom the information is to be released. The remainder of the form consists only of boxes to be checked, boxes with labels such as educational history, employment history, military service, medical history, credit record, police record, honors and awards, and any other classes of information about the individual which the files might contain. The individual's signature, verified by a notary's seal, would be required before the form would be honored.

Such a process, needless to say, would be simpler than that of filling out forms; the organization receiving the information would benefit; the individual's privacy would be protected. This is only a hypothetical possibility, but it serves to show that the centralized, computer-based storage of personal information which is viewed with apprehension by so many commentators is not necessarily an unmixed evil, or uncontrollable.

Some maintain that the society of the next generation will be a "learning society," in which individuals continue to absorb new skills and knowledge throughout their lives instead of (in most cases) obtaining the great bulk of their education during a formal, restricted period. In the learning society there would be less emphasis on learning as a means to obtain gainful employment, and increased emphasis on obtaining fuller enjoyment from life and personal dignity based on newly important criteria such as creativity, community leadership, and general erudition. This interesting subject is beyond the scope of this book, but it is evident that if continuing individual education grows, better tools must be provided to make it possible. Indeed, better tools must be provided even to keep up with our present level of education in the face of the population explosion and the general shortage of competent teachers. This is nowhere more critical than in the field of continuing management education. Many such tools are possible: closed circuit television, microfilm-based information retrieval devices, and audio-visual programmed teaching systems are among the most important. The computer will also be an important tool insofar as it is helpful in information retrieval, programmed teaching, and in supporting the learning of individual skills. Some individuals have already benefited from the application of the computer to their education and training; surely many more will in the future, regardless of ones' view of the level of educational material the computer is capable of handling. As we have seen, the computer is already in widespread use as an educational tool supporting vehicle simulators used to train pilots and astronauts. In this area computers have already provided very significant benefits to individuals.

CASE 12C

◀ The X-15 experimental rocket airplane operated by NASA requires skillful piloting; it reacts so fast to the pilot's actions and to changes in the environment that pilots must have extremely rapid—almost instinctive—reactions if they are to be able to fly the plane safely. Individual flights of the X-15 are expensive, and budgetary restrictions have dictated that most of the available flights be devoted to the research program rather than to the training of pilots. As a result, from the beginning of the X-15 program it was anticipated that a computer-controlled flight simulator would be used to train pilots so that by the time they made their first flight they would already be reasonably expert in handling the X-15.

During one actual X-15 flight the pilot was faced with an emergency situation which had never been encountered before by him or any other X-15 pilot. Fortunately, the situation was one which the computer controlling the flight simulator had been programmed to reproduce, so the pilot had previous "experience" with it and reacted successfully. Aware from his training in the simulator that the situation had to be corrected in two seconds if he were to make a safe landing, he reacted sufficiently quickly and landed the research craft back at the field without injury to himself or damage to the aircraft. It may be presumed that without the experience in the simulator he would have been unable to diagnose the situation and react sufficiently quickly, and the story would not have ended happily.*

In the highly likely event that computer-controlled simulators are used more extensively in the future to teach manual skills and the operation of complex machines, cases such as this where personal injury or damage were apparently averted by training in the simulator will become more common.

Computer-controlled simulators can apparently be applied to many other kinds of educational requirements. For example, a computer-controlled simulation of a human is in experimental use in California for the training of anesthesiologists; the simulator "responds" to anesthetics and other conditions just like a human.†

The promise of individual benefits from computer-assisted instruction may be bright, but even the most enthusiastic must agree that it will be realized only slowly. Apart from the development of knowledge and technology still required, there is the matter of cost: a recent study‡ indicated that the cost of suitable equipment for the entire public school system will be between $10 and $25 billion per year.

It is interesting to observe that most of the opportunities the computer offers to the private individual involve increasing the convenience and ease of doing things he wants to do. Computer-based systems retrieving information about reservations or security prices are a simplification of present methods. Organizations' customer-oriented systems that perform more services for the individual or enable him to obtain the desired action faster (e.g., payment of a welfare benefit) make life more convenient for him. Computer systems storing files of personal information enable the individual to release certified information selectively and easily, and computers assisting in the teaching of information or skills make it easier, faster, and (hopefully) less expensive for the individual to acquire them. To the degree that the individual or manager feels harassed by the myriad of clerical details involved in modern life, such simplifications made possible by the computer should be most welcome.

INDIVIDUALS IN ORGANIZATIONS

The individual has been affected more by the computer in his job than in his private life, and apparently he will be further affected. As we have seen, some

---

* *SDS Interface 15,* Scientific Data Systems Corporation, Los Angeles, July 1968.
† A. Paul Clark, H. Loberman, and L. Arthur Hoyt, "SIM–1, the Model Patient," *Datamation,* August 1968.
‡ *Electronic News,* August 12, 1968.

of the major effects of computers on organizations (and on their employees) are only beginning to appear but are clearly predictable.

Managers

We have observed that the computer has not yet had much impact on the job of the top manager, and it has been suggested that in important areas it never will; that the top manager is often concerned with intangibles—predicting the more distant future and the possible performance of candidates for management—concerns with which the computer is unlikely ever to be of great assistance. However, other aspects of the top manager's job are more susceptible to help from the computer-related techniques broadly encompassed by the term "system analysis," particularly those for choosing among possible alternative resource allocations. We have seen that the use of the computer for modelling and simulation of business ventures has been rather slow to get started. There are several reasons for this: lack of knowledge among managers, imperfect computer programs, and (above all) insufficient data describing the "systems" to be modelled. Increasingly, however, computers are accumulating the data needed. Increasingly, general-purpose languages for simulation and selective reporting are being developed. Cases illustrating and demonstrating these developments have been presented earlier; there is no need to cite more here. In brief, it appears that the much-heralded opportunity for the manager to obtain current and complete data about his business, and to use a simulation to help him evaluate alternatives, is finally emerging.

This may lead to an entirely new environment in business organizations, one which Professor Fano of M.I.T. calls "information rich."* Through remote input-output devices the computer becomes accessible to all authorized employees; its files and its prestored simulation programs become as much at the service of a management trainee as of the chairman of the board. What is to prevent a junior manager, having conceived a better way to meet the demands of his particular job, from exploring its implications as thoroughly as anyone in the organization? Now, information follows narrow channels and is generally either difficult or impossible to get. Quantitative techniques are not used, so experience (sometimes just seniority) becomes the criterion for testing a new idea. In the new environment of quantitative pretesting of proposed changes, the facts can speak for themselves regardless of the seniority or position of the individual who develops them.

This may lead to the concept of "flickering authority" introduced earlier, which would make it possible for the authority to initiate plans to move freely among the employees of an organization. Since he who is most in-

---

* *The General Electric Forum*, General Electric Company, New York, Winter 1967–1968.

terested in a particular issue will have access to the computer and its programmed tools to help him explore it, he will be tempted to do so whether or not the organization has explicitly authorized him. (It is to be hoped that most, appreciating the value of this, will provide such authorization.) This is not entirely a new idea or trend; it perhaps arises as much from changes in the structure and complexity of organizations, and the popular philosophies of management, as from the availability of computer-related tools. For example, there is an increasing trend toward delegating planning authority to "study groups" often having "project leaders" who may be quite junior. The idea is also compatible with the observations of other observers of organizational trends. Professor Forrester of M.I.T., for example, says,* "I think that in the long run—certainly no more than ten years—we're going to see a trend toward a form of industrial democracy with freedom that will be far more satisfying to the individual instead of a trend toward more centralization with restriction of the individual."

Because "flickering authority" depends on the availability of computer files and programs which are only beginning to be perfected by a few pioneers, there are no cases which clearly exemplify it in full form. However, some advanced users of computers are approaching it.

CASE 12D

◀ A large, diversified forest products company has emphasized the development of comprehensive information systems exploiting the computer's capability throughout its organization. Since these information systems have been available there has been a significant change in the structure of decision-making within the company, which was not planned but has management support. There has been a movement upward in the organizational hierarchy of the authority to make some decisions, accompanied by a downward movement for others.

The class that has moved upward deals with supporting services, such as transportation, data processing, purchasing, and research. It appears that the new ability to coordinate information across the organization's divisions makes it possible to make integrated plans for research allocations, support facilities, and purchases that accommodate the needs and experiences of all divisions, plans more economical and effective than those formerly made at division level. As a result, the authority for such plans and decisions has naturally (without advance intent) moved upward from the divisions to the corporate staff.

---

* Jay W. Forrester, *The Impact of Computers on Management,* M.I.T. Press, Cambridge, 1967.

The class of decisions that has moved downward deals with the operational direction of the divisions. The managers of the divisions are now provided with better information not only about their own divisions but also about the relationships between their divisions and the others. They are now able—either singly or in concert—to make decisions that would formerly have been passed up the line. At the plants, for example, the managers have information about the production schedules and relative efficiencies of their own and all other plants, so new demands on any one can be met with the assistance of all the others. Allocations were formerly made by the corporate staff, but they were frequently unaware of local problems and viewpoints. Now, those with the most at stake make the decisions. Again, this was not planned; the managers began insisting on making the decisions as soon as they had enough information to do so, and the corporate staff was quite happy to be rid of the problems involved. ▶

In this case authority does not "flicker" from one individual to another in the free manner we have described. Instead, it has "migrated" from previous levels which were established by the organizational hierarchy to the levels where each decision can most efficiently be made, where the greatest knowledge and interest in the problem reside regardless of the level in the hierarchy. It may be that this is an alternative version of, or a precursor to "flickering authority."

"Flickering authority" is not to be confused with any change in the pattern of responsibility. The project leader using the computer to develop the consequences of an idea and the plan for executing it will probably not have the right to decide to implement it. As now, this decision will be reserved for the level of management responsible for custody of the organization's resources. Only those formally designated as custodians of resources should be able to commit them; to have "flickering responsibility" as well as "flickering authority" would be to invite chaos and is not necessary. "Flickering authority" alone, if widely practiced, will bring all the ideas and plans of subordinates that pass the test of simulation to senior management's attention for review and approval. This should at the same time permit wide freedom of action and retain control.

It would seem, then, that all levels of management are likely to receive increasing benefits from the computer. The senior managers are likely to get more help in at least some of their areas of concern, and will be provided with more and better developed ideas from their subordinates. Furthermore, decisions which are passed up the line to them today but which could be better made by those most concerned will apparently migrate to their rightful level, thus lightening their loads. The more junior manager benefits even more directly, because his authority becomes the authority naturally associated with his position and the authority he is able to command through his creativity; he is no longer allowed only the authority arbitrarily assigned to him by his position in the organizational hierarchy.

Employees

Computers will increasingly issue instructions for individuals to carry out at an operational level. This was indicated by the considerations of the computer's strengths and of the benefits organizations are striving to obtain from it. The negative effects of this relationship, the dehumanization, elimination of supervisory positions, and loss of flexibility, have been explored. We have also explored certain positive effects which result, however, not only in the operational efficiency of the organization (the basic reason for employing the computer) but also on the employees involved. With the computer as "watchdog" against mistakes, some of the heavy responsibility employees must bear for proper operation of expensive machinery is relieved, and they appear to welcome this relief. For example, almost every new electric generating plant is equipped with a computer which, among other things, controls and sequences the complex processes of plant startup and shutdown. This process involves strict sequences of opening and closing valves, applying power, closing switches, and the like, each step in the process to be taken only after certain temperatures, operating speeds, or loadings have been achieved. Errors in following the process may result in damage to very expensive machines, and the "mindless" process of following the instructions rigidly every time is both irritating and anxiety-producing. Employees in such plants usually are pleased to have the computer perform this watchdog function for them. The computer can also be observed performing such functions for complex businesses where many detailed rules must be followed.

CASE 12E

◀ Computer manufacturers must offer very extensive product lines to be competitive and serve a sufficient variety of prospective customers. We observed in Chapter 7 that in 1956 the most popular IBM medium size computer was offered in two models with five options, while in 1967 the corresponding newer computer was offered in fifty-four different models with ninety-one options. For technical and market reasons there are various restrictions: certain of the options are available only with certain models of the computer, the use of certain options precludes the use of others, and often special adapter units (with their own model numbers and prices) must be interposed between computers and optional equipment. Each manufacturer-supplied program is written presupposing a certain configuration of equipment, and no customer having less than this configuration can use it, so programs are also a factor in selecting equipment. All this poses a problem for the computer salesman. When he induces a customer to order a computer system, he must submit a contract for acceptance that specifies the configuration and price of equipment ordered, and the manufacturer-supplied programs that he has committed to the user as part of the sale. Despite the fact that the salesman has reference material and training that equip him to prepare an accurate contract, it is still entirely understandable that he may make occasional mistakes.

Such mistakes can be serious. At a minimum, they involve an embarrassing call on the customer in which the error is confessed and the customer is asked to accept modifications to a contract he has already signed. At worst such errors may lead to erroneous information being used in manufacturing planning and money being invested—even deliveries being made—before anyone realizes that the details of the contract do not match the commitments made by the salesman and the customer's expectation.

In order to eliminate these salesmen's errors in configuring computer systems, all manufacturers employ personnel specially trained in the subject to review and verify drafts of the contracts. This prevents erroneous manufacturing commitments but the embarrassing return call on the customer may still be necessary, delays are involved in the review process, and the review personnel represent a significant cost.

One computer manufacturer, anxious to avoid the delays, embarrassments, and clerical costs involved in reviewing contracts, developed a computer program to verify the salesmen's configurations automatically. The salesman, having developed the configuration he believes correct, transmits the details and identifications of the programs he has promised the customer to a computer at the home office from a remote input-output terminal located in his branch office. The computer checks the configuration against its files and verifies that the configuration is correct, or if it is not, identifies the required change. In some cases the computer can provide active assistance by suggesting a lower cost configuration that will operate the required programs as well as the one the salesman has proposed.

The salesmen were delighted when the service became available, because it provided them with assurance that their contracts would be correct the first time without imposing significant time delays. Management was also pleased because of the improvement in the "image" presented by the salesmen, and also because the central computer, while checking the configuration, would also collect timely new order information for sales statistics and manufacturing planning as a by-product. ▶

We have seen that improved scheduling performed by computer can reduce peak loads on the employee, reduce overtime, and help him provide more responsive service to the customer. The computer is also a tool that can be used directly by the employee for computational and data handling tasks incidental to his regular work. Many time-sharing services now make available input-output terminals at reasonable costs for employees of organizations who must do mathematical work in the course of their jobs. They are convenient when the calculations to be performed by statistical clerks, actuaries, and engineers exceed the capabilities of desk calculators, but when access to and programming of a centralized computer is inconvenient. With the time-sharing terminal such computations can be performed easily and quickly. Furthermore, many time-sharing services also offer text editing services to employees writing reports or preparing catalogs or letters that are similar but vary in detail. In such services the employee sends the original draft of his document to the remote computer by typing it into his remote terminal. Later he keys in changes, additions, and corrections using an "editing language" which makes it easy for him to inform the computer what kind of change is desired and where it fits in the text. The computer automatically makes the required change in the original draft and is ready at any time to produce a hyphenated, justified version of the text suitable for reproduction or mailing. The repetitive retypings of a report as it is edited and improved are reduced to a single, initial typing with later typing for only new material. Similarly, a document to be prepared many times with only small changes need be typed into the machine once and then as the changes for each version of it are typed in, the computer can produce a finished document for each version.

As time passes and computers and their programs improve, a wider variety of less expensive "tools" will become available. Entrepreneurial firms interested in making a profit by providing such tools will introduce more and more of them, and as they see fit organizations will subscribe to the services, benefiting both the organization and the employee who uses the tool. The manager will be the greatest beneficiary, both because of improved direct services and improvements in the organization managed.

Scientists and engineers

The increased opportunities offered by the computer to scientists and engineers have been discussed in Chapter 9. Most of the new services that will be available to the next generation of technicians have already been conceived and are under development in laboratories and universities, but the perfection and widespread implementation of them will apparently take many years. To recapitulate briefly, the individual will be able to do more in less time by using the computer for his calculating and drafting—probably combining both into a single operation. He will be able to test ideas using the computer's simulation ability, and thereby be able to both shortcut expensive experiments and pilot plant operations and investigate areas otherwise impossibly difficult. Computers have seen limited use for all these purposes but limits have been imposed by the high cost of computer time, delays associated with using computers, and the language barrier (e.g., difficult programming and the absence of previously perfected programs and data). As these limits are relieved and the versatility and convenience of computer programs for specific disciplines in science and engineering improve, the opportunities offered will increase accordingly.

The effect of the computer on many engineering and scientific disciplines has been so profound that it cannot fail to have an eventual effect on the individual practitioners. Whether this will be seen in the next generation or not is difficult to foresee, because so far the potential of the computer is only beginning to be realized; there is little evidence to suggest what a generation of technicians who have grown up accustomed to it will be like. Surely they will be more *systems oriented,* more accustomed to viewing the interacting characteristics of a dynamic process as a whole rather than (as in the past) breaking down a system into its elements and then struggling with the interactions on an element by element basis. The methods of orderly, step-by-step development of a design will become less important; increasingly, emphasis will be on successively approximating ideal solutions to the total problem with the computer simulating the behavior of each approximation. There will be less emphasis on learning "cookbook methods," i.e., formulas worked out by experience that can be applied without analysis to classes of design problems. There will be less emphasis on learning applied mathematics, the computational tools engineers have had to learn for working out formulas and solving equations. Mathematical programs are now available for all computers and in the more advanced systems they will be "embedded" in computer-aided design complexes that will automatically execute them, perhaps without the engineer's explicit knowledge. He will have to spend less time on mathematics both during his work and during his education, but will be unable to use the mathematical methods now employed. This may be a loss, but it is inevitable: navigators are rarely proficient in celestial navigation in this age of LORAN and electronic aids, and (to take a more extreme case) very few housewives today know how to butcher a chicken, though they all did not so long ago!

The interactive sharing of an experimental investigation or design task between a data processing system and a human has profound implications, but it is far from existence yet in most disciplines and has had little cumulative effect on them. We must leave the question open then, and conclude that the next generation of scientists and engineers will still be exploiting the fundamentally new opportunities offered by the computer and only slowly adapting to it in ways not yet clearly foreseeable. Managements of organizations employing them must patiently help them adapt; false starts are to be expected, but in the long run great gain is hoped for.

ORGANIZATIONS

As we have seen, most organizations have used the computer to achieve savings and improvements in operations. For many it has clearly made operations more efficient and responsive, by making possible optimum scheduling and fast responses employing the complete information files of the organization. Initially, most organizations have applied these capabilities to reducing inventory levels and providing faster turnover of capital. However, it also appears that organizations using computers extensively become free to diversify their authority and organizational structures. Case 12B described a company which found that automated information systems permit decision-making to move both upward and downward in the organization to the logical levels, where those qualified to make the decisions are to be found. We have also suggested that some organizations may go even further and have no fixed authority structure; rather, they may employ "flickering authority" to take advantage of the varying pattern of capabilities and ideas within the organization's fixed structure of responsibility.

Some organizations take advantage of computer and communication systems to centralize management to a greater degree (Chapter 6). In the Department of Defense the degree of centralization is extreme, and in most cases it seems that some functions (such as data processing planning) will generally become highly centralized. However, we reviewed many problems which will cause most organizations to be wary of extreme centralization. The motivating and rewarding of personnel, the training of future professionals and managers, the disorientation of employees deprived of personal supervision and subject to an accelerated pace of change, the desire in many organizations to provide flexible and personalized customer service, the need to modify purely rational decisions based on knowledge of local conditions and backgrounds, all combine to render extreme centralization undesirable to most organizations.

A spectrum of compromises is more likely. A clue to one form of compromise appeared in our discussion of the evolution of computer manufacturing companies as they endeavor to respond to competition and customers' demands. Case 7A reviewed a typical computer marketing organization which incorporates a widespread network of branches and completely centralized information handling and scheduling functions. However, it also includes regional offices to deal with the branches' problems and support them. The regions are equipped with consultants who provide expert assistance to the branches in areas ranging from advanced technical questions to legal and policy matters. They provide maintenance support when unusual or difficult problems are encountered, and they provide schools for training branch staff and for the more advanced customers. Perhaps more important, the regions embody a management level in a position to evaluate the performance of field representatives, to guide and advise them in personal development, and to be concerned with their motivations and rewards. It may be that many organizations will follow such a path, establishing centralized information systems for storage and retrieval of company data as well as for overall scheduling, but providing decentralized support and personnel management in a relatively small number of regional staff groups. The next chapter will explore the overall organizational structures that may result from the combination of this and other factors.

The computer will offer almost every organization an opportunity to collect and utilize more useful information than ever before. We have spoken mostly of its utilization, but computers also make possible data collection systems that are revolutionary in nature, such as the surveillance satellite. Surveillance satellites are highly developed because of their use for a number of years in military applications, and they are now beginning to be applied to peaceful ends. The Nimbus satellite, for example, was designed primarily to collect oceanographic and meteorological data but is so general in purpose that it can handle a great variety of information. In its polar orbit it passes over every point on earth each day, and it interrogates instruments on the surface by radio as it passes them. These instruments, designed to work with it, gather data of any kind and store it as electrical signals. Upon interrogation by the satellite they transmit the data to it by radio. Then, later in its orbit when the satellite is passing over a ground station, it will be directed to transfer all the information accumulated during its last orbit to the ground.

The Nimbus satellite is a general-purpose data gathering system for quickly transferring data gathered remotely at any point on earth. In addition to instruments collecting weather and oceanographic data, many other kinds could obviously be used. They may track the movements of animals or icebergs, collecting data from transmitters attached to them; they may track the movements of fish, using floating buoys that detect their sounds. In addition to Nimbus other types of satellites carrying their own sensors view the earth's surface in visible, infrared, and other wavelengths. Such satellites are expected to be useful in measurements of vegetation and land use and in geological explorations, because large scale rock formations can be perceived well from space. Also, they may observe the movements of vehicles or even groups of people or animals (e.g., nomadic tribes in the desert) for demographic studies. Of course computers are essential to the operation of satellites both to direct them and to "unscramble" the masses of data they gather. Computers will be equally essential to other types of data gathering systems of more specific industrial use (e.g., oil well logging systems).

The computer most often helps organizations to obtain better data by storing and processing quantities of previously available information formerly too voluminous for convenient use. Some organizations are already developing data banks of information about their markets, customers, competitors, and the economic conditions which affect their business.

CASE 12F

◀ The Honeywell Corporation* has established a centralized marketing information service staffed by specially trained marketing, systems, and computer personnel and supported by three computers, microfilm equipment, and a library of specialized computer programs. Basic identification and location information on approximately 500,000 firms in the United States is stored for each firm as well as a description of its activities, size, products, and finances. For organizations with which Honeywell has had direct association (e.g., customers or vendors) additional information includes the nature of the past association, the volume of past business, and the names of appropriate individuals to contact. In addition to these basic computer files, a large variety of ancillary information (e.g., annual reports) is retained in microfilm files, indexed in additional computer files.

The system can retrieve information about specific companies, but it also processes the information in a number of ways. For example it can relate the company information to a mathematical model of the U.S. economy, selecting firms representing potential markets for a product or involved in activities related to one specified by the questioner. The files can be searched to produce the names of all companies of a given type in a given area; the system is able to prepare mailing labels for promotional efforts. The range of studies and analyses the center can perform in support of market research is very broad, and Honeywell expects that it will grow in scope and usefulness. ▶

Such systems are quite common nowadays. Obviously with such files completed and convenient computer programs available to retrieve and analyze information, an organization's ability to plan its future ventures will be enhanced.

---

* Honeywell Marketing Information Service, Document No. 59–0826, Honeywell Corporation, Minneapolis, November 1967.

Computers enable organizations to vary the products and services they offer without giving up the benefits of mass production and of automatic data handling. We have reviewed a number of examples of this such as Case 4G, which described an automobile company that has been able to offer a much greater variety of models and options because it uses computers to control and schedule its manufacturing and can handle more variations in the information. There are limits to this, of course; every option and variation of the product must be within the framework of product designs and manufacturing plans the company has already developed, and the individual order may not be so unusual or large that it is outside the pattern of conditions for which the computer was programmed. Within these limitations, though, it is apparent that a great deal of flexibility can be obtained.

We have also seen that the computer offers the organization an opportunity to become more responsive to its customers. The kind of responsiveness the computer makes possible is not always the kind desired, however.

CASE 12G

◀ The government of one of the Carribean Islands maintains an office in New York for the purpose of encouraging tourism. The office receives many inquiries, almost all for standard information: brochures, names and rates of hotels, schedules of transportation media. In order to reduce its clerical costs for handling these simple requests, the organization installed an experimental telephone answering device containing a variable program which could recognize inquirers' words to the extent of separating "yes" from "no." The device would answer the telephone, identify itself as a recording and ask the inquirer to please answer "yes" or "no" to each of the questions it would ask him. First it would ask, "Are you a travel agent or a private individual?" Based on the "yes" or "no" answer to this question, it would branch to either of two sequences because the prerecorded answers differed for the two. The machine would then ask a series of questions such as, "Do you want hotel brochures?" For each "yes" answer it would go into further detail until the specific hotel, airline, steamship line, etc., was identified. If the inquirer wanted only general information, the proper sequence of answers would cause the machine to branch to general information questions leading to the mailing of general brochures or answers the machine was prepared to give over the telephone. If the questioner attempted to say anything other than "yes" or "no," the machine would say, "I did not understand you," and repeat the question. Upon two failures it would ring the receptionist in the office who would take the call.

In every case, after the sequence of questions was completed the machine summarized for the caller the actions that the sequence of "yes" answers had indicated (e.g., "We will send you the brochure for Hotel X."). Finally, the machine would say, "At the tone you will have 30 seconds to record any additional message you wish to leave," so that questions that had not fit into the program's structure or any comments or additional requests could be reviewed later by the office staff.

The experiment did not work, and the machine was removed after a few months' trial period. There was no trouble with the machine and the large majority of questions did fit well with the answers programmed into it. However, the persons calling refused to submit to its discipline. If they had business other than requesting information, they became impatient for the machine to get through its questions and were often irate by the time the machine either connected them with an operator or was ready to record the message. Also, as people began to be aware of the machine's existence crank calls and curious children began to overload the incoming lines. It was finally decided that although the machine had been satisfactory technically, it was a failure sociologically; the machine was removed. ▶

This case sounds a note of warning: defenseless machines should not be exposed to a mischievious public! It is likely that in most cases where an information system is to deal with the general public a human will have to take the call and operate the computer. This is still a great advance over earlier information systems which took days or weeks to locate required information, however, and will be satisfactory to most organizations.

Last and perhaps most important, the removal of organizational constraints made possible by the computer permits a flexibility in people's roles which is unprecedented in the structured organizations of our time. If the authority structure is allowed to vary or "flicker," many more opportunities develop for employees interested in demonstrating their creativity or their fitness for managerial positions. Those interested in routine but interesting jobs will also find the computer has improved their lot: the customer service agent provided with computer-based information, for example, spends more time dealing with the individual customer and less time searching files, filling out forms, and "shuffling papers." Likewise the advertising agent, buyer, personnel manager, interviewer, or salesman teamed with the computer can spend more time on the interesting and interpersonal parts of the job and eliminate the dull and repetitive ones. The technician or professional benefits from the availability of the computer to make his existing computational work easier and to broaden the scope of work he can do in the future.

Even those interested in routine, repetitive jobs (of which it appears there will always be some) will be accommodated. We have seen that the automated factory, in which no employees appear, is a rarity. A number are still ordinarily needed to tend the computer-controlled machines, to provide variations in the processes that are too complex to program for the general run of operations, and to be on the watch for emergency conditions or interferences in the flow of work. Such routine jobs, apparently more pleasant than earlier routine jobs, will remain available. There will also be service and maintenance jobs in increasing numbers as the complexity of machinery increases, and there is a tremendous and increasing number of jobs in computer data preparation and control which will apparently always be available.

Some commentators such as Professor Forrester* believe that this is the greatest opportunity of all: the opportunity for the individual employee of the large, bureaucratic organization to develop a freedom and flexibility in determining his own role that was never before available.

SUMMARY

This chapter, as the title implies, is intended to be one of optimism. It is right to be optimistic; surely Mr. Eppert's quote at the beginning of the chapter is not entirely unfounded and this enumeration of the opportunities offered by the computer is bound to impress. On the other hand, it is well to end with a note of caution. It is easy to become carried away by the possibilities offered by the computer and gloss over the difficulties of realizing them and the dislocation and unhappiness caused in the process. The magnitude of the technical and economic difficulties of realizing these opportunities must be recognized, as well as the problems inherent in the pace and scope of the changes involved.

The period of experimentation leading to slow exploitation of the opportunities offered by computers will surely be many years long, perhaps covering more than an entire generation. The outcome at the end of that time can be partly foreseen by a simultaneous consideration of the opportunities offered and the concessions demanded by the computer, the subject of the concluding chapter.

---

* Jay W. Forrester, *op. cit.*

CHAPTER 13

NEW DIMENSIONS OF FREEDOM

*"Academies should return to wisdom study in tree groves rather than robot study in plastic cells."**
ALLEN GINSBERG

"Machines should work; people should think."
IBM CORPORATION

The preceding chapters have shown that if we wish to fully realize the potential of the computer, we must make concessions in our familiar habits of thought and ways of doing things—indeed, in our valued privileges of individuality and privacy. In return, we will be offered stimulating and far-reaching opportunities to simplify and enrich our activities. The changes that occur will reflect a combination of concessions made and opportunities realized. While we can foresee them only to a limited degree, we have learned that the difficulty of developing and absorbing the new systems is so great that even this limited foresight probably spans a whole generation.

This chapter attempts to forecast the changes caused by computer systems by combining the findings of the previous chapters into the most probable patterns. They will be presented as a series of hypothetical cases, each depicting a fully realized computer-based system and its effect. None of these exist today, but each is foreshadowed by cases we have already cited. Furthermore, none of them involves any new technology; in every case, the perfection and widespread implementation of already proven technology would be enough. They should, then, provide useful guidance for the manager or computer user interested in intelligently adapting to and controlling this process of change.

---

* *Time,* July 12, 1968.

THE NEXT GENERATION OF BUSINESS ORGANIZATIONS

Computers will be used to direct operations to a greater degree than now, even though progress has already been substantial. Most organizations have yet to undertake the laborious data collection and mathematical analysis that underlies decision rules the computer can implement, so most are not ready to use computers for routine decision-making. However, because some organizations are doing so, the nature of the process involved is clear, as are the changes that follow in the organization and its employees. The effects of applying the computer to operations—the changes it causes in the process— are no longer matters for speculation but for reporting as fact. The facts have been recorded in Part II. In the next generation, the most likely development is simply the further extension of computer-assisted decision-making to more organizations and more wide use of it in present computer-using organizations, with the ensuing changes more widespread.

A more novel use of the computer is its application to the competitive process of making the organization's product more attractive to the customer. We have reviewed cases where this has been done, but it has rarely happened and only to a modest degree. The following hypothetical case illustrates the degree to which business organizations in the next generation may use computers to improve their services.

CASE 13A (hypothetical)

◀ An automobile dealer of 1980 offers standard models he has acquired for inventory, in order to meet the demand for immediate delivery to customers who do not want unusual features. However, in the more normal case where the customer wishes to specify the characteristics of his car and is willing to wait for its manufacture and delivery, the agency offers a "Custom Design Service" which works as follows.

The potential buyer and the salesman sit together in front of a computer input-output terminal connected to a remotely located regional computer owned by the company, and proceed to design the car the customer wants. Depending on the customer's interests, either the mechanical design or the body design may be attended to first. If the customer wishes to start with the body design, the salesman operates the keyboard of the terminal so that the computer causes pictures of available body sections to be displayed one by one on the TV-type screen of the terminal. The customer is shown a choice of grills, hood designs, fenders, body styles, and rear end configurations. He chooses the one of each that seems most attractive to him and the salesman informs the computer of his choice. The computer verifies the acceptability of combining the body segments the customer has selected (obviously not all combinations are possible; a convertible rear end could not be combined with a station wagon body, for example). If the selection is unacceptable, the computer will so indicate and suggest alternatives as close as possible to the style initially selected. When this "dialogue" is complete, the customer has selected all the necessary body sections and specified colors, and the computer has verified that it is mechanically possible to combine them. The computer then displays on the screen the image of the resulting car for final review and approval by the potential buyer.

This done, the buyer and salesman then turn to mechanical aspects of the car. The chassis and suspension must be selected; the computer will again pass on their suitability for attachment to the selected body. Engine, transmission, steering, brakes, heating and air conditioning, and accessories follow in order. In each case, the computer displays for the buyer and salesman the available options (always considering the restrictions made necessary by previous choices) including their characteristics and costs. As each is selected, it is added to the list of previous selections in the computer's memory until the last selection is made and the design is complete. Then the computer displays for the prospective buyer the final appearance of the complete car together with information about total price, weight, and overall performance characteristics. If the result is attractive to the buyer, he and the salesman then turn to negotiation of the "deal" considering the usual factors of discounts, trade-in allowance, and financing. This remains a purely interpersonal process.

If a deal is satisfactorily concluded, the salesman enters this fact together with the terms of the transaction into the computer, which then performs a variety of data processing functions. The salesman and the customer are each provided with a copy of a purchase order printed by the computer detailing all the selections, the final price, and the delivery date so that each may have a written record of the transaction. The information about the order is transferred from the computer to the manufacturer's machine for use in manufacturing scheduling and accounting. The details of the financial transactions are transmitted to the record-keeping programs of the dealer for his accounting and (possibly) to the data processing system of the finance company which the customer will use to finance his purchase, if the parties involved happen to have worked out a system for automatic interchange of data. The customer, of course, is still permitted to finance the purchase any way he likes. ▶

No major change in the automobile manufacturer's way of doing business would be required to make this service possible. He already manufactures standard chassis, engines, body parts, and the like and assembles them into individual models as the market demands. The only novelty involved in this hypothetical service is allowing the customer to assemble them to suit his own desires rather than the prejudgments of the manufacturer's product designers. This service has not been possible because the manufacturing scheduling is much more complicated; a much wider variety of combinations must be scheduled on the assembly line. But as we have seen, the use of computers has already permitted automobile manufacturers to greatly proliferate their combinations and this service requires only a further step in the process.

Such a service is attractive because it offers greater freedom and convenience to all parties, while requiring almost nothing in the way of additional concessions. The buyer, if he wishes, can design a very individual car with components studied and selected in great detail. On the other hand, he can accept a standard model with no more effort than is involved in today's car purchases. All parties benefit because of the simplification in the paper work and accounting involved: the customer because the information about his order is immediately transmitted to the manufacturer's manufacturing complex so that delivery time may be reduced; the dealer and manufacturer because of the immediate capture and processing of the information at no additional cost in data preparation. The only concession involved is the effort required by the salesman to learn to operate the keyboard of the computer terminal, but this should be very little more difficult than his present effort to learn to use his sales manual.

It is easy to imagine many other possible examples of this increased flexibility in service being offered to customers. Furniture, prefabricated houses, clothing, appliances, and many other consumer goods could be provided with such an increase in flexibility without increasing the complexity of the manufacturer's production process, if only the information needed to produce the personalized product could be communicated among the buyer, the salesman, and the manufacturer—a communication now made possible by the computer.

Businesses are already using computers to provide better information for their employees. In the last chapter we reviewed the Honeywell Corporation marketing information system; there are many comparable examples. Some large banks, for example, who deal repeatedly with business customers have found it advantageous to establish centralized data banks in which all of the information about the bank's dealings with customers is stored. Thus, any employee having dealings with any representative of a customer company may easily be appraised of all the past history of the bank's association with the company, regardless of location and type of transaction. At present a great deal of time searching through the records of various departments might be needed before complete information could be obtained; even then it might be out of date because all the records might not be equally current. This is another well-established computer application whose evolution in the next generation is likely to be simply an extension in frequency of use and scope of coverage.

The concessions involved in using such a system include the necessity—usually only irritating—of abiding by the standards, and loss of the right to withhold information and keep it proprietary. The latter concession should not be serious within an organization, but if (as is sometimes true) the same system serves a number of firms, the loss of secrecy can be serious.

CASE 13B (hypothetical)

◀ In 1985 it has become possible and convenient for any individual to buy or sell any kind of security or medium of investment—stocks, bonds, commodities, mutual fund shares, and even some types of real estate—in direct negotiations with any other trader anywhere in the country, eliminating the middleman. It has been found necessary to license such individuals to avoid fraud and failures to pay or deliver, however; every registered trader must post a bond or evidence of sufficient capital to cover any debt he may incur, and must submit to examinations of his records to indicate that his dealings have been conducted in a legally acceptable manner. (In practice, this means that only a few private individuals have the motive to become registered traders on their own accounts. Almost all registered traders are employees of brokerage firms, mutual funds, bank trust departments, or other institutions doing quantities of trading for their own accounts or for the accounts of retail customers.)

Every registered trader subscribes to a computer communication service which employs a nation-wide network of computers and communication lines. Each subscriber is provided with a terminal device connected to the network, having a keyboard, a display screen, and a printer. There is also a printed directory (revised weekly) to be used with it. When the trader wishes to buy or sell any investment, he looks up the identifying code for it in the directory and then enters the code into the keyboard of the terminal. At this point the display shows him the current price (if any) for the property, and also the names of all individuals who have previously entered into the computer a desire to either buy or sell it together with their bid prices for buying or selling it. If the trader's intention is to record a bid of his own, he may enter his identifying code and the bid or asked price at which he is willing to trade. The computer will then display his bids along with the others to inquirers. If the trader wishes to buy or sell, he reviews the list of dealers' bids and selects an interesting one. To learn which trader has entered the bid, he looks at the identifying symbol on the display which is an abbreviation of the trader's name or company affiliation. He may recognize it immediately if he does business regularly with the individual or firm, or he may have to refer to the directory to identify it. Then, to negotiate his purchase or sale he contacts the firm whose quote he has selected as the most interesting. He does this by using the computer system as a telephone or teletype switch, entering in the keyboard the identification of the trader being called and noting whether he wishes to converse with him via the keyboard and page printer or via a telephone attached to the terminal. The computer system connects the two traders' telephones or teletypes, and they discuss the terms of the transaction. If they arrive at an agreement and have used the teletype, the computer automatically selects the necessary details (identity and amount of the property, price, identification of the two parties, etc.) from the final message, and enters the transaction in its records. If they used the telephone, they must key in this data. The page printer at each trader's terminal then prints a confirmation of the transaction and (if the trader subscribes to the optional accounting service offered by the computer complex) proceeds to enter the information into his accounting records.

This system is not speculative, but is almost certain to be realized in much this form. The NASDAQ system, now being implemented for the National Association of Securities Dealers, will provide services almost identical to this for the network of dealers in over the counter stocks, and it is anticipated that the system will also include at least bonds and perhaps mutual fund shares. It is already a matter of controversy whether stocks listed on the exchanges will also be included in this system (thereby providing an alternative market for them); it seems likely that under some arrangement this will eventually be done. There is, in fact, no intrinsic limit to the variety of properties that can be quoted in such a system, or to the parties using it, as long as they are willing to pay the price and to trade in a responsible manner. ▶

The opportunities offered by this system are great. Any trader of any size, anywhere in the country, has immediate access to all other traders' bids. Every property of interest to a trader anywhere is "advertised" to all others, and all are assured of equivalent prices because all trade on the basis of bids advertised to all. Furthermore, because all traders share the cost of a single system, its cost to each is very low.

The concessions demanded by this system are equally great. The very nature of today's brokerage and trading firms is challenged by this system, as is the reason for existence of stock exchanges themselves. They all exist for the primary purposes of bringing buyers and sellers together and conducting trading in an orderly way; the system (with regulation) would do this instead. There are unquestioned advantages to today's orderly markets in which a relative few control price movements and trading rates, and there are perfectly honorable trading opportunities that depend on privacy of information about customer orders, one's own position, or differences in prices being quoted by different dealers. These would be obviated by such a system. It is not too much to say that the securities trading industry would be revolutionized by the full implementation of such a computer-based system, with new opportunities for all but with disastrous loss of the very reason for existence of many. Managers in other industries would do well to remain alert for signs of similar changes.

Whether information comes from outside the organization, inside it, or both, its ready availability combined with the computer's ability to process it provides new opportunities for all the employees and managers of the organization. Specific items of fact can be requested, or a great variety of collections or analyses of them. An executive responsible for the manufacture and sale of a product can obtain regular and special reports on all events throughout the company that pertain to that product: its raw materials and manufacturing cost, its sales, its reliability and service record, etc. Using the same data elements but putting them together in different ways, managers can review the performance of organizational units such as the sales and service experience of all products within the territory of a sales branch. Data elements can be grouped in other ways, too: a salesman interested in the company's relations with a particular customer can obtain a report summarizing all data elements containing references to that customer regardless of what function in the organization dealt with him or what product was involved.

Combined with this facility for grouping data elements in varied ways will be the computer's ability to simulate or model—its ability to predict the outcomes of possible actions based on a model of the interactions occurring within the company, and between it and its environment, expressed in the form of mathematical relationships. All of this will make possible—indeed, may make inevitable—emergence of the "flickering authority" explored earlier which in principle will enable every employee of the organization to undertake the planning and decision-making roles for which he is qualified and interested, regardless of his position in the organization.

This does not mean that every employee and manager will become expert in using the computer. Over time, more and more of the organization's employees and managers will indeed become familiar with it assisted by the improving languages available for preparing programs, but it seems unlikely that all executives will be prepared and willing to use the computer directly for the foreseeable future. Also, when the problem to be posed to the computer is complex, even the fully computer-trained executive will probably require the services of specialists. Most organizations will probably employ a group of specialists in formulating problems, collecting and relating data, and programming the computer, who will help management use it. This group will probably be derived from the programmers and system analysts of today, but having less concern with the elements of the machine as it becomes easier to use, and more with management problems and the interactions embodied in the increasingly sophisticated problems they will study. This group, the "interpretation staff," will interpret the manager's more complex needs for the computer and interpret its results for the manager. The interpretation staff (which may serve well as a management training area) should reduce the concession required of the manager in learning about computers, and enable the company to wrestle with problems more complex than the level of knowledge achieved by either the managers or the computer people alone would permit.

All these developments will work together in the organization of the next generation, and the result may be typified by the following hypothetical case.

CASE 13C (hypothetical)

◀ A junior executive performing production scheduling for a computer manufacturing company has, by 1978, become familiar with computers because he has participated in the evolution of a computer-based production scheduling system for the company. By now the system has reached a high stage of perfection and is nearly automatic. The daily work load of detailed decisions formerly required of executives in production scheduling has been greatly reduced, so the junior executive has time to concern himself with other matters.

He reads in a computer journal about experiments with computer-controlled internal combustion engines, where functions of mixture control, ignition timing, cooling, lubricant flow, and transmission control have been programmed for small computers directly controlling engines. The computers have been programmed to record and integrate all the factors that determine the setting of the engine's controls: the speed, output torque, mixture, fuel flow, manifold pressure, engine and coolant temperature, atmospheric temperature and pressure, and composition of the exhaust gases (pollution control is a primary objective of using the computer). The computer combines all these conditions using preprogrammed relationships which indicate the optimum setting of all the engine's controls under all possible combinations of conditions. The article in the journal reports that experiments with computer-controlled engines have had promising results, and suggests that there will be a sizeable market for them because of their efficiency and long life.

The production scheduling executive thinks this area might be a new market for the computers made by his company. The article suggests the size and complexity of computer that would be needed, so he turns to the company's own computer system to obtain an estimate of the manufacturing cost of such a computer; a suitable estimating program is available. A profit simulator program is also available; it forecasts the profits which would result from combining the assumed manufacturing, programming, and marketing costs of a proposed product with assumed sale prices and volumes. He experiments with the cost estimates provided by the estimator program, relating them to various sales volumes and prices. He obtains a series of curves which seem to promise a favorable result at what look like reasonable assumptions of sales volume, price, and cost: the specialized computer for engine control appears to be a highly profitable product. The production control executive then prepares a report incorporating these curves and submits it to management with a recommendation that the product be developed and introduced.

Management, reviewing the report, is impressed with the profit forecasts but is not certain that the estimates of either costs or sales volumes are reliable. Therefore, management starts an engineering design study to determine the actual cost of manufacturing the computer; the engineering staff goes to work with their computer to simulate and then predict costs for the actual logic and memory circuit functions that would be needed for such a machine. Management also instructs the interpretation staff associated with the company's central computer to study the possible sales volume at the forecast prices. The interpretation staff, for a fee, obtains access to a computer-based data bank of automotive industry information from which they obtain data about the characteristics, operating costs, and sales volumes of the different kinds of engines currently manufactured. Obtaining results from engineering about the actual cost of the proposed computer, they perform another study which compares the lifetime acquisition and operating cost of engines equipped with the computer to that of engines equipped with conventional controls. They perform a series of computer runs using the volumes and costs for different types of engines for automobiles, trucks, locomotives, aircraft, and other uses. The results of these computer runs tell them with more precision which type of engine would obtain the greatest benefit from the computer, which specific area represents the computer company's best market.

The interpretation staff reports back to management that the results do indeed look favorable, but only in the areas of large truck and locomotive diesel engines. Only they have a favorable enough combination of circumstances to make it likely that early sales will be enough to support the manufacturing volume level at which the sales will show a profit. Six weeks have now elapsed since the production control executive read the article.

Management approves the introduction of the engine control computer but restricts the marketing effort to the manufacturers of the larger diesel engines. The executive originally suggesting the idea is rewarded for his effort, and several of the participants start exploring ideas that have developed during the study for using small computers to control other forms of power generating machinery. ▶

This hypothetical case shows how a number of new data processing developments are likely to come together in a business. It shows the "flickering authority" which enables a junior production control executive to suggest a major new product line. It shows the use of a computer in forecasting the financial outcome under various conditions. It shows the use of computer based data banks (in this case, one containing automotive industry data) by an organization needing the information but not ordinarily collecting it. Finally, it demonstrates one example of how interactions might occur between the individual with the idea, management, the engineering staff, and the interpretation staff responsible for complex computer studies and data analysis. Is it realistic? Almost certainly, because the process followed is closely akin to that presently practiced by companies considering the introduction of new products. The differences are that more accurate data and forecasts are available, that the initial analysis of the idea can be performed anywhere in the organization, and that the whole cycle of initiation, study, and decision about the idea can take place far more rapidly than today. However, no revolutionary change in how people work, in the nature of the planning process, or in technology is implicit in making this hypothetical case a reality.

This kind of activity could only occur in a large organization because it requires the availability of computers with a wide variety of programs and data bases, and of an interpretation staff having the time and ability to obtain data and perform studies of previously unfamiliar subjects. What of small organizations, then? Small organizations will still be unable to support complete data processing facilities of this magnitude on their own, because of the cost of computers and data preparation and (most importantly) because of the cost of skilled personnel. They have less need for complex simulation models and for "flickering authority," because their very smallness enables their personnel to form a more coherent group with better intercommunication, and it is less necessary to establish mathematical models of interactions which are more obvious on the smaller scale. However, surely some of the information needed by the large company (such as automotive industry data, internal manufacturing cost data, and the profit forecasting model) would be needed as much by a small organization as by a large one to perform a similar study.

We have seen that many "community of interest" data processing services are coming into existence to serve groups of smaller organizations who effectively share the development and operating cost of each service. The automotive industry data bank might be one such service, available for the same fee to either the small or large organization and providing the same quality of data. The profit forecasting model developed by the large organization might be generalized to many companies; a small one might, for a fee, obtain a series of computer runs of a general-purpose forecasting model which applies with sufficient accuracy to its situation. Through subscription services the small organization may find itself on an equal footing with the larger one in taking advantage of the new opportunities offered by the computer, but it must unquestionably make concessions in doing so. The small organization must so order its operations and its problems that they fit into the structure of the existing subscription services, and in relying on them for part or all of its data processing it will lose control of the details of this function. This loss of control may become serious for many.

The large organization, too, must make concessions to use simulations. Perhaps most important, the range of possible new products which could be investigated using the computer's models and data bases is restricted to the area in which previously developed models apply (e.g., computers similar in general design to those the computer manufacturer is already producing). If the production control junior executive had developed an idea for a revolutionary child's toy, for example, his company's computers would have had no information about the manufacturing costs of toys, their marketing and distribution costs, their profit margins, and all the other financial elements necessary to make a business decision. It would have been impossible for the process to have occurred efficiently, and over the long term this restriction in the organization's flexibility because of the restrictions in its computers' programs and files may have ominous implications.

Inevitably, organizations using the computer in such a manner will change. We have examined many cases of changes in the structure of organizations as they accommodate to the computer: the centralization of the data processing planning function, the reduction in the number of levels of authority for operations, and the increasing association between the organization's branches (or "agents") in the field and a centralized information center from which they obtain their detailed instructions.

Several kinds of overall organizational structures might emerge from these changes. What may be the most typical can be derived from a consideration of the computer manufacturer discussed at length in Chapter 7, the overall organization of which is depicted in Fig. 13–1.

The company still retains the traditional functional divisions between manufacturing, engineering, marketing, and finance. Each, however, interacts in many ways with the centralized data processing facility developed and oper-

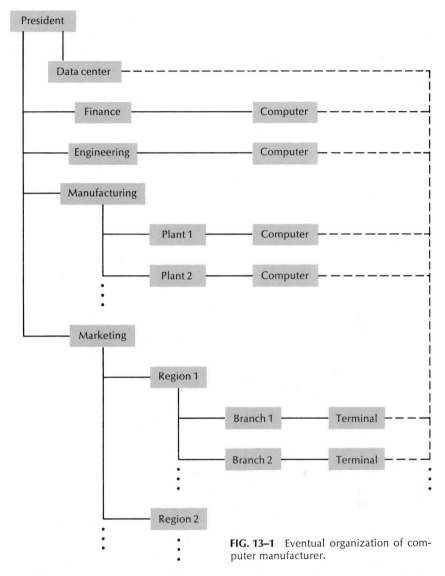

FIG. 13–1 Eventual organization of computer manufacturer.

ated by an interpretation staff reporting to the central management of the company. The company is large, so computers for internal use are to be found at various locations within the functional elements. They are, however, all related to the central facility by common data and programming standards. The more than 100 branch offices responsible for sales, customer support, and service are also connected by remote input-output terminals to the central computer complex and (when needed) to the functional division computers for such purposes as entering and verifying orders, administering sales plans, and accounting and administration of all kinds. However, because of the continuing need for supervision over the branches—supervision of personnel development, monitoring their performance, providing technical support and service, solving customer problems, and providing training facilities both for the company's staff and for customers—a series of regional offices also exist to which the branches report, and from which they obtain many kinds of assistance.

On the surface this organization is very little different from those of today; the chart shows only occasional eliminations of levels of management or responsibility. This superficial view would be misleading, however, because the pattern of information flow and decision-making has changed greatly. Information flows through an integrated and standardized network having only two basic levels, the centralized complex at company headquarters and the many locations where operations of all kinds are performed. Day-to-day transactions and decisions are conducted through this network, bypassing entirely the chain of command which is no longer concerned with them. The intermediate levels in the chain of command, no longer responsible for details and day-to-day administration, are still responsible for satisfactory overall performance, new developments, and problem-solving. People work with people in dealing with "people-type" problems; machines work with machines in dealing with "machine-type" problems.

Another more radical alternative could permit two simultaneously existing structures in a single organization. The administrative and planning structure would remain traditional, with managers at the vice presidential level for each functional element supported by professional staff groups reviewing performance and planning future improvements. The operating structure, however, would be "self-organizing," with groups from all the functional elements of the organization forming and changing adaptively to meet the demands of the day (e.g., practicing "flickering authority"). Such an unstructured, adaptable operations organization would normally collapse in confusion and inefficiency, but with the computer providing resource and administrative information it becomes possible. The structure and functioning of such an organization is illustrated by the following hypothetical case.

CASE 13D (hypothetical)

◀ A medium size manufacturing company specializing in foundry and machine work is able to supply either complete mechanical products or subassemblies to order. It obtains most of its business from the automotive and aerospace industries, selling few products directly to end-users but often making major assemblies that go into the products of others. In order to remain

ADMINISTRATIVE
STRUCTURE

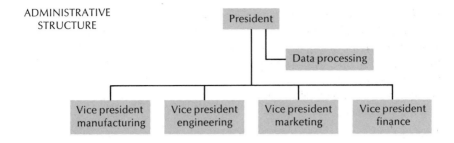

OPERATIONAL
STRUCTURE

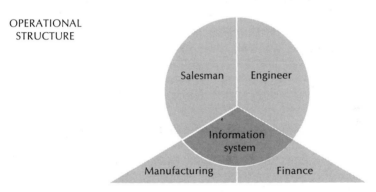

FIG. 13–2   Structure of hypothetical organization employing "flickering authority" in operations.

competitive it must simultaneously emphasize efficiency of operation, rapidity of response, and soundness of design: these are its three formal objectives.

Administratively, the organization is structured as shown in the upper part of Fig. 13–2. Each of the four major functions—finance, marketing, engineering, and manufacturing—is a separate division headed by a vice president and measured according to its performance in meeting the three objectives. Within each division training operations are performed, personnel are evaluated on performance and capability, and planning of new techniques, new facilities, and new personnel policies are performed by the vice president assisted by his staff.

This structure is not responsible for the day-to-day operations of the company. These are performed in an unstructured manner depicted schematically in the lower part of Fig. 13–2, as follows.

1   When a salesman obtains an order, he quotes a delivery time and price. To do this, he must work with a design engineer familiar with the type of product and they must jointly consider the availability of the required engineering and manufacturing resources. The salesman may either go directly to an engineer he knows or ask the organization's centralized information system for the name of a qualified engineer who has time to consult with him. The two (or more if necessary) confer and ask the computer for relevant information about comparable past jobs. They also consult the computer's manufacturing schedule to develop the delivery quote.

2 If the order is obtained on the basis of the quote, its description is entered in the computer so that a reservation of manufacturing time may be made and the initial accounting transactions generated. The engineer then proceeds to design the product, again using the computer's computational support. Since the company has found it advantageous to employ numerically controlled machine tools extensively, the engineer frequently develops his design largely or entirely in computer language, and computer programs generate punched paper tapes which will control the machine tools.

3 When the design is completed, the tapes and the detailed production schedule are delivered to the manufacturing division, which carries out the schedule under the final control of its supervisory personnel.

4 At all stages, necessary accounting and administrative information is prepared by the computer and incorporated in the management reports of the divisions. When the manufacturing process is complete, the computer is able to produce shipping documents, invoices, and cumulative performance statistics for all three operating divisions. ▶

This organization is hypothetical, but some not too different already exist. It is attractive from an operational standpoint because when a new demand is made, the individuals and resources form an "agglomeration" to meet it without delay or administrative waste, as the availability of resources permits. When the job is done the agglomeration automatically dissolves, and each of the individuals and resources moves to such other tasks as may have appeared in the meantime. Without the aid of the computer, such organizational fluidity would be impossible; administrative chaos would result. But with the computer to keep track of the nature and availability of the resources, and with its ability to schedule operations and collect administrative information, the evident desirability of such freedom from organizational constraints becomes possible.

The type of organization depicted in Fig. 13–1, with centralized information systems but decentralized regional management, would seem to apply to a larger service or manufacturing organization with many customers and more or less standard products. The type of organization depicted in Fig. 13–2, employing a "free-form" operational structure, would more likely be a small one with varying products or services. Probably other variations in authority structures will apply to other types of organizations; indeed, with the freedom from prior constraints made possible by the computer, infinite variations become feasible. During the next generation many organizations will experiment with many patterns and some preferred ones for organizations of given types will probably emerge. The above may be among them or they may not; there will probably also be others. The one prediction we can confidently make is that a period of organizational experimentation has started which may lead to surprising results and will be interesting and challenging for all involved. Managers involved in this process will find it difficult to discard their traditional attitudes, but once they do so they may find their new environment more interesting and stimulating.

The "atmosphere" in organizations changing along these lines will surely be somewhat different. Because of the new emphasis on quantitative planning and the "flickering authority" that has resulted from the availability of the computer to all, there should be less distance between higher and lower levels of management. The authority a manager can exercise should be more determined by what he is able to do (which may vary) than be assigned to him by his place in the organizational structure (which is fixed). A manager's suggestions will be weighted according to the evidence he can produce rather than by his seniority and reputation. This is obviously a more attractive environment for junior managers and it simplifies the jobs of senior managers too. Instead of traveling through an endless round of conferences at which unsubstantiated opinions are aired, the senior manager (aided by improved communications) can stay in his office and make only those decisions which he is naturally best equipped to make about issues which have already passed quantitative tests.

The prices the organization must pay for this are several. First (as we have seen) flexibility in the organization is constrained to the flexibility of the accumulated files of data and completed programs. The "dead hand" of previous generations of programmers is bound to constrain the organization's future potentialities. Second, there is a danger of overreliance on the computer's forecasts and simulations. Many decisions must necessarily be made on the basis of intangibles, and senior management must still be able and willing to weigh these accurately in light of their accumulated experience and judgment. Third, while the manager's environment will be more fluid and offer more opportunity, it will also be more complex and "exposed." Relationships with other managers will be less structured, so a higher degree of sensitivity and tact will be needed. Rank and experience for its own sake will be valued less. Every manager must be prepared to have his performance and ideas evaluated without deference to his position. These conditions will be unattractive to many line managers of the traditional type; in fact, the "nakedness" and insecurity inherent in this environment may be unwelcome to most people. Perhaps this is the underlying reason why the computer has caused the confusion and anxiety among managers noted in earlier chapters. It is not yet clear whether this has occurred more because of the climate of change which has accompanied the computer, or because of a permanent change caused by the computer.

THE SOCIAL SERVICE AGENCY OF THE NEXT GENERATION

Social service agencies (schools, hospitals, police, and welfare agencies) have benefited less from the computer than businesses and scientific establishments, partly because they have less money for computers or to hire and train programmers. They have also been delayed because they have less control over their data processing than businesses do; much of what they must collect, process, and report is established by law or by their interaction with other agencies and with governments at all levels. It is difficult for them to establish data processing systems independently of one another.

These conditions are changing. It is more difficult to develop cooperative data processing systems for multiple users than it is to develop them independently, but it is not impossible. "Community of interest" data processing services are being developed by many parties. Nonprofit organizations through which social agencies already coordinate their work (e.g., state education departments, hospital associations) develop services, as do computer manufacturers who hope to enhance sales and Federal Government agencies interested at the same time in helping state and local bodies obtain greater efficiency and in obtaining more rapid and standardized reporting. Profit-making firms are also providing community of interest data processing services for social agencies. Some now provide classroom scheduling and student record services for schools and prepare payrolls for hospitals. These firms add broader and more sophisticated services as their experience grows. More fundamentally, the economics of data processing for social service agencies is changing. As the cost of providing every kind of social service expands explosively, the pressure to find more economical and efficient methods increases and the expenditures necessary to support data processing are increasingly justified. Experience, investments, and commitments are all growing, and it seems certain that the next generation of social service agencies will benefit from the use of computers to at least the same degree that businesses already have in reducing clerical costs and increasing efficiency of operation.

But social service agencies are not businesses, and it is not to be expected that they will show the effects of computers as businesses do. Present trends suggest that some novel adjustments to data processing will develop in social service agencies, which will be illustrated by descriptions of hypothetical cases.

When a social service agency deals with a client, whether he be a welfare applicant, patient, student, or suspected criminal, it must ordinarily spend time and effort to collect data about his relevant background, whether the data is in its own files or in those of other comparable agencies with which he might have been associated. As case 12B showed, efforts are already being made to develop statewide or regional information systems which contain data banks of such experience. It seems certain that pressures of efficiency and economics will expand the scope of these efforts until they are national if not international in scope, and cases such as the following will become typical.

CASE 13E (hypothetical)

◀ In 1982 an unemployed immigrant enters a welfare office in New York City to apply for unemployment compensation. He explains that he has recently arrived in the United States and has been unable to find work, and that his records of personal history and past employment are all in his native country.

As a first step in the application process, the applicant is asked to complete a release form for personal data which will permit the Federally supported National Welfare Data Bank to release to the agency any records it has about this applicant. He may refuse and still be eligible for unemployment compensation, but then the burden will be on him to produce documentary evidence that he is eligible. He consents, however, completes the brief form illustrated in Fig. 12–2, and has it notarized by the notary public in the welfare office. He is then asked to return the following day to learn about the disposition of his application.

The form is filed, and the essential data on it is transmitted via a remote computer terminal to the National Welfare Records Center. The day's accumulation of similar requests is processed overnight and the results are transmitted back to the terminals at the inquiring welfare offices.

In this case, the information the applicant was asked to release concerned his employment history and his history as a welfare recipient in his native country and in the United States. The computer's records show that instead of being a recent immigrant (as he claimed) he had in fact resided in Miami for more than a year, and had been receiving unemployment compensation. Because he was unwilling to accept employment opportunities offered to him in Miami, he exhausted his eligibility for unemployment compensation there.

Armed with this information, the welfare office is able to disapprove his original application immediately, and prepare an alternative proposal for him involving much tighter restrictions on his freedom to reject employment. The applicant is offered the right to file a statement disputing the accuracy or applicability of the data. However, surprised that the New York office has been able to discover his falsehood so rapidly and now convinced that his record will follow him to any city, he reevaluates his position. ▶

Social service agencies taking advantage of these common data banks will have to make major concessions. They will have to adopt common methods of identifying information, common reporting forms, and common operating procedures even though these might not seem best to the particular agency. Perhaps more painful, they will have to make extensive investments in converting their existing files to machine readable media so that the computer's files may be established in the first place, and then they must report all subsequent information in the same media. This process (particularly the initial conversion) will be enormously laborious and expensive and will slow the pace of development of such systems.

The individual must also make a concession in dealing with such systems. He must be willing to accept the status of "a number in the system"; he must be willing to conform his individuality to the common pattern of information storage of the system. This concession, while severe, is not novel; in dealing with today's social welfare agencies recipients have already been forced to make it.

We have seen that it is possible for computer-controlled systems to perform simple, repetitive operations in schools and hospitals for which professional staffs are now required. In order to relieve the pressing shortage of professionals, and buoyed by the hope that the never-failing uniformity of the computer's operation will often lead to better service being provided in routine matters, it is to be expected that many routine dealings of such agencies with individuals will become almost entirely mechanical.

CASE 13F (hypothetical)
◀ In 1978, a woman enters a large, progressive city hospital and asks for treatment of a worsening respiratory condition under the Medicaid program. She is asked for two things: an information release which will permit the hospital to have access to records of her Medicaid eligibility and to her medical history, and a description of her symptoms. Since she is upset about her condition and desires attention as soon as possible, she is asked to sit in a waiting room until a doctor can see her.

The clerk then turns to a computer input-output device and queries the city Medical Records Data Bank. It confirms that the woman's medical history and Medicaid record are contained in its files and that she has no records in other cities' data banks. (In this case it has been found more economical to maintain records in cities and regions than to keep them centrally, because the medical records are relatively voluminous and the frequency of requests to transfer them between jurisdictions is not very high.) The computer responds that the patient is eligible for diagnostic services under the Medicaid regulations in effect, and asks for the statement of symptoms, which the clerk then sends to it through the terminal. The computer combines the statement with the medical history according to a simple decision-making program, and finds that they indicate the patient has emphysema or a similar condition. The computer causes the terminal to print a copy of this "diagnosis" and the medical history. The clerk then indicates an immediate demand for a suitably qualified doctor. The computer, having the day's schedule for all the doctors on duty at the hospital, identifies the man suitably qualified for this type of ailment who will be available the earliest. The computer transmits a call to him through the hospital's central paging desk, and delivers his name and the time of the patient's appointment to the clerk, who informs her (freeing her to leave and return if she so desires).

The doctor meets the patient in an examining room to which the copy of her medical history and the tentative diagnosis have already been delivered. He verifies the diagnosis through further questioning and tests, occasionally using the services of the hospital's computer via an input-output terminal located in the examining room to associate data about the patient's condition with prestored probabilities about the nature and severity of the condition. Deciding that she does indeed have a serious case of emphysema, he advises her to return to the hospital for admission the following morning. He informs the hospital's computer of his decision, and it reserves a bed in a suitable ward and informs the ward staff of the anticipated admission. (If no suitable space had been available in the hospital, the computer would have passed the request to computers in other city hospitals so that an immediate admission could have been obtained at one of them.)

When the patient reports for admission the following morning, she proceeds directly to the indicated ward because the necessary admission forms have already been prepared. Instrumentation to monitor the progress of her condition has been reserved automatically; a sensor which will monitor her respiratory condition and automatically signal the nursing staff of any major changes has been attached to the bed she will occupy. By the time the physician who will treat the patient first talks to her, charts recording the progress of her symptoms have already been started by a computer recording the output of the sensor devices connected to the bed, and all the related papers are available at the nurses' station in the ward. ▶

The benefits of this kind of automation will be felt most by the administrators and professional staffs employed by hospitals, schools, and other agencies taking advantage of it. These professionals now suffer from quantities of routine administration and paper work, completing forms with data already available elsewhere. They also waste time because of imperfect scheduling. With the computer taking over most of this, they should be able to devote more of their time to complex cases demanding their professional skills, and more efficiently allocate their time among less demanding cases. This will presumably be more satisfying to them, but the benefit to the public is more important. If the computer produces an important increase in the effectiveness of social service agencies, society should benefit, both in the quality of care administered and in the convenience to the individuals involved.

Many years will be needed for most agencies to change to this degree, primarily because great costs are involved in acquiring and installing the necessary equipment. (Most of the theoretical work needed to support the services cited above has already been done.) There is also a welter of laws, regulations, and customs at all levels that will require modification. Changes of this magnitude are not likely to be absorbed overnight by all the parties involved.

Among the parties likely to object to these changes are many members of the public itself. Obviously a significant concession in the individual's self-esteem must occur, and his fear of the unknown must be alleviated, before he will be willing to deal as directly with machines as the above case implies he must. Patients must be willing to trust the system not to misdirect the initial diagnosis so seriously that the physician will be misled, and must be willing to submit to the potentially frightening prospect of monitoring by automatic machinery. Many individuals who have not grown up having this kind of association with the machine will probably never accept it; it is likely that for those able to afford them, hospitals and schools emphasizing purely human contact and care will exist indefinitely.

The social service agency of the next generation should look more like a machine, then, but it should be more responsible, more responsive, and more effective. The computer-based systems will not be as inflexible as those of today, so the requirement that clients deal with them may be acceptable to most. The machines will be backed up by professional staffs who should have more time to deal with the individuals who really need their help. The freedom to obtain extensive personal service from personally selected professionals will unquestionably have been constrained, but the freedom to obtain adequate overall service from the combination of machines and professionals will have been extended. For those able to adjust to the new situation, the trade should be a beneficial one, but in any case there is little choice. The rising pressures of demand, complexity of services, and costs make this evolution absolutely mandatory whether it is abstractly desirable or not. The choice is between using the computer and collapsing under the pressure of demand.

So far the discussion of social service agencies of the next generation has dealt with kinds of agencies already in existence. A fascinating though more speculative possibility is that entire new dimensions of social service may be made possible by information systems using the computer, and while few of these are likely to have matured within the next generation, interesting development work indicates that some may come quite quickly.

The planning of urban development has become a necessity. Republicans, Democrats, Socialists, and Communists alike must accept the obvious fact that uncontrolled evolution in today's complex cities will inevitably lead to chaos and collapse. Urban planning has advanced very far, but it has always been handicapped by the sparseness of necessary data: data about traffic flows, economic and demographic statistics, and data about the sociological dynamics of ethnic and economic groups residing and working within metropolitan areas. As time passes, more data is collected, and the record of successes and failures leads to greater understanding of additional data and information needs. As the situation improves, urban planners can begin to speak in terms of "models" of cities in which the dynamics of economic, physical, and sociological interactions are portrayed with reasonable accuracy, making possible the study of proposed projects' effects on the city's organism. Such models would almost surely involve computers for the storage and manipulation of data. The number of individual quantities to be stored will be enormous, and for the results to have useful detail, a great number of individual interactions will have to be considered. When such tools become available (as they unquestionably will) they will support a new "urban dynamics" (perhaps popularly abbreviated "urbanamics"?): a science of quantitative city planning so well based in accurate information and understanding that the full economic and sociological implications of every proposed project can be known with reasonable accuracy ahead of time.

CASE 13G (hypothetical)

◀ By 1990 the wave of enthusiasm for professional soccer has shown that in the city of Boston a new stadium of at least 100,000 seats will be necessary to accommodate the crowds. The 60,000-seat stadium constructed in 1975 for the professional football team is inadequate, and there are schedule conflicts between the football and soccer teams. Private financial support is available to build the stadium contingent upon its being in a suitably accessible location; the Boston city planners are faced with the task of attempting to locate such a site.

The problem is passed to the City Department of Urbanamics for study. Their simulation model already contains data about the effects of sports events on the city's transportation and utility system, so they are in a position to simulate the effect of any proposed location for the stadium on the existing city. Each of the proposed sites is already in use: some are commercial and industrial areas, others are residential areas of varying economic and ethnic nature.

The Department decides that the first questions to be answered are economic and sociological. No site will merit further study unless the apparent economic benefits to the city from locating the stadium there at least offset the economic penalties involved in relocating the present activities. Also (where the areas considered are residential) a sociologically acceptable accommodation for the people displaced must be available.

The model can deal directly with the economic question, because projections of the economic benefits resulting from the stadium are available and data about the values, tax revenues, and business volumes in each area are already in the model. The economic study of each area leads to a series of analyses, however, because alternative secondary areas must be considered for the relocation of the activities displaced. Relative costs of land and buildings, availability of markets, costs of transportation, and availability of work force are all quantitative factors available in the model for all segments of the city, so that these analyses are simply a matter of enough computer runs.

The sociological implications involved in relocation of residential areas cannot be evaluated so explicitly, but the model is still helpful because it contains accurate descriptions of the residential makeup of all areas and a file of background data about the broad desires and past reactions of all the ethnic groups that might be involved. With the help of expert sociologists, then, it is possible for the Department to predict with some accuracy what relocation alternatives are likely to be acceptable to the groups involved.

For those sites passing the initial tests, the requirements for utilities and (above all) for access by both public and private transportation must next be studied. They can be determined precisely from past experience, so for each surviving site the planners perform a series of "worst case" runs. Some involve flows of traffic to both the new stadium and the existing one assuming simultaneously scheduled events; others involve coincidence of stadium traffic with commuting traffic peaks; others involve the effects of bad weather. In each case, the model is able to explicitly describe the effects—the traffic loads on the streets and subway lines leading to the site being studied, the duration and magnitude of traffic jams expected to result, and the resulting pattern of transportation times between the stadium and the areas from which the stadium's patrons are expected to travel. None of the sites is already equipped with completely adequate access roads and transportation facilities, so the planners must consider the new facilities needed. Again using the model for testing repeated alternatives, they consider the sociological, economic, and physical problems of building new access roads, public transportation lines, and utility lines to each of the proposed sites and the availability of economically and sociologically satisfactory relocation sites.

In six months the Department of Urbanamics has been able to fully evaluate the implications of ten proposed sites for the stadium. Each of the evaluations has involved scores of alternatives for the relocation of those displaced, and hundreds of variations in transportation and utility services for the site. The Department is then able to develop its recommendations, and to present the precise results of following both the recommended plan and all conceivable alternatives for political and public decision. ▶

It has also been suggested that computer-based systems may have an impact on political structures. One possibility that could be implemented during the next generation is a system for polling all registered voters immediately on any issue. Given access to remote terminals connected to computers and an ability to intercommunicate standard data, it would be possible for every voter to quickly and easily register a vote from his home or place of business and to tabulate the results in an hour or two. The use of the social security number or some other identification mechanism established for credit purposes would enable the computers to verify that each vote is valid and not duplicated. Whether such a system is desirable for legislative purposes is debatable, however. Some maintain (including the drafters of the Constitution) that there is an advantage in having elected representatives of the public, rather than the public directly, make such decisions. Even if the votes are not binding, however, such a system could serve as the ultimate opinion polling service. Dr. Carl Hammer, Director of Scientific and Computer Services for Sperry-Rand Univac Federal Systems Division, says,* "We could then immediately learn the opinions of the U.S. adult populace on national issues, and social scientists would have a complete computer analysis of how the preference related to segments of society." How the legislative system might evolve in the presence of such immediate and perfect information is an interesting subject for speculation.

On an even broader scale it appears that perfected information systems of the type already in development have implications to the size and scope of governmental units. Very large governments should become more efficient and (at least in run-of-the-mill cases) more responsive to the desires and needs

---

* *Business Automation,* July 1968.

of individual citizens. Thus, the computer unquestionably makes large governmental units more feasible and efficient. On the other hand, the cost of establishing computer-based systems to provide such services will not be excessive. States, large counties, and cities of 1,000,000 or more inhabitants would be able to afford the facilities needed to provide services at least as responsive as those provided by giant governments. Apparently citizens could choose relatively small governmental units without sacrificing the services offered them by large ones. The computer seems to widen the individual's freedom to choose the size of governmental unit he wishes to support, though at the same time constricting his freedom to interact with that government in a personalized manner using his own choice of language and definition of service. Of course the size of governmental units is fundamentally an economic, political, and military matter rather than one of availability of service, but for whatever it is worth, existing constraints will apparently be relieved.

THE NEXT GENERATION OF SCIENTISTS AND ENGINEERS

Scientists and engineers will become more productive as the support they receive from computers improves. This is obvious; if there is any doubt, the cases cited in previous chapters provide convincing evidence. Differing scientific disciplines will receive varying degrees of support, however, depending on the applicability of the computer to the particular discipline and on the amount of investment likely to be made in developing advanced programs in the area. In some disciplines the improvement in computer support that can be confidently expected within the next few years is nothing short of astonishing.

CASE 13H (hypothetical)

◀ By 1977 the problem of insecticide contamination of crops, waterways, and public lands has become severe. Heavy pressure has developed to reduce the amount of chemical insecticide used so that contamination may be held down, yet the requirement to control the insects that attack crops is as great as ever. Researchers have discovered that a number of plants and trees secrete substances which deter predatory insects by emitting odors or making the plants seem to be inedible. These substances, naturally produced and compatible with the biology of the plants producing them, have no contaminating effects and represent ideal substitutes for chemical insecticides. Because of the severity of the problem and the size of the markets involved, the companies producing insecticides have invested large amounts of money in research into natural insect deterrents, and the development of tools to assist this research.

A research scientist working for an insecticide company has isolated a substance secreted by a fruit tree which, he believes, deters predatory insects. Before he can test its effect and determine whether it is a possible product, he must synthesize a quantity of the pure substance. Before he can synthesize it, though, he must analyze it to determine its molecular structure. The substance is a complex organic molecule, until recently impossible to analyze. The scientist has obtained a tiny sample of the pure substances in crystalline form; it has taken him months to collect even a little of the tree's secretions and carefully isolate the molecules of the substance in question without damaging them. However, the scientist is equipped with a new 1977 model x-ray analysis system which can work with a tiny sample of only a few milligrams. The scientist inserts the sample in his x-ray crystal analysis system and starts the machine. The pattern of x-rays diffracted by the crystal is displayed for him on a television-type screen, and from the pattern and his previous knowledge of such molecules he makes a guess about the overall structural form of the molecule. A mathematical analysis of the diffraction pattern is then performed by the specially programmed computer within the system. It determines whether the assumed structure could have produced the observed diffraction pattern. If the assumption was correct, the result of the mathematical analysis will be a "fuzzy" model of the molecule displayed on the screen that can be refined by further assumptions and mathematical analyses of the original diffraction pattern. If not, no meaningful pattern will be displayed. The scientist makes many assumptions, the majority of which turn out to be wrong, and has the system perform the mathematical analysis of each in its built-in computer. At the end of each analysis the resulting change in the model of the molecule's structure is displayed for the scientist on his cathode-ray tube display, and he decides whether he is closer to the fully detailed model or not. After dozens of trials over a period of several days (he has left the machine several times in order to think up new ideas and to let other researchers use it) he derives a precise model of the molecule being analyzed which perfectly matches the x-ray diffraction pattern. He can then proceed with the subsequent steps of synthesis and testing. ▶

This hypothetical case may not seem remarkable to those unfamiliar with the area, but to organic chemists of the recent past it would seem absolutely fantastic. The mathematical analysis of each of the assumed molecular structures is extremely laborious; when the molecule of vitamin B-12 was successfully analyzed by x-ray diffraction in 1955, eight years of continuous labor had been devoted to the calculations.* What took eight years of work for a relatively simple molecule thirteen years ago will probably take a day or two

---

* Lawrence Bragg, "X-Ray Crystallography," *Scientific American*, July 1968.

for much more complex molecules seven years from now. This is almost miraculous progress, which tremendously widens the scope of organic chemical research.

Another striking feature of this hypothetical case is that no part of the "x-ray crystal analysis system" is novel; every part exists today. The computer, the programs, suitable display devices, and the basic x-ray crystallographic unit all exist. All that is needed is further refinement and assembly of the pieces. (No minor task, though: the computer speed required is at least equal to that of the largest machine of today, the programs to produce the required types of displays are still in development, and the "language" for intercommunication does not exist.) Nevertheless, even a conservative forecast for the development of data processing and instrumentation technology over the next eight years indicates that such systems as this appear to be a virtual certainty. Obviously the managements of organizations likely to benefit from such scientific computing developments would do well to watch them with great interest; the profit potential could be enormous.

The power of such tools is so prodigious and the scope of research they make possible is so much greater that the scientific discipline involved will be greatly advanced. Other disciplines will not gain so much: tools of great value in organic chemistry presumably are of no use to archeology, for example. But archeology, in common with every other known branch of science, is developing steadily more powerful computer-based tools and methods and it is only a matter of degree which benefits most.

We have seen that scientists in increasing numbers are using the computer as a substitute for costly and slow experimental processes by setting up mathematical models of the systems they wish to study, and simulating their behavior in computers. The above case illustrates a combination of direct experiment (an actual sample of the substance being analyzed was used) together with computer simulation (models successively closer to the actual molecular structure were compared by the machine to solutions of the x-ray diffraction pattern). In other cases, such as Case 1F where models of the interiors of stars were constructed by researchers for manipulation by computers, the process of simulation is a purely abstract one. More progress in less time and at much less cost will result in those areas such as particle physics and meteorology where experiments are expensive or impossible.

Engineers designing machines, structures, and the like will also be helped by similar tools. The scientists who "converses" with a computer in designing a model of a molecule's structure which matches the characteristics of its x-ray diffraction pattern is different only in detail from the engineer who "converses" with a computer in designing a model of a petroleum refinery that makes the most economical use of heat, or the structure of a bridge having the necessary strength while using the minimum quantity of steel. The engineer who must also consider costs in his design studies will be further helped by the existence of data banks and cost models derived from experience. In Case 13G, for example, the engineers designing the new stadium for the City of Boston were provided with detailed costs of alternative public transportation systems for possible stadium sites. The engineer in the "job shop" manufacturing company of Case 13D, who worked with the salesman in developing the price quote, the manufacturing process, and the delivery estimate for the product desired by the customer, took advantage of the company's computer files to develop a rapid and accurate estimate. He then used the company's computer to help him design the product: to perform the myriad laborious calculations involved in producing the precise instructions required to operate machine tools performing the actual manufacturing steps. The combination of the numerically controlled machine tool and the computer for automatically preparing the specific instructions for driving the machine is already widespread and increasing rapidly. The result will not only be great savings in engineering costs for the entire manufacturing industry but also a change in its nature, as its ability to produce unique, small-lot products at the same cost as large lots improves and as lead times between conceptual design of the product and delivery shrink sharply.

What concessions and penalties accompany this bright picture? There are several. First, there is the obvious fact that despite decreases in the cost of computers, the systems we have described for computer control of experiments, for complex simulations and analyses, and for the application of data banks to design studies will still be expensive. A sizeable investment will be required before any organization can participate in the scientific or engineering discipline for which the tools have become necessary, and the technological gap between the small organization and the large one may widen. As in the case of business organizations, the small organizations may find it possible to share the cost of such facilities, either directly or through service companies—small colleges often share the cost of expensive research tools today—but such sharing can be inconvenient. Another concession required of the scientists and engineers will be that they must learn the operating procedures, limitations, and shortcomings of their new tools. Such knowledge, frequently at the detailed and irritating level of "how to prepare a sample for the model XXX analyzer," will be a necessary part of the scientist's training however little interest he may have in it.

This requirement that the professional learn the language of the machine may have a more subtle but more profound negative influence. Having learned its language and become accustomed to working with it, he may lose his ability to work without it. It has been widely observed that engineers

Another essential aspect of the home terminal is a facsimile transmitter and receiver through which pieces of paper can be exchanged. This would be necessary for the exchange of business documents, receipt of tickets and stock certificates, and every kind of receipt or evidence of transaction. Today, public facsimile transmission facilities are available at prices ranging from $5 to $8 per page transmitted. These costs will also drop, but again only proportionately to communications costs. There are other essential components of such a home input-output terminal, too, for example the credit card reader which is fraud-proof, providing a positive identification both of the validity of the card and of the person using it. No such mechanism has yet been invented at any cost, and it may be presumed that any becoming available will be relatively complex and expensive.

Other costs are the central costs: computers, file maintenance, and programming. The individual user will presumably be asked to pay a portion of their cost, as in the case of present stock quote services and remote time-sharing computing services. Today's users typically pay between $300 and $600 per month for these services; it seems unlikely that the very few dollars per month the average homeowner is likely to be willing to pay will be realistic for a very long time. Not the least cost problem would be that associated with standardization of information systems among stores, financial institutions, and travel companies of all kinds. Before the forecasted kinds of services could be made available, most or all such firms must be able to interchange information in standard form and coding. As we have seen, the cost of file conversions can be extremely high, and it is unlikely that all institutions and businesses will be willing to make them within the next generation.

The language barrier is another problem with the home terminal concept. We have seen that to use computers people must conform precisely to the terminology and operating procedures specified by the programmers. We have also seen that individuals have trouble doing this consistently. Few are able to use all the facilities offered by the direct telephone dialing system, for example, without making errors or obtaining operator assistance. In using a network of varied computer services via a home terminal, individuals would be asked to conform to the languages of not one but many such systems, perhaps hundreds. It would seem difficult if not impossible to ask the casual user in the home to deal with them all faultlessly. Furthermore, as Case 12G showed, malicious or frivolous misuse of such systems is likely to be a problem when they are exposed to the public without constraint. This misuse is, of course, likely to become fraud whenever devices and programs permit it.

For all these reasons, it seems unlikely that universal data and communication systems communicating with home input-output terminals will be realized in the next generation. This is not to say they will never be—costs will eventually decline to an acceptable level, particularly if the input-output terminals are combined with the electronic entertainment facilities of the home so that components and subsystems may be shared. Also, in time more and more private individuals will become familiar with computer systems during their schooling and in their work, and may be relied upon to handle them more accurately. Finally, the programs and devices available for such systems will steadily improve in flexibility and sophistication, so the language barrier will become less severe and protections against fraud and mischievous misuse may become adequate. However, these improvements seem to require long, evolutionary processes.

A compromise appears much more likely, with individuals being offered the services of computer and communication systems through terminals convenient to but not in their residences. The concept of a "local terminal office," located in shopping centers, travel agencies or bank branches and therefore easily accessible to most people, appears more feasible. Such an office could also be staffed by employees familiar with the information systems the individual will be dealing with, either to help him or to operate the terminal for him. The employees could also be trained to handle cash, check credit or identification, and otherwise learn to protect the systems from improper use.

CASE 13 I (hypothetical)

◀ John Doe, having decided that for his 1975 vacation he can afford a trip to Europe, goes to a travel agent near his home to arrange the trip. He discusses possibilities with the travel agent, and as they are reviewed, the travel agent displays brochures and photographs from a microfilm file. The same microfilm file contains up-to-date airline schedule and fare information, and at the end of the conversation a tentative itinerary has been established. Then the agent turns to his input-output terminal and places a series of calls to the central reservation service, reserving the desired airplane seats, rooms at selected rates in each of the preferred hotels, and rental cars where Mr. Doe wants them. Since he has also selected sight-seeing tours in certain cities where he prefers not to drive himself, reservations are also made for them. Being a music fancier, Mr. Doe has arranged his itinerary so that he can attend several music festivals for which reservations are also made. Since some of Mr. Doe's first choices are not available, a conversation involving himself, the agent, and the machine is needed to develop alternatives.

The reservations made, the computer is then requested to print a statement of the total cost of Mr. Doe's vacation and its breakdown among the carriers, hotels, and others providing the services he has reserved. Since it is unacceptably high, another three-way conversation takes place to reduce it. Finally, Mr. Doe writes a check for the total.

Because Mr. Doe does not have a current passport, the travel agent assists him in filling out a release form for personal information to be transmitted to the central records file containing his personal data, directing that the necessary information be released to the nearest passport agent. The travel agent, a notary public, is able to certify the release form and administer the oath associated with the passport application. It is unnecessary for Mr. Doe to visit the passport agent; the valid passport will be issued to him directly by mail.

After Mr. Doe leaves the office, the travel agent (who was not previously acquainted with him) calls the computer system of Mr. Doe's bank from the terminal and requests a verification that his check is valid. Upon confirmation, the travel agent with a single message instructs the system to inform all parties that the reservations are paid for, and that tickets and confirmations should be issued. After all of these messages have been delivered overnight and acknowledged, the computer system causes all the individual documents to be printed automatically by the travel agent's terminal for delivery to Mr. Doe.

Mr. Doe spent two hours with the agent, and at the end of this single visit every detail of this trip was arranged. The following day all the tickets and confirmations are delivered, and he is ready to go. ▶

Systems such as this are clearly more feasible than alternatives that would deal directly with the individual in his home yet seem to offer him almost equal convenience, adding only the inconvenience of a single local trip. It is interesting to speculate what forms they may take, and how far they may be developed. Will the businessman be offered local "automated conference rooms" equipped with input-output terminals, television, and facsimile systems which he can rent in order to confer with colleagues in other "automated conference rooms" in other cities? Perhaps; the only apparent barriers are economic. In any event, it appears that some compromise between the extremes of opportunity offered the individual by computer systems and the concessions required will lead to very attractive new services in the next generation. The hospital patient in Case 13F would benefit because of more rapid and directed attention with much less paper work. The bank's customer in Case 12A receives automatic budget accounting services which save him time and trouble. The individual whose records are stored in the Federal Central Records Service of Case 11C would forever afterward be freed from the chores of filling out forms duplicating information already recorded.

Each of these cases cites a single service, attractive to the individual by itself. There is nothing to prevent an organization providing multiple services, and integrating functions now traditionally considered separate, if the computer makes this possible and the result is competitively attractive. The following hypothetical case describes such an integrated service for the individual. It appears to be attractive and is certainly technologically feasible (though not now legally so).

CASE 13J (hypothetical)

◀ Mary and John Smith, married in 1975, began to deal with many organizations interested in participating in the new family's financial affairs. A variety of insurance companies variously offering life, casualty, automobile, disability, and health insurance; several kinds of savings institutions, including banks and savings and loan companies; finance companies; commercial banks with several checking account and automatic credit plans; mutual funds; and stockbrokers all entered the picture eventually. As they dealt with more and more of these institutions, the resulting proliferation of bills, payment plans, alternative investment rates and plans, cash values, and balances caused them increasing confusion, and they became irritated at the volume of paper work involved in all these relationships. So, when a representative of the Universal Fiscal Management Company approached them in 1984 offering to cut through the complexity at one stroke, he found them a willing audience.

The Universal Fiscal Management Company, actually a bank holding company owning a variety of financial institutions in addition to banks, asked the Smiths for both their checking and savings accounts, and for first consideration when they needed credit beyond the limit automatically extended along with their checking account. In addition, it asked for all their financial records and limited powers of attorney. In return, it offered the following services at no additional charge:

1 It would provide consolidated monthly statements of the family's "net worth" with balances, cash values, and equities totaled on one side of the statement and debts and liabilities on the other.

2 It would consolidate all inflows and outflows of cash so that they would be sent a single invoice monthly for all amounts due on insurance policies, mutual fund and stock purchase plans, debt repayments, and interest and tax payments due. Provided with a single lump payment, the company would undertake to apportion it among the various recipients. Indeed, should the Smiths want the additional convenience, the company would automatically charge their checking account with the amount due without bothering them with an invoice, and inform them later.

3 Should the Smiths want either to withdraw money or invest it, free financial consultation would be automatically available. Considering the relative rates of interest and their indicated desires for cash and equity savings and insurance protection, the company would advise them whether a withdrawal should best be made from savings, by a personal loan, by selling securities or mutual fund shares, or by taking a policy loan on the cash balance of an insurance policy. Should they wish to increase their savings or protection, they would be advised on the most attractive type of investment considering rates of return and their existing pattern of coverages and assets.

4 At all times the company would act as the family's financial "watchdog," informing them immediately if their position should vary from the pattern they had initially specified, or if their future liabilities appeared to exceed their established pattern of payments.

The salesman explained that their financial guidance would be provided by automatic computer analysis rather than by a member of the bank's staff, but assured them that their family's financial pattern was a familiar one, well within the range that the computer's programs had been prepared to handle; in their case the automatic analysis was almost sure to be superior to anything they could do for themselves unless they were unusually expert. ▶

A number of existing trends point to the likelihood of such personal financial services. Automatic budgeting services are already offered, combined checking and small loan services are being offered by banks everywhere, and many arrangements already exist for automatic payment from checking accounts of regular charges such as insurance premiums. Life insurance companies already perform computerized family financial analyses, as we saw in Case 9E. All of these, further developed and supported by improved and more economical computers, point toward the emergence of such services. The managers of such financial institutions would do well to consider evolving in this direction.

It seems certain that many of the irritating complexities of paper work, record keeping, information seeking, bill paying, and financial management that the individual now puts up with will be simplified in the next generation. This simplification will surely be welcome to most, but it is appropriate to stop and consider the price that must be paid.

In all cases, individuals will have to conform to the language of the system with which they deal. Concessions to organizations' systems may not be as severe as with the reservation and information retrieval systems reviewed above, because customers are likely to deal repeatedly over extended periods with the systems offered by organizations and may become accustomed to them. Nevertheless, it is always irritating to have to put up with such constraints.

The requirement for conformity with the systems' capabilities is perhaps more serious. If the individual's case does not fit the pattern encompassed by the computer's programs, it cannot be handled at all. If the financial structure of a family departs in any significant respect from those assumed by the programmers of the Universal Fiscal Management Company, that family will be unable to use the company's services and will be completely "on its own." Perhaps people are not so lazy that they will let such considerations determine their choices, but certainly there will be an increase in the already weighty pressures for individual conformity with the norm. If the computer's programs are sufficiently broad and flexible (as may be presumed given enough time for evolution), the scope of the norm may be very broad; it may in fact encompass almost every variation individuals may choose. The idealist would say that a prison is still a prison no matter how roomy it may be. The pragmatist, on the other hand, would say that any constraint you do not feel is effectively nonexistent; that a prison as broad as the world is no prison at all.

The most serious concession of all may be the increasing dependence of the individual on these systems. The individual whose reservations and tickets are all obtained through an automatic system will not know how to obtain them directly on his own. The family whose financial affairs are regularly monitored by a computer program may forget how to manage them without the computer. The engineer or scientist whose computations are always performed by a machine may forget (indeed, he may have never have learned) the mathematical techniques necessary to do them for himself. The manager relying on simulations to guide his decisions may become dependent on them. Modern man has, of course, already accepted the necessity of relying upon specialists and machines for many of the services and products he needs; none of us is completely self-sufficient. It may be argued that these additional dependencies on computer-based systems are no more than an additional step in the same direction, and may bring no more harm as long as the systems all work. But systems sometimes fail, and the larger and more interdependent they become, the more resounding and serious their failure could be. (For example, the Northeast power blackout resulted from cascading failures of interconnected systems.) We have argued that if the Federal Central Records Service becomes an actuality, the individual's privacy may be protected by a system of selective release of information, in which the individual has complete control over the release of his personal data to government and business entities with only legal action able to override his lack of consent. However, we have not considered the implications of such a system suffering complete breakdown. Surely few individuals or organizations would bother to keep complete duplicate records, and in any case they would not have the certified authenticity of those coming from the Center. If the system failed, credit ratings, criminal records, and welfare records would disappear, and many essential processes would inevitably come to a halt. With luck and sufficient forethought such increases in dependency may prove harmless, but as the overall mechanism becomes more complex and the individual's capability to conduct his affairs decreases, the risk of failure and the sensitivity of the whole to perturbations presumably increases.

The fear most commonly heard is that the individual will become depersonalized; that he will "become a number"; that the pressures to conform will be so strong that individuality will be crushed. Our case studies have shown emphatically that this need not be true and probably will not be true, as long as the evolution of computer-based information systems is responsive to the pressures of competition, voters' demands, and other forms of consumer pressure. Perhaps this responsiveness may be lacking, and in the interests of uniformity and minimization of development cost, flexibility will be slighted and the systems with which we will be forced to work may become harmfully constraining. But the case studies show no sign that this is happening to any important degree now, or that it will happen in the future. To be sure the individual will be forced to conform, but in doing so at trivial levels he will apparently obtain new dimensions of freedom resulting from a great increase in the scope of his options. In adopting direct distance dialing, the telephone system requires a trivial loss of individuality of us all because we must address one another as numbers, but the increase in our freedom to communicate because of decreased cost and increased responsiveness in the system is infinitely more important. The employee and manager of a company must learn the language of the computer in order to deal with it, but in return he is offered flexibility, "flickering authority," and an entirely new freedom of personal attainment.

We conclude that if present evolution continues, the next generation in return for relatively trivial concessions will be offered an expansion of scope and a simplification of irritating detail in personal and business life which will be far more important. For a small price the individual's freedoms may be multiplied and expanded; the hectic pace of simply keeping up with affairs may be reduced; the scope of human values may be widened. Such a widening of values is exactly the goal of the growing body of protest represented by the quote from Mr. Ginsberg at the beginning of this chapter. The protesters feel that to enhance humanistic values, the progress of mechanization must be reversed, but perhaps the opposite is true. Perhaps a strange and unexpected alliance is forming between two forces apparently antithetical—the protesters against the mechanization of society, and the mechanizers. The IBM Corporation's slogan "machines should work; people should think" is evidence of a basically similar viewpoint. The next generation may (if we are lucky) see the attainment of the protesters' goals through the very process they decry, and the enhancement of freedom.

LIST OF CASES

LIST OF CASES

INDEX

INDEX

ABCDE69